The Essential Guide to Lesbian and Gay Weddings

Tess Ayers and Paul Brown

alyson books
los angeles | new york

THE ALYSON BOOKS EDITION OF "THE ESSENTIAL GUIDE TO LESBIAN AND GAY WEDDINGS" CONTAINS SOME CHANGES TO TEXT AND GRAPHICS THAT ARE A REVISION OF THE FIRST EDITION.

MANUFACTURED IN THE UNITED STATES OF AMERICA.
PRINTED ON ACID-FREE PAPER.

THIS TRADE PAPERBACK IS PUBLISHED BY ALYSON PUBLICATIONS INC.,
P.O. BOX 4371, LOS ANGELES, CALIFORNIA 90078-4371.
DISTRIBUTION IN THE UNITED KINGDOM BY TURNAROUND PUBLISHER SERVICES LTD.,
UNIT 3 OLYMPIA TRADING ESTATE, COBURG ROAD, WOOD GREEN,
LONDON N22 6TZ ENGLAND.

FIRST EDITION PUBLISHED BY HARPER SAN FRANCISCO: JULY 1994
FIRST ALYSON BOOKS EDITION: FEBRUARY 1999

00 01 02 03 a 10 9 8 7 6 5 4 3 2

ISBN 1-55583-484-1
(PREVIOUSLY PUBLISHED WITH ISBN 0-06-250271-9 BY HARPER SAN FRANCISCO.)

LIBRARY OF CONGRESS CATALOGING-IN-PUBLICATION DATA
    AYERS, TESS.
        THE ESSENTIAL GUIDE TO LESBIAN AND GAY WEDDINGS / TESS AYERS AND PAUL BROWN.
        INCLUDES INDEX.
        1. GAY COUPLES—UNITED STATES. 2. GAY MARRIAGE—UNITED STATES. 3. WEDDINGS—UNITED
        STATES—PLANNING. I. BROWN, PAUL. II. TITLE.
    HQ76.3.U5A94 1994
    395'.22'08664—DC20   93-45967 CIP

TEXT DESIGN BY SUSAN SAROFF.

▼

The Essential Guide to Lesbian and Gay Weddings

For Janey, My Light

and

For Rick, Without Whom . . .

CONTENTS

CONTENTS

ACKNOWLEDGMENTS

Our love to the friends and family who guided and supported us through it all: Charlotte Sheedy, Roz Wolpert, Jay Wolpert, Bea and Morris Mitz, Vincent Price, Polly Anderson, Penny Stallings, Mike and Val Ayers, Dana and Catherine Ayers, Robin Mitz, Steve Hook, Jenny Sullivan, and Martin Gage. Our thanks to our editor, Kandace Hawkinson, and everyone at Harper San Francisco, especially Andrea Lewis, Matthew Lore, Jennifer Boynton, George Brown, Joan Olson, and Carl Walesa; and our love to our parents, Bob and Esther Ayers and Stan and Lyn Brown, for planting the seeds that made us who we are today.

We would also like to thank the following people, who were kind enough to share their experiences or their expertise with us:

David Craig; Joe Timko and Randy Neece; Naomi Caryl; Dr. Gwynne Guibord; Stanley Siegel and Joey Smith; Barry Michlin; Michael Arden; Susan Saroff; Laurie Pincus; Lynn Houston; Nancy J. Robbins; Judy Rudin; Allan Rich; Ann Volkes; Patti Levey and Beth Saltzman; Sandra Scoppettone; Bob and Rod Jackson-Paris; Stephanie Blackwood; Seema Weinberg from P-FLAG Washington; Adele Starr from P-FLAG Los Angeles; Rabbi Julie Greenburgh of the Jewish Renewal Life Center of Philadelphia; Ben Bakus; Barry Douglas; Mike Anders and John Chambers; Martin McCauley and Jeff Robertson; Susan Teisciero and Mary Huggins; David Bruner and George Ziemer; Michael Franco and Bob Shores; Norman Nichols and David Williams; Michael Snell and Michael Tonda; Ben Shivley; the Reverend Eduard Perry of MCC Tucson; Naomi Tomashoff; Geoffrey Fidelman; the Reverend Mary Grigolia of the Strongsville, Ohio, Unitarian Universalist Church; Father Mike Tueth; Marianne Muellerleile; Peter Passell from the New York *Times;* Roxy Ventola and Matthew McGrath; Ellen Hulkower; Rupert Holmes; James Lafferty from the National Lawyers Guild; Jennifer Press; Barbara Safrin from Write on Third stationery; Charlotte Booker; Debbie Grunfeld; Rachel Solasz; Randy Tomme from Bloomingdale's gift registry; Howard Mandelbaum from Photofest; Time-Warner, Inc.; Tina Esposito; Don Roe; George Pyle, editor of the Salina, Kansas, *Journal;* the Reverend Kit Cherry of MCC Los Angeles; the Reverend Dusty Pruitt of MCC Long Beach; Lydia Segal of MCC Toronto; Shaun Newton of MCC Dallas; David White and Blake Derry; Fran Ruth and Sandy Moldafsky; the Reverend Victoria Lee; Mark Metzen and Tom Nolasco; Shirley Scott and Betty Barr; Don Campbell and Russell Windall; Boomer Kennedy; Demian from Partners Task Force; Nancy Seaton; Bob Mills and Jeff Wright; Mark Bower; Shelly Peters and Sandra Pearce; Pol and Andy Sandro-Yepes; Peter Tatchell of Outrage!; Craig Dean and Patrick Gill from the Equal Marriage Rights Fund; the Reverend Rosalind Russell; Babs Daitch from Olivia Cruises; Cindy Cesnalis and Clay Reeves from Shocking Gray; Bonnie Gruszecki and Maggie Wynne; Joel Hecht; Bobby and Kay Smith; Michelle Lifer and Nancy Ferron; Dr. Betty Berzon; Judith McDaniel and Jan Schwartz; Dianne Greenberg-Dilena from the Hotel Bel-Air; Jane Lockhart from Sweet Lady Jane Bakery; Hannelore Hahn, editor of *Places;* Diane Goodman; Suzanne Sherman; Pat Allen, Jim Kepner, and Jeff Hagedorn from the International Gay and Lesbian Archives in Los Angeles; the June Mazer Collection; Wayne Whiston, editor of *Our World;* Sandy Pinney and Carma Liperr from Sandy's Printing Services; Beverly Kopf; J. Kenneth

Poe from the City of West Hollywood; Sandy Sprung; Carlos Stelmach, Sara Hart, and Cookie Kinkead from *10 Percent;* Brian Smith and John Beitner; Janice McQueeney; Michael Mitz; Myla Fahn from the Beverly Hills Doll Company; Tony Cook; Rabbi Marc S. Blumenthal of Temple Beth Chayim Chadashim; the Kit McClure Band of New York City; Donald Kreindler of 21 West Catering, Beverly Hills; Elaine Holliman; Heidi and Debra Stern-Ellis; Pam Putch from Earth Angels; Barbara Held from Barney's New York; Mary Micucci from Along Came Mary Catering; Maria Sumnicht from Precision Software; Andrea Thomas from Royal Hawaiian Weddings; Susan Feniger from City Restaurant; Marcelina Martin; and Greg Richmond. Thanks to those who helped on this new edition: everyone at Alyson Publications, especially Greg Constante, Scott Brassart, Julie Trevelyan, and Kennette Crockett and her wife, Monica Warden; Patricia Lee and Vanna Pecoraro at Family Celebrations; DJ Davis Photography; and Linda Dozoretz.

And our admiration and congratulations to every gay and lesbian couple who have ever had a wedding ceremony and to every couple who ever will.

Introduction

Shortly after the first edition of this book went to press, the TV show *Northern Exposure* aired an episode culminating with a gay wedding. No, we didn't see the grooms kiss, but the show was a sure sign that same-sex weddings were riding the wave of a national zeitgeist. In rapid succession, *Roseanne* had Martin Mull's character Leon reuniting with and marrying his old flame Scott, and *Friends* had Ross's ex-wife Carol marry her lover, Susan. And the MTV generation supported the union of Pedro Zamora and Sean Sasser on *The Real World*.

All of this commitment on the tube was a reflection of what was happening in the real, real world. It wasn't just gay and lesbian television characters becoming visible; it was your everyday garden-variety boy- or girl-next-door gay man or lesbian finally beginning to be perceived as a real person in search of love and commitment.

When we started researching the book back in 1992, the idea of a same-sex wedding planner was borderline nervy, maybe even radical. The good news is that now, six years later, more and more people have had, been to, or at least heard of a gay commitment ceremony. There's less of a tendency for a jaw to drop when you say the words "lesbian wedding."

The bad news is that as of this writing, gay and lesbian marriages are still not legal anywhere in the United States. But a quantum leap has been made in the hearts and souls of the American people, and we're still moving forward at an incredible rate. In just the last few years:

- Domestic-partner offerings by corporations, cities, and universities across the nation have gone through the roof, with more than 600 employers offering coverage for millions of same-gender domestic partners.
- Four countries offer gay marriage-like partnerships: Denmark, Iceland, Norway, and Sweden.
- Query "same-sex marriage" at <u>amazon.com</u>, and your search results bring you not only this book but also dozens of others dealing with the various political and social aspects of same-gender unions.
- Religious participation in gay unions is more commonplace: leading Episcopalians have called for liturgies for same-gender ceremonies, and Reform rabbis are considering sanctioning the blessing of same-sex unions.
- On the Web there are home pages of couples featuring albums of their commitment ceremonies, as well as many gay honeymoon packages for Hawaii.

When this book was first published, we hoped that maybe, just maybe, some of the more enlightened bookstores would place it not just in their Gay and Lesbian Studies sections but right there on the same shelf next to *Weddings* by Martha Stewart. And sure enough it happened across the country.

This book was written because it was difficult to maneuver your way through straight wedding planners to try to make them work for gay ceremonies. For our purposes, some of the old wedding rules just don't apply, and others seem antiquated. We thought we could do better. So we set out to write a how-to book that would not only give you information concerning same-sex weddings but that also helps free you from the bounds of what you may think a traditional wedding is supposed to be.

But this doesn't mean that when we say "same-sex wedding" we're adding an asterisk after *wedding,* with a note of apology that it's really not a wedding and that because same-gender marriages are not legal, we're going to take the posture of second-class citizens and make our celebrations "less than." No, when we say wedding we mean wedding. Yes, there are many styles of weddings, and you can pick and choose what you want to. But since this is a wedding book, equivalent to the books that your straight friends might read, we have included everything that, in a different world, a better world, a more equal world, would be part of a gay wedding.

The couples we interviewed brought something new to the party. What they all had in common was that they had fallen in love and wanted to share their lives with each other. Wedding was interpreted differently by each couple, for reasons sometimes having to do with their cultural, religious, or ethnic background, and sometimes not. Some did their weddings just like their parents had done; others made it up as they went along. But they all approached their weddings with pride and a sense of humor.

We originally approached this book as if same-sex marriage were suddenly legal. And even though as of this third printing, it still isn't, we are closer than ever. Six years ago we dreamed of a day when gay and lesbian couples could legally marry, but it did feel like a dream. Now, however, lawsuits filed by gay couples seeking marriage licenses have reached the supreme courts in three states: Hawaii, Alaska, and Vermont. But there has also been a backlash, with 28 states officially banning gay marriage over the last three years. Congress has done the same with the odious Defense of Marriage Act. National politicians make public pronouncements against gay marriage in order to polish their credentials with the religious right. But we think (on our optimistic days anyway) that this is all a good sign—that the only reason this is all happening is that they're running scared because things are changing. Recent polls bear this out; the number of Americans who favor same-sex marriage is growing steadily.

In the words of Ninia Baehr, who is a participant in the same-sex marriage lawsuit in Hawaii, "It is now the subject of a conversation that's going to be happening in the nation's living rooms and in the courts and in the legislatures for many years to come. I think that just in that sense we are far ahead of where we were six years ago. To me that is a very big victory."

If you're buying this book to plan your own ceremony, congratulations to you. If you're buying it for a friend or child or nephew who's gay and considering a wedding, thank you for your enlightenment. And if you're a gay or lesbian teenager who's buying it just so you can daydream about the guy or girl you're going to marry, well, that just about says it all.

Tess Ayers and Paul Brown
Los Angeles
September 1998

Part I

Waxing
Philosophical

▼ # WHY BOTHER (IF IT'S NOT LEGAL)?

nce upon a time, there were two women who fell in love. They lived together for a few years, and then one night, one of them got down on one knee (we think it was her left one) and asked the other one to marry her. The following June they went down to city hall and got a marriage license, and then they had a huge church wedding, wearing long bridal gowns with trains. They had eight attendants in matching fuchsia dresses, and three hundred guests. At the reception that followed (paid for by both sets of parents), each bride danced with her new mother-in-law and father-in-law, and both were toasted by various friends and relatives. This was all announced in the "Weddings" section in the local newspaper. Soon afterward, each became eligible for the other's health insurance from work; and the following year, they filed a joint tax return.

A fairy tale? Not totally. Same-sex couples have been celebrating their unions in various ways for centuries. Some of the events in this "fairy tale" are actually happening with some frequency in cities all over the country. True, gays cannot, anywhere in the United States, be legally married; they can't get a marriage license or file a joint tax return. But is that any reason to avoid making a public commitment? We think not. (Obviously, since we've built an entire book around this premise.)

And while this book is designed to help you plan your wedding, before we can deal with the wedding part we need to address the issue of why same-sex couples would want to be married in the first place. Anyone can have a wedding, but if you're not legally married, why bother? Does the pursuit of marriage rights reduce us to little more than heterosexual wanna-bes? And anyway, isn't "gay marriage" the ultimate oxymoron—a contradiction in terms? To some, the combination of these two words might seem odd. "Gay" has a contemporary ring to it, like some postmodern

And when Pat Buchanan thundered, and I quote: "We stand with George Bush against the amoral idea that gay and lesbian couples should have the same standing in law as married men and women," I wondered, who is Pat Buchanan to pronounce anybody's love invalid? How can he deny the profound love felt by one human being for another?

—BARBRA STREISAND,
speaking at an APLA fund-raiser

Photo: Nancy J. Robbins

idea—though of course it's not; and "marriage" sounds so traditional and stodgy, something that lesbians and gays wouldn't really want to get into.

And as a heterosexual institution, isn't marriage under attack from all sides? Let's hit the rewind button and take a look at its history.

It all began with cavemen claiming their brides or stealing them from other tribes, and then gradually evolved into its own little cottage industry, with the bride's father negotiating her price. (In fact, this is the origin of the word we still use for the celebration; in Anglo-Saxon society the groom was required to give a "wed" of money, goods, or domestic animals in exchange for a bride. Festive, huh?) Then in medieval times, along came Saint Augustine to suggest that mutual agreement just might be a better foundation for a marriage than stealing or bartering. The idea of romantic love didn't really catch on until the eighteenth century, but even then if the relationship soured, people often stayed married for economic or social reasons—marriages of convenience.

In the twentieth century a lot of the rules have changed, yet the bonds of matrimony undeniably remain a centerpiece of Western civilization's social structure.

IF THE CLUB WON'T HAVE US AS MEMBERS, WHY WOULD WE WANT TO JOIN?

When you add the history of gays into the mix of the history of marriage and begin to talk about gay marriage, you'd better believe you're sitting on a powder keg. There are several emotionally charged issues at play here, both within the gay community and in society as a whole.

First of all, there is the concept of marriage itself. There are those who maintain that marriage is a convention that has not weathered well over time, and that the word *marriage* comes with too much baggage, including undesirable and outdated concepts like "ownership," and expectations of a picture-perfect existence à la Donna Reed. One can argue that today's through-the-roof divorce rate is proof that marriage as an institution has not treated men or women very kindly.

Well, why can't lesbians and gays take the best of what marriage has to offer and discard the rest? It's been observed that many gay relationships are more egalitarian than heterosexual relationships; just granting us the right to marry doesn't mean we'll have to lower our standards.

And consider the question of same-sex unions as a gay political issue. Some may wonder why, after years of being unaccepted (even damned) by society, gays and lesbians would want to participate in an archaic tradition that has "straight world" stenciled all over it. By entering into gay marriages, are gays engaged in a misdirected attempt to adopt traditional heterosexual institutions for themselves instead of encouraging tolerance for divergent lifestyles? After all, Kurt Russell and Goldie Hawn had kids together and chose not to get married; why shouldn't gays have the same option?

The response to this concern is that gays should fight for marriage laws because they offer a certain road to complete equality. Nobody's saying that if you're *allowed* to get married, you *have* to get married; but until lesbians and gays have exactly the same legal rights as heterosexuals, we will always be second-class citizens. After all, gay cohabitation is legal in all but about a dozen states; by denying same-sex couples the choice to legally wed, society is encouraging those relationships to be undeveloped and insecure.

And finally, there's the issue of lesbians and gays seeking the right to validate their unions in a society that is often resistant to change. The notion of legalizing same-sex unions challenges the morals and insecurities of the status quo. Acknowledging a committed gay relationship and saying that it is just as valid and acceptable as a nongay relationship just plain scares the hell out of some people.

Well, even a reluctant social structure can adapt. Only twenty-five years ago it was still a crime in some states for a black woman to marry a white man. We can only hope that twenty-five years from now, society will find it just as incredible that at one time two people of the same sex were not legally entitled to marry.

BIRDS DO IT, BEES DO IT

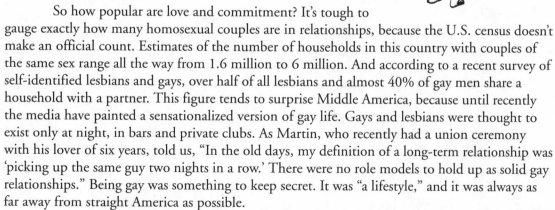

While there are any number of important political reasons to support legal marriage between same-sex couples, we like to think that straight people and gay people alike get married for pretty much the same reason: love. And love and commitment are so rare in this world that it seems absurd to thwart them.

So how popular are love and commitment? It's tough to gauge exactly how many homosexual couples are in relationships, because the U.S. census doesn't make an official count. Estimates of the number of households in this country with couples of the same sex range all the way from 1.6 million to 6 million. And according to a recent survey of self-identified lesbians and gays, over half of all lesbians and almost 40% of gay men share a household with a partner. This figure tends to surprise Middle America, because until recently the media have painted a sensationalized version of gay life. Gays and lesbians were thought to exist only at night, in bars and private clubs. As Martin, who recently had a union ceremony with his lover of six years, told us, "In the old days, my definition of a long-term relationship was 'picking up the same guy two nights in a row.' There were no role models to hold up as solid gay relationships." Being gay was something to keep secret. It was "a lifestyle," and it was always as far away from straight America as possible.

But as playwright Harvey Fierstein has said, "Gay liberation should not be a license to be a perpetual adolescent. If you deny yourself commitment, then what can you do with your life?" And fortunately, the times they are a-changing. After decades of free love and living for the moment, many straight couples are now choosing to nest, as are gays and lesbians. The C-word—*commitment*—is on the comeback trail for a number of reasons, including the increase in lesbian and gay parenting and concerns over safe sex. But perhaps the most important reason is that the fight for advances in gay and lesbian civil rights is bringing awareness and newfound determination to many. The result? The confidence to march out of the closet and down the aisle.

While there are no records at city hall that can tell us how many gay and lesbian unions have been celebrated, we do know that they're on the rise, with reported numbers multiplying geometrically each year. There are religious ceremonies in churches and temples; ceremonies performed by clergy who bless the unions but cannot sanction them under the laws of their church; and thousands of civil ceremonies that are not reported to anyone except supportive friends and family. All over the country—in banquet halls, on cruise ships, and in national parks—guys and guys, and gals and gals, are saying "I do," tossing bouquets, and driving off in Jeeps.

ASK NOT FOR WHOM THE WEDDING BELL TOLLS; IT TOLLS FOR THEE

Okay, you say, commitment is one thing—but a wedding? Why bother? Because we humans love to mark milestones with celebrations. From baptism to a sweet-sixteen party to a retirement party, we take stock of our lives with rituals. By planning a wedding ceremony, you are participating in an age-old rite that honors the purest and most basic union between two people. A wedding is part of a universal language that says "turning point," and as human beings we need to feel a part of the pageant of history.

A wedding is also about saying to society, "This is a relationship that is of the deepest importance to us. Help us carry it forward." John Spong, the Episcopal bishop of Newark, is on the front line in the fight to acknowledge homosexual couples. Here's his take on the struggle: "We have to bless gay unions because, I think, these relationships are holy. . . . I don't think there's a heterosexual marriage in this country that would exist with the absence of support that we give to gay couples. So the very fact that some gay people are able to forge lifetime relationships is to me almost a miracle." When you declare your love in front of your friends and family, you're asking them to support and bless you in this relationship.

Weddings also offer the couple a sense of emotional security. When we asked Randy if getting married changed him, he said, "Not the next day. But over the years I felt the importance of having a ceremony. We had made such a public commitment to each other that, the few times we've had trouble, it wasn't so easy to just walk away from Joe."

And guess what? Getting married is a lot of fun! Almost every couple we interviewed spoke about what a great time they had on their wedding day, calling it one of the high points of their lives. Sounds like a pretty good deal to us.

Looking back on it, I spent most of the ceremony holding back the tears; I didn't think it would affect me in such an emotional way. Then afterwards at the reception, we danced wildly for four hours. . . . I haven't danced that way in years.

—VINCENT

WHAT TO ANSWER WHEN YOUR MOTHER ASKS, "WHY IN THE WORLD WOULD YOU WANT TO DO THAT? IT'S NOT LEGAL."

Choose one or more of the following responses:

"We've entered into a relationship that is too big and too meaningful to deny."

———

"It's a celebration of our lives together."

———

"If Cousin Bernice can get married, why can't I?"

———

"We're formalizing our relationship to the outside world."

———

"We want to create an occasion to gather the diverse people who are important in both of our lives."

———

"I'm expressing to my partner the ultimate in commitment and responsibility."

———

"We're participating in an age-old tradition."

———

"I'm making a political statement."

———

"We want to raise a family, and we'd never consider having children unless we were married."

———

"We're doing this to hurt you."

When George asked me to marry him, I didn't know that he meant get married and go to a church, and tuxedos—the whole ball of wax. It didn't click. I mean, who would do that?

—DAVID

I feel there is a truth to the idea that when you commit in a ceremony, legal or otherwise, your subconscious adjusts to the fact that you're committed for life to this person. Gay people always have an out, just as straight people living together do. Why do we look with awe at a gay couple in their sixties who have been together for thirty years? It's a rarity in our world. Part of that is because there's no marriage.

—ELLEN

YOU CAN SAY "I DO,"
BUT THE LAW STILL SAYS "YOU DON'T"

Now, before you start making your guest list and hyphenating your last names, we again want to remind you that it's not legal, and that you will continue to lose out on a number of benefits that your cousin Bernice automatically had coming to her when she got married. Parents and Friends of Lesbians and Gays (P-FLAG) uses the phrase *heterosexual privilege* to describe these perks, which include: employee benefit-plan coverage (health insurance, bereavement leave, pension plans), joint income-tax filing, Social Security survivors benefits, reduction of estate taxes, visitation rights, child-custody rights, tenancy rights, conservatorship, reduced auto and homeowners' insurance rates, community property, and even jurisprudence (if Bernice's hubby robs a Häagen-Dazs store, she can't be forced to testify against him). All this because Bernice married Don and not Donna.

But there is some good news—a sort of compromise status called *domestic partnership* that's being sanctioned by a number of cities, corporations, and universities. The recognition of domestic partnerships marks an official acknowledgment of nontraditional families, with the loosest interpretation of *nontraditional family* being "cohabitants who have a stable relationship and are financially interdependent." Depending on the specific situation, domestic partnership can qualify you for anything from taking over the lease on a rent-stabilized apartment to sharing in your significant other's dental insurance policy; in Ithaca, New York, for instance, you get cut rates at the city golf course. In other cases, domestic partnership is purely symbolic, and people sign up for political or emotional reasons.

Domestic partnership was unheard-of ten years ago. But with companies like Levi Strauss, MCA-Universal, and AT&T—as well as dozens of cities from Berkeley to Minneapolis to Cambridge—now offering domestic-partnership benefits, it's obvious that something is going on. In the words of Ruth Berman, a 59-year-old grandmother who registered in New York City with her companion of 18 years, Connie Kurtz, "We're taking another step to make a statement. We wish we still had greater rights as a couple, but this is a start."

STRUCK BY A THUNDERBOLT

We can cite Kinsey till the cows come home, but statistics just never get the point across the way stories do. Here are a few personal insights into the decision to get married.

👤👤 George and David knew each other a year and a half before getting married in the Church of Religious Science, with eighty guests in attendance. They've been married for two years.

I didn't know the moment we met, but almost from the time we met. . . . I knew that this is the man I want to grow old with and spend the rest of my life with, and all that corny stuff that you hear. I can't really explain it, but I knew it. —George

👤👤 Joe and Randy moved in together and exchanged wedding rings soon after they met. They had a union ceremony on the fifth anniversary of their first date, and have now been together for almost ten years.

If someone were to ask me what was the best day of my life, it would be the wedding day. Maybe it's because of the planning that goes into it. For three months you didn't think of anything else, so there's that anticipation. We had the white tuxes, we had the boutonnieres, and both of us just looked so great that day. The weather was perfect, the exotic flowers, the view of the coast. . . . It was the most perfect day. —Joe

👤👤 Jane and Peggy had dated for ten years and had lived together for four before they committed to committing.

Look, we figured, we're not getting any younger. We wanted to have some kids and settle down. Having a wedding finally made sense to us. —Peggy

👤👤 Both Victoria and Shirley had previously been married. Shirley proposed to Victoria after they had been dating for a few months. They had their wedding a year later, and have now been married for three years.

I'd had weddings before, but this was the wedding I'd always wanted. —Victoria

Just because it's not legal and it's easy to get out of doesn't mean that you should take this step lightly. If you want your wedding to mean anything to the other people in your life, it had better mean something to you first. Here are some of the less compelling reasons for a couple to get married:

SEVEN BAD REASONS TO GET MARRIED

♥ All of your friends say you bicker like an old married couple already.

♥ You need a new toaster oven.

♥ You think you look really great in a tuxedo and don't get enough chances to wear one.

♥ Since meeting last week, the two of you have not had a single disagreement.

♥ Both of you name *All About Eve* as your favorite movie of all time.

♥ She's the best two-step partner you've ever had.

♥ "Because I wanna."

The way I am, I knew when I met her that this was going to be forever. We went to pick out an engagement ring, and when I brought it home, I got down on one knee and said, "Victoria, I love you with all my heart. Will you be my bride?" —Shirley

👤👤 Eric and Josh met in college and lived together—off and on—for twelve years. They had a union ceremony two years ago.

There was a lot of water under our bridge, and we always felt that although we had a great thing going, what if something better came along? Maybe it's because we met so young, and we wanted to give each other time. After twelve years, the time was up, and we realized this was the relationship we both wanted. —Eric

There's been a common thread in the stories of all of the happily married lesbian and gay couples we've interviewed—a moment when each person looked at his or her mate and thought, "This is the one." For some couples, this moment came the first time they laid eyes on one another; other couples went through some rocky years before it hit them. Some couples made homes together for a decade before deciding to take the plunge; others moved in on the first date and never moved out. The amount of time doesn't really matter; if this is the person you're destined to spend the rest of your life with, you'll know it. But look, marriage isn't for everybody. As Mae West once said, "Marriage is a great institution, but I'm not ready for an institution yet."

SOMETHING OLD, SOMETHING REALLY NEW

Perhaps at this point you're a bit confused about terminology. *Webster's* says that a wedding is (among other things) "the act or an instance of harmonious blending." We think that's applicable. In this book, we go all the way with the idea of a *wedding*—including options such as something borrowed, something blue; best men losing the rings; bridesmaids enveloped in turquoise tulle; and guests fighting over the centerpiece. But we'll also give you a whole range of possibilities on the less traditional end of the scale.

Whichever way you ultimately decide to celebrate, we've found that calling the event a wedding makes some people a little uncomfortable or nervous. As a public service, we've compiled the following list of terms that other same-sex couples have used to describe the event that heretofore in history has been referred to as a wedding.

OTHER THINGS YOU CAN CALL THIS EVENT

♥ *Lifelong Commitment Vows*

♥ *Lifetime Commitment*

♥ *Celebration of Commitment*

♥ *Commitment Ceremony*

♥ *Permanent Partnership Ceremony*

♥ *Affirmation Ceremony*

♥ *Ceremony in Celebration of Our Lives Together*

♥ *Ceremony of Heart*

♥ *Life Partnership Ceremony*

♥ *Bonding Ceremony*

♥ *Union Ceremony*

♥ *Holy Union*

♥ *Blessing of the Relationship*

♥ *Blessing of Love*

♥ *Rite of Blessing*

♥ *Joining*

♥ *Tryst*

♥ *Handfasting*

♥ *Relationship Covenant*

♥ *Covenant of Love*

THE QUINTESSENTIAL WEDDING TOAST

At our wedding, Jane and I were fortunate enough to have in attendance a dear friend, Jay Wolpert, who is undeniably the world's finest toast-maker. He happens to be heterosexual, but he so completely understood the Big Picture—the essence of why we chose to get married—that I couldn't have articulated it any better than Jay did in our wedding toast.

—*Tess Ayers*

When we first found out that Tess and Jane were getting married, my first reaction was, very frankly, What for? To prove their love to each other? I mean, they've been together for eight or nine years; that would seem to me proof enough. To underscore their commitment? Okay, but this is the ninth decade of the twentieth century, and the sad truth is, marriage doesn't always mean commitment. Well then, I thought, it must be for the legal protection that marital status affords their relationship. Now, I'm no lawyer, but it seems to me that whatever legal protection their relationship enjoys at this hour today, it probably enjoyed at this hour yesterday.

So, what's it all about? What it's all about is Tess and Jane taking what's theirs. And what's theirs is the right to partake in a ritual that has been held by the straight world for its exclusive use for thousands of years, even though gay people have been around for as long as straight people. What it's about is Tess and Jane not going gently into a sexual ghetto, but instead insisting on the recognition of public ritualistic articulation of love being everyone's right. It's about exchanging rings that symbolize that love. Finally, it's about being willing to endure the awkwardness, the insensitivity, and the abuse that will almost certainly come from the wearing of those rings.

Now, I think that's kind of gutsy. Maybe even a little heroic. Because maybe there are two people in this room today who, because of this wedding, will say, "Let's do this too." And maybe then two people who, after witnessing that wedding, will get the confidence to do the same thing in their own right. And maybe pretty soon a shibboleth disintegrates, and maybe pretty soon a wall falls, and maybe pretty soon the happy day arrives when what used to take guts takes no guts at all.

You know, many years from now, when humankind bursts out of the jungle onto the clean, green veldt of tolerance and understanding, no one will remember, or perhaps ever have known, about the billions and billions of microseconds that came before wherein something occurred that just nudged the human parade one inch further through the thicket. And as long as we're here, I would submit to you that maybe this is one of those microseconds.

Not only do we thank you, Tess and Jane, for the happy times with which you have buoyed us; the insights with which you have enlightened us; the kindnesses with which you have sustained us; and the talent with which you have enriched us. We thank you also for the courage with which you inspire us. And if it is your fate never to have your parents take pride in that courage, be assured that one day your child will.

I looked up a word in the dictionary a couple of days ago, and as I suspected, what the word has come to mean is only its fifth meaning. And the number-one meaning is the one I had hoped it would be: "a woman noted for her courageous and daring acts."

So finally, here's the toast: To Tess and Jane. May they be forever what they are today: heroines together!

—JAY WOLPERT

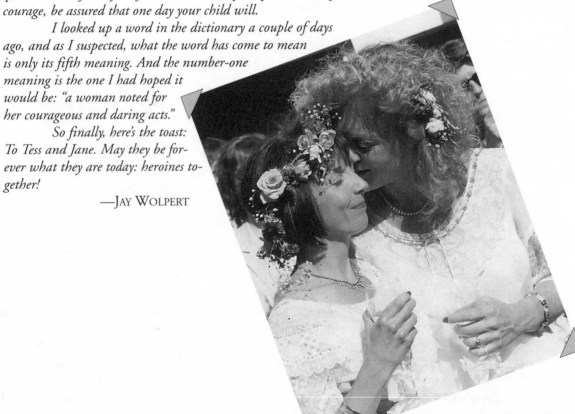

Photo: Lynn Houston

God knows this book is not intended to be Homo History 101. But if all of this gay and lesbian wedding stuff seems incredibly "now" to you, and you think it's just too too trendy, consider what your lesbian and gay ancestors have done throughout the ages.

A TIME LINE OF SAME-SEX COUPLINGS

▼ **SECOND CENTURY A.D.:** Iamblichus writes the novel *Babyloniaca,* which includes the characters of Berenice, the queen of Egypt, and the female lover she married, Mesopotamia. At the same time, Lucian writes *Dialogues of the Courtesans,* in which Leaena describes a woman of (where else?) Lesbos who is married to a woman from Corinth.

▼ **DURING THE ROMAN EMPIRE:** Male soldiers are often wedded to one another prior to battle.

▼ **BEFORE EUROPEANS ARRIVE IN THE NEW WORLD:** 133 North American tribes (including the Navajo, Mojave, Lakota, Eskimo, Yuma, Klamath, Crow, and Blackfoot) commonly accept alternative gender roles involving cross-gender or same-sex behavior, including same-sex marriages.

▼ **1368–1644:** A form of male marriage develops in China's Fujian province during the Ming dynasty. A younger man moves into the household of an older "adoptive brother," whose parents treat him as a son-in-law. Many such marriages last twenty years or more.

▼ **THE NINETEENTH CENTURY:** The exclusively female Golden Orchid Associations are common in the Guangzhou province of China. Within these groups, lesbian couples can marry. After exchanging ritual gifts, the couple hold a wedding feast; later they are allowed to adopt young girls.

▼ **1855:** Edwin Denig publishes a paper documenting a Crow "woman chief" who has taken four wives.

▼ **1863:** The Englishwoman Mary East, disappointed by the opposite sex, and an American woman who feels likewise agree to pass the rest of their days as husband and wife. Who should be the "husband" is determined by lot. They remain together for thirty-four years.

▼ **1878:** "Mrs. Nash," a laundress for Custer's seventh cavalry, dies. She has been married to a succession of soldier husbands, staying in the service even when her husbands are discharged. When some of the garrison ladies prepare the body for the wake, they discover that "Mrs. Nash" was a man.

▼ **The Late Nineteenth Century:** In New England, "Boston marriages" are common. Women choose other women as life partners, and together work toward a feminist vision of social justice.

▼ **1901:** The *New York Times* of January 19 reports that Murray Hall, a prominent Tammany politician, was a woman who masqueraded as a man for more than a quarter of a century. "Furthermore, Murray Hall is known to have been married twice, but the women to whom she stood before the world in the attitude of a husband kept her secret as guardedly as she did."

▼ **The 1920s:** In Harlem, black lesbians in butch/femme couples marry each other in large wedding ceremonies that include bridesmaids and attendants. Couples obtain marriage licenses by masculinizing a first name or having a gay male surrogate apply for the license. The licenses are placed on file with the New York City Marriage Bureau, and the marriages are often common knowledge among Harlem heterosexuals.

▼ **1930:** The autobiography of the pseudonymous "Mary Casal" is published in Chicago, presenting an extraordinarily frank sexual and affectional life history of a lesbian. Concerning her future wife, she writes, "We decided that a union such as ours was to be could be made as holy and complete as the most conventional marriages, if not more so. I suggested that we read the marriage ceremony together as a sort of benediction to our union."

▼ **1957:** The Daughters of Bilitis sponsors a public discussion entitled "Is a Homophile Marriage Possible?" The keynote speaker, a psychotherapist, answers yes: "Any marriage is possible between any two people if they want to grow up."

▼ **1960s:** "Covenant" services are conducted for some gay and lesbian couples by clergy involved in the Council on Religion and the Homosexual.

▼ **June 1963:** *One* magazine ("The Homosexual Viewpoint"), has a cover story entitled "Let's Push Homophile Marriage."

▼ **October 6, 1968:** The Reverend Troy Perry founds the Universal Fellowship of Metropolitan Community Churches (MCC), which welcomes gays and lesbians and recognizes the sanctity of a same-sex union. Twelve people attend the first meeting.

▼ **June 12, 1970:** In what is described by the *Advocate* as "the first marriage in the nation designed to legally bind two persons of the same sex," Neva Heckman and Judith Belew are married by the Reverend Troy Perry in Los Angeles. It also notes that the Reverend Mr. Perry "said he had no immediate candidates for a second wedding, but his lover, Steve Jordan, caught the bride's bouquet." The marriage is later ruled to be not legally binding.

▼ **1971:** Donna Burkett and Manonia Evans, two lesbians in Wisconsin, file a class-action suit against the Milwaukee county clerk for refusing to issue them a marriage license.

▼ **JANUARY 7, 1975:** Two gay men in Phoenix, Arizona, legally obtain a marriage license and are wed in a ceremony at the local Church of Christian Fellowship. A superior court judge, citing the Bible, later voids the marriage. Soon afterward the Arizona House of Representatives votes thirty-seven to three to pass an emergency measure specifically banning same-sex marriages.

▼ **MARCH 26, 1975:** After the local district attorney rules that there are no county laws preventing two people of the same sex from getting married, a county clerk in Boulder, Colorado, issues a marriage license to two men. Over the next month, she issues five more licenses to same-sex couples. "I don't profess to be knowledgeable about homosexuality or even understand it," says Clela Rorex, "but it's not my business why people get married. No minority should be discriminated against." In late April, the Colorado attorney general rules that gay and lesbian marriages are illegal and orders Ms. Rorex to stop issuing licenses to same-sex couples.

▼ **1976:** Two Chicago women, Nancy Davis and Toby Schneiter, are arrested for the fourth time for staging sit-ins at city hall, insisting upon their right to a marriage license. They spend a year in the state penitentiary for their final conviction.

▼ **OCTOBER 11, 1976:** Dr. Tom Waddell and Charles Deaton are the first gay couple to be featured in the "Couples" section of *People* magazine. The article's subhead reads, "We have the same problems as any other couple."

▼ **JUNE 30, 1984:** The Unitarian Church votes to recognize and approve ceremonies celebrating the union of gay and lesbian couples.

▼ **DECEMBER 5, 1984:** Berkeley becomes the first city in the United States to extend spousal benefits to gay city employees' live-in lovers. To qualify under the new program, applicants must fill out and submit an "Affidavit of Domestic Partnership."

▼ **1987:** The American Civil Liberties Union passes a resolution supporting the legal recognition of lesbian and gay marriages.

▼ **OCTOBER 10, 1987:** One thousand gay and lesbian couples exchange vows in a mass wedding held on the steps of the Internal Revenue Service building in Washington, D.C.

▼ **JUNE 22, 1989:** Professional bodybuilder Bob Paris marries fellow bodybuilder and model Rod Jackson in a highly publicized formal ceremony.

▼ **OCTOBER 1, 1989:** Denmark legalizes same-sex marriages.

▼ **MARCH 19, 1992:** Four lesbian and gay couples file applications for civil marriage at Westminster Registry Office in London—the first such attempt in Britain. Their requests are denied.

▼ **APRIL 24, 1993:** On the day before the second massive gay and lesbian march on Washington, D.C., "the wedding" takes place on the steps of the IRS building. More than 2,000 couples are united in the ceremony.

▼ **MAY 7, 1993:** In a decision concerning a lawsuit filed by three same-sex couples, the Hawaii supreme court declares that the state has to prove that prohibiting same-sex marriage does not violate the couples' constitutional rights.

▼ **JUNE 13, 1994:** The annual wedding cover of *The New Yorker* magazine features two men posed in front of a cake topped with two grooms.

▼ **JANUARY 2, 1995:** Hans Jonsson and Sven-Olav Jansson become Sweden's first gay couple to legally marry under that nation's new legislation.

▼ **FEBRUARY 5, 1995:** "A Commitment to Love," an event billed as "the World's Only Gay and Lesbian Wedding Fair" is held in Chicago. An estimated 1,000 people attend.

▼ **SEPTEMBER 1996:** In anticipation of Hawaii's decision to legalize same-gender marriage, the U.S. Congress passes and President Clinton signs the Defense of Marriage Act. This defines marriage as the union of a man and a woman and ensures that other states will not have to recognize same-sex marriages.

▼ **DECEMBER 1996:** A Hawaii circuit court rules that barring same-gender couples from receiving marriage licenses is unconstitutional sex discrimination.

▼ **APRIL 17, 1997:** The Hawaii House and Senate approve a plan to let voters decide on an amendment to ban same-sex marriages but give gay and lesbian couples some rights and benefits available to married couples.

▼ **JANUARY 1, 1998:** A registered-partner measure granting gay couples every right of matrimony except access to adoption and artificial insemination goes into effect in the Netherlands.

▼ **FEBRUARY 12, 1998:** First National Freedom to Marry Day. Lesbians, gay men, and straight people participate in events across the country calling for an end to discrimination in civil marriage.

▼ **MARCH 1998:** The Methodist Church puts the Rev. Jimmy Creech on trial, charging him with violating Methodist rules for having blessed the union of two women. The jury acquits him. Ninety-two Methodist ministers release a statement of support saying they will perform "rites of union with all couples, regardless of gender."

OTHERWISE ENGAGED

THE ENGAGEMENT

*T*his chapter is about the period immediately preceding and following that moment when one of you decides this wedding stuff is for you and you're ready to act on it. You know: the Engagement. Because for some, *engagement* is a silly word and conjures up images of bygone eras—cucumber sandwiches and white-glove debutante balls— we tried and tried to come up with an alternative term, to no avail. (Imagine, two gay people not being able to come up with an alternative.) So if you feel like it, go ahead, call it "the Engagement." Or, if you prefer, "Not the Engagement."

We can't give you any hard statistics to back this up, but we're pretty sure that most gay men and lesbians do not "save" themselves for the wedding night. Chances are that if you're gay and you decide to have a wedding, you're already living together. This is also a fairly common, almost expected practice in the straight world these days. Some couples even look upon moving in together as the beginning of the engagement, because it's when they're preparing for the ultimate commitment. And if you're gay and in a serious relationship, with no option of legal marriage, living together is what you do.

If you do live together, your lives have most likely already melded in some areas; you have friends in common, and you've probably met most of the people that your lover considers important. So maybe you sorta-kinda think of yourself as married already. You may have gone to other union ceremonies together; you may have made oblique references to marriage in the past; you may have actually said that if you were ever to get married, it would be to the person you're with. But now that you're seriously thinking about having a wedding, how do you get the ball rolling?

How about proposing?

TONY CURTIS: . . . Why would a guy want to marry a guy?

JACK LEMMON: . . . Security.

—FROM BILLY WILDER'S *SOME LIKE IT HOT*

A DECENT PROPOSAL

A proposal proclaims the end of dating, living in sin, or whatever you two are doing that will soon be replaced by "ever after." The proposal is the true beginning of the wedding. Think proposing is too corny? Too old-world? Too politically incorrect? What's next, asking a father for his daughter's hand? You're saying, hey, I'm gay, why do I have to imitate the straight world? If you don't want to, fine, don't. But the act of proposing, or the experience of being proposed to, is a wonderful occasion that need not be passed up. You don't want to look back on the moment you decided to get married and be unable to distinguish it from the moment you decided to get HBO. ("Oh, look, they're having an installation discount. All our friends have it and we've been thinking about it for a while, so let's get it over with and just do it.") No, no, this will never do.

It isn't mandatory to get down on one knee, although we know of some who have. The proposal is your own private opening ceremony, before the rest of the planet becomes involved with your union, so why not make it a Hallmark occasion? What's this all about if not making memories? David put a fake engagement ring in a jack-in-the-box, which he then presented to his lover, Brian; the clown popping out of the box was David's way of popping the question. Emily sent a dozen long-stemmed roses to Angel's office with a proposal inside. Mitchell rented a billboard saying, "Jim, Will You Marry Me?" Tina gave Cindy a roll of Lifesavers in which she had carefully inserted an engagement ring right next to the lime Lifesaver. Bob asked William to marry him by writing his proposal in the sand on the beach at Fire Island. We've known the question to be popped through a personal ad, and many have returned to the scene of their first date or the place they met in order to re-create the magic.

There's also the possibility of Spontaneous Agreement. This occurs mostly among couples who have been together a long time; maybe one day they're doing the dishes and it becomes simultaneously obvious that this is The One. Charlotte turns to Miranda and says, "Why don't we get married?" Miranda says, "I can't think of any reason not to. Is it my turn to wash or dry?" We find this occurrence kind of charming, but also suggest that if you find yourselves in such a situation, you might want to mark the occasion in a romantic way. Cook a special meal, shut off the phones, and spend the evening in. Go shopping together for engagement rings if you're going to wear them, or buy a commemorative object for your household that you've both been wanting. (How about that antique bed you've been eying, or a set of new sheets?) Steal away for the weekend. Go to a ball game and arrange to have congratulations flashed on the scoreboard. Just do whatever it is you most enjoy doing together.

It's also possible that when the question is finally posed, your loved one will say, "What, are you crazy?" or "Come back next year and ask me again." If this happens, don't despair, and don't give up! Fran told us that she tried to get Sandy to marry her for three years before Sandy finally agreed to say "I do." That was seven years ago, and they're still happily married.

At any rate, we're going to proceed on the assumption that however you've gotten there, the answer at this point is "Yes."

ALWAYS RING TWICE?

Judy, sweetheart, you're engaged? Congratulations! Best wishes! Oh, I know you'll be so happy together. I remember when your uncle and I got engaged. I felt so hopeful, so fresh. So she's a nice girl? Let's see the engagement ring! What?!? No ring? She didn't buy you a ring? You young lesbians are so modern. . . .

Heaven knows you don't need an engagement ring to enter into the (Not the) Engagement. Traditionally, in the straight world, a man proposes with engagement ring in hand, and when his beloved accepts, he immediately slips the ring onto her finger. However, an engagement ring doesn't say, "I owe you one wedding ring"; rather, it is symbolic of your intentions. If you've always wanted that rock on the fourth finger of your left hand, and you're both willing to spring for it, here's your chance. It's not uncommon to see two lesbians wearing matching diamond rings these days; in fact, engagement rings are becoming popular with gay men as well. It really doesn't matter what kind of a ring you wear, unless it's important to you that the general public is aware of your engagement.

If neither one of you plans on wearing an engagement ring but you're sentimental, you could get a beautiful ring box from a jeweler and put one or more of the following items inside: a pipe-cleaner ring; a little slip of paper with the words "Will you marry me?"; or a tiny print of your favorite photograph of the two of you. Present this to your partner when you propose, and we can practically guarantee you a dramatic response.

In 1993, Crown Prince Naruhito of Japan formalized his engagement to former diplomat Masako Owada by sending gifts of fish, silk, and sake to the family of the future empress. You might choose to give another type of present to mark the occasion. How about turning your little black book over to your loved one, or framing a book of matches from the restaurant where you had your first date? You might exchange identical watches or give a family heirloom, a romantic piece of art (either bought or made), or an engagement puppy or kitten (for confirmed animal lovers only, please)—or, if appropriate, something phenomenally expensive, such as a Ferrari.

Marriage is like pantyhose. It all depends on what you put into it.

—PHYLLIS SCHLAFLY

SHOUTING IT FROM THE ROOFTOPS

Some couples prefer to wait a bit before telling anyone that they are betrothed to one another; it gives them a chance to get used to the idea and to prepare the proper response to questions such as "How's your girlfriend?" (The proper response being, of course, "She's no longer my girlfriend, she's now my fiancée.") Other couples fling their windows open and scream to the world, "Hallelujah! We're engaged!" For some couples, who they tell about their decision and how they tell those people may be the most anxiety-ridden phase of this whole process. But it doesn't have to be that way. This should be a time of tremendous celebration and joy. Let's see how you can help that along.

Historically, the first people to learn of an engagement are the couple's parents. However, because many gays and lesbians make their friends into their true extended family, and those friends will probably be jazzed to hear your news, you may elect to tell members of your chosen family first. Odds are they'll give you the kind of thrilled reaction you may not get from your biological family. This can build a wave of confidence and good feelings, and give you the support you need to make the announcement to your folks.

You may discover that after telling just a few of your closest friends, you've created a buzz and a telephone tree is passing the good news for you. Or you might decide to have a dinner party, each of you inviting your closest friends, and between courses, instead of serving sorbet, tell them of your momentous decision.

In terms of public announcements, well, that's really up to you. While there are some mainstream newspapers that now publish gay wedding announcements after the ceremony has taken place (see chapter 22, "The Aftermath"), we've not yet seen a gay engagement announcement. If "firsts" intrigue you, be our guest; give it a try. Our guess is that many newspapers will begin to come around on this one. And if you really want to spread the word, you can always take out an ad in your local gay newspaper or run a personal ad in one of the national gay magazines.

Two interesting footnotes here—footnotes you should take with the proverbial grain of salt. The American Gemological Institute recommends that a man spend two to three months' salary on an engagement ring. And according to *Bride's* magazine, the average engagement ring today costs $2,200.

ALL IN THE FAMILY

With a gay wedding, if, when, and how you tell your parents of the big step depends of course on how good your relationship is with them. And their reaction to your news will on some level depend on how accepting they are of you, of your being gay, and of your significant other. So how have other gay couples fared in this area? May we present to you three scenarios:

❶ When David and Phil decided to get married, David called his mother and said, "Mom, wish me *mazel tov.* I'm getting married." His mother replied, "No, *you* wish *me mazel tov.* I'm the mother of the groom!"

❷ When Susan and Sharon decided to get married, Susan called her mother and said, "Ma, give me your blessing. I'm getting married!" Her mother replied, "You mean you and Sharon? That's nice. But maybe we'd better not tell your father just yet."

❸ When Michael and Allan decided to get married, Michael called his mother and said, "Mother, congratulate me. I'm getting married!" His mother replied, "Thank God, you finally found the right girl."

Parents are supposed to be happy when their child decides to get married because it means he or she has found someone to love and to share life with. But it doesn't always happen like that; remember the Capulets and Montagues? (And their kids were straight!) If your parents have had problems in accepting your gayness or your relationship, this announcement may momentarily make the situation all the worse. But it may also allow them to finally come to terms with the fact that this is not a phase you're going through. And you should realize that this is the point at which they might have to do some "coming out" themselves, to their friends and business associates. So try to be patient.

In a 1992 issue of the Washington *Blade,* Seema Weinberg wrote about her reaction to her gay son's impending wedding:

> *I shared the up-and-coming occasion with only a few of my friends who know my son is gay. Working in a very homophobic office, I could not openly indulge in the normal luxury of imparting my news. Ironically, at the same time one of my co-workers was in the throes of preparations for her daughter's wedding. Every day we were privy to blow-by-blow descriptions of the proceedings, mingled with her effervescent enthusiasm. I went through terrible feelings of guilt, living with my "secret."*

In the long run, having a wedding ceremony and getting married can help demystify your relationship in your parents' minds and make you more like a "regular couple." So give them some time and maybe they'll end up thinking as Ms. Weinberg eventually did: "When I now meet new people and we exchange social credentials, I proudly answer the inevitable question 'Are your sons married?' with no hesitation. "Yes, one is a straight marriage and one is a gay marriage."

When your relationship with your folks is a 10 and they live nearby, the ideal situation is to tell them of your new status in person, together. If they live at a distance, a phone call to share the good news is just fine. On the other hand, if you anticipate a lukewarm or negative reaction, you may be better off informing them privately, and alone. Or if you feel you can express yourself more clearly in writing, you might consider sending them a letter, which has the added benefit of giving parents time to process the news at their own pace.

If you're not out to your parents, you have two options. First, you can use this situation as the foundation for a whole new arena of honesty with them. For example, if you've been living with the same "roommate" for years, and you know that your parents know there's something more there but they don't really want to hear about it, this may be the time to face the music by telling them about your romantic involvement and your decision to "settle down." Or, second, you can choose not to tell them anything at all about your wedding. When there's not much of a relationship between parents and children, this may be the best for all concerned. The one situation you should avoid at all costs is not telling your parents anything about your commitment, but continuing to bring your spouse to family functions and pretending that he or she is something other than your spouse. This can only lead to lots of resentment and tension in your marriage.

This will be the point in time when you can begin to gauge what kind of financial and emotional input your parents will have in your wedding. If you're among the very fortunate, one or both sets of parents may offer to help pay for the wedding. (That's right, both. Traditionally, the bride's parents pay for the wedding. Because you're gay and there's no precedent, you have twice as many potential "investors.") Clearly, this is extremely generous and signifies an acceptance on some level. Good for you! It's also possible that even if they don't do so initially, as the preparations progress and excitement builds, they'll offer to pick up part of the tab or give you a check to start you out on your new life together.

THE BAD NEWS

**Your parents probably won't become as fully involved
in your wedding
as they did in your sister's wedding.**

THE GOOD NEWS

**You don't have to deal with a mother who is trying to relive
her own wedding.**

And if your parents have never met your future mate, you really should try to arrange it before the ceremony. The more you make this like the real world, the more legitimately everyone will treat your relationship. (Well, nine times out of ten, anyway.)

If both sets of parents have been informed and they're okay with it, they might want to meet each other. This is kind of a traditional thing: the groom's mother or father calls the bride's mother or father to welcome the new daughter into the family. Needless to say, that rule doesn't apply here, so anyone can make the first call. If you can't picture the two families in the same room, or the mere thought of it makes your skin crawl, you might give it a shot anyway. You may be surprised; perhaps your mothers will start going to P-FLAG meetings together or even plan joint family dinners.

NOT KIDDING AROUND

Now, what about children? If either of you has children who aren't aware that you're gay, you'll have to deal with that issue first, and that's a whole other book. If you have children who are involved in your life and accepting of your relationship, you'll want to sit down with them and discuss your plans. (If the children are yours from a previous relationship, you'll probably want to do this independently of your intended spouse—unless you are coparenting.) Talk about what you feel marriage is, and why you're getting married. Talk about the child's place in the new family, and what changes, if any, this might represent. Talk about your spouse's integration into the family and what this might mean. Even though your spouse will not be a legal stepparent, your marriage ceremony recognizes the possibility that he or she will become, or already is, an important figure in the child's life. If the situation is right, someday this person may be considered a second mommy or a second daddy.

It's common to have children of all ages involved in a union ceremony. With children, as with parents, a wedding has the potential to be a crossroads of acceptance. We know of a case where a son gave his father away and one where a daughter toasted her birth mother and her new stepmother. And small folk are always perfect as, and thrilled to be, ring bearers and flower children.

Every time I mentioned our wedding plans, my mother's mouth would become like a zipper and she'd immediately change the subject. When I finally got her to talk about it, she declared that she found the event to be "theatrical," that there was no reason for us to get married because it wasn't legal. To her, we were flaunting ourselves. She wanted us to be closeted, and marriage is just the opposite of that.

—JULIE

The first time I met James's parents we were all uncomfortable and uneasy. We had them over for brunch, and nobody said too much at first. I tried to put them at ease and let them know that my wife and I wanted to recognize our son's partnership as we would any marriage. The more time we spent together, the less awkward it was; we stopped talking only about our sons and began to get to know each other. I let them know that the only thing I dislike about their son is the fact that he roots for the Phillies. The last time James's parents came to town, they stayed with us. What more do you want from in-laws?

—STAN

My oldest daughter from a previous marriage gave me a lot of trouble when she was in her teens. She hated the fact that I was a lesbian, and she'd say things like "I can't stand you, Mom." Over the years, we've kept working on it. When I called her to tell her about the wedding, she honored me with the best wedding gift I ever could have had: she flew three thousand miles to be my matron of honor at our ceremony.

—VICTORIA

LET THE GAMES BEGIN

Somewhere along the way here you may decide to throw yourselves an engagement party, or perhaps some of your friends might host one for you. Custom has dictated that the bride's family give the first party; everything from teas and brunches to barbecues and bowling parties follow, all in honor of the bride and groom. Although it may seem otherwise, engagement parties aren't about receiving gifts; in fact, according to the etiquette gurus gifts are not necessary at these occasions. The parties are about friends and families widening their circles to include the newest members.

Even though these frilly affairs may strike you as being a little creaky, don't be too hasty in your judgment, because lots of good can come from them. Everyone likes to be supported and honored, and to feel reinforced that they've made the right decision. An engagement party can be a good way to break the ice, and can even be a sort of trial run for the big day. The more comfortable people are at this party, the better time they'll have at the wedding celebration itself. It can be the first meeting of the two families if you so choose. It's the perfect opportunity for different groups of people to mix it up a little; for example, your father may find himself in a fascinating conversation about his German shepherd with your dog trainer, Lora, and her lover, Toria. Your group therapist, who's become a good friend, may finally get to meet your brother, and with any luck your brother will start sessions next week. The girls from the office can meet the girls from the bar.

Since the main purpose of this engagement party is to welcome the newest family members, one of the highlights is the toast, or toasts. One of the best toasts we've heard about was given by a woman's father, who put a twist on a traditional salute when he said, "I'm not losing a daughter, I'm gaining a daughter."

GETTING TO KNOW YOU (EVEN BETTER)

The window of time between your engagement and your actual wedding provides you with the opportunity to prepare yourself for married life. The average engagement in the United States lasts for 11.6 months, and it's possible that those months can be filled to the max. Between being feted at numerous parties and interviewing potential best men and women, you should give some thought to redefining your relationship and considering what it's about to become.

If you choose to have a ceremony that is performed by a member of the clergy (we'll talk a lot more about that in chapter 9), he or she will almost certainly insist on your coming in for some kind of premarital discussions or counseling sessions. This may surprise you; it may even annoy you. But it's the highest compliment a gay couple about to be married can be paid, because you're being treated just like any other couple. If you don't have a clergyperson officiate, give some thought to the counseling process anyway. We're not saying it's necessary to get help if you're particularly skilled at facilitating this sort of dialogue. But in the same way that diets always have that little disclaimer that says, "Before you start any diet or exercise program, consult your physician," it may be in your eventual best interest to consult some sort of experienced professional before you take the marriage plunge.

Allow us to digress for a moment here and speak to the idea of second thoughts. We can almost guarantee you that you will have some. Little habits and idiosyncrasies of your loved one that you used to find endearing will suddenly begin to gnaw at your very core. (Funny, you never before noticed how loudly he chews in the movie theater and how quickly he polishes off that bucket of popcorn.) As you get closer to each other and reveal new layers of yourselves, you may hear more than you ever wanted to ("Did I ever mention that I was once married and I have a daughter who's older than you are?"). You may suddenly realize, "Oh, my god, this is the only person I'll ever sleep with for the rest of my life!" and everyone from the stock boy to the exterminator will begin to look really good to you.

What can we say except chill out and put it in perspective. This is absolutely normal. It happens to straight people all the time, and as a wise friend of ours once said, "Just because we're gay doesn't mean that we don't act like heterosexuals sometimes." All of these feelings of insecurity and doubt can and should be discussed during the engagement period, which is why counseling can be helpful. Premarital therapy allows you to place your doubts on the table, and put them into perspective by talking about them. It also gives you a common vocabulary for dealing with all that lies ahead.

In any case, the following are some questions that might be posed to you during counseling.

You might know exactly how you feel about some; others may be totally foreign to you; and still others may strike you as being just plain stupid. Note that, unlike the results of a compatibility quiz in *Cosmopolitan,* there are no right or wrong answers here; no points are tallied, and no prizes will be awarded.

THIS IS NOT A TEST

1) How possessive are you about your personal things? Do you consider things to be "mine" and "his," or are they "ours"? Does this include things you've bought together since you've shared a household?

2) How important is your career? Your partner's career? What would happen if one of you were to get a job offer in a city a thousand miles away? Does either career require a great deal of travel?

3) What body of water does your lover remind you of?

4) What are some things you've planned together for the future? Do you want to live in another state or in a foreign country? Do you want to create a dream house?

5) Do you each have your own groups of friends that don't overlap?

6) How close do your families live to you, and does it matter?

7) Do you share chores? Does one cook and the other clean up afterward? What are the consequences if you don't play by the rules?

8) What are your household habits? Is one of you incredibly neat and the other one sloppy, and have you come to terms with that?

9) Do you have the same taste in furnishings? If there is a disagreement over which lamp to buy, how is it settled?

10) Will your financial arrangements change after you get married?

11) How do you feel about remaining friends with ex-lovers?

12) Is either of you interested in raising kids? If you plan on being parents, have you discussed the arrangements and possible legal complications?

13) Do you feel that you've maintained a sense of self? What about your sense of being part of a couple?

14) Do you have basically the same ethics concerning large issues? Do you lean the same direction politically? Religiously or spiritually?

15) Do you hate nose rings?

16) Do you have separate interests? Is either of you threatened or insulted by the idea of time spent away from each other?

17) What's the deal-breaker in this relationship?

18) How would you dissolve this relationship if you decided it wasn't working?

The point is this: the more you think of yourselves as a couple or single-unit team, the more it helps strengthen your bonds to each other and to the world at large. We like to think of this process as "moving in together emotionally."

WAYS TO FORMALIZE THE RELATIONSHIP

Once you're feeling secure about your decision, there are a variety of things you can do to formalize your relationship. You may have taken some of these steps already, while you may not be ready, willing, or able to consider others. That's okay; just make sure the two of you discuss the formalities so there will be no misunderstandings.

☛ Draw up and have notarized a *relationship agreement.* This doesn't have to do with property; it has to do with personality—sort of a contract of what each of you expects from the other person emotionally.

☛ Open a joint savings account, checking account, or charge account.

☛ Have both names on all club memberships and subscriptions. Don't forget the automobile club, health clubs, and frequent-flier clubs.

☛ Choose a doctor for both of you, who in effect becomes your family physician.

☛ List your partner's name on medical records as your husband or as your wife. Do the same with credit companies.

☛ Have address labels or a rubber stamp made up with both your names on it.

☛ Make donations in both your names.

☛ Include each other in your wills.

☛ If your city or employer doesn't offer same-sex benefits or recognition of any kind, you can always register with the city of West Hollywood as domestic partners. This is a purely symbolic gesture, of course, but at least you're being acknowledged by an official body. (See the Resource Directory at the end of this book for the address to write to for an application.)

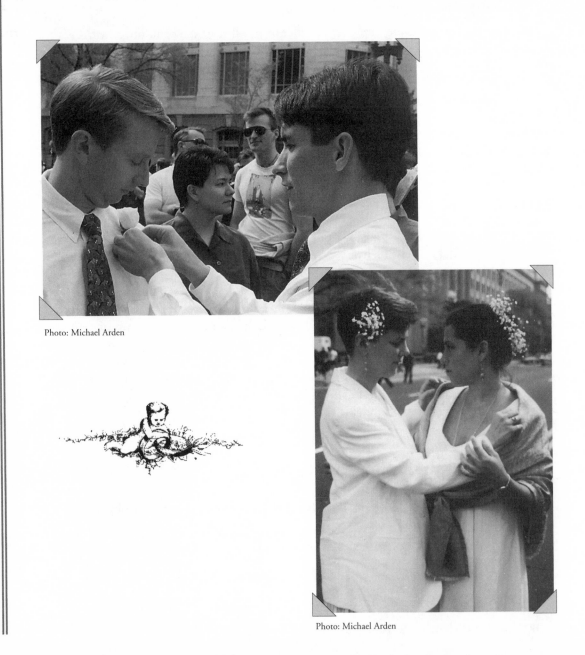

Photo: Michael Arden

Photo: Michael Arden

▼ # IT'S A STRAIGHT STRAIGHT STRAIGHT STRAIGHT WORLD

DEALING WITH THE OTHER 90 PERCENT

This chapter is different from most of those that follow. It's not exactly a how-to, but a what-to-do. It's not about how to register for china or choose a floral arrangement, or what to serve the guests for hors d'oeuvres. It's about being gay in a straight world. And what, if anything, you want to tell that world.

When you're a same-sex couple about to get married, you are, as someone we know once said, "coming out over and over again." Not only are you telling your family and coworkers; you're spreading the word to everyone—from friends and florists to caterers and clergy. And often this continuous coming out gets pretty frustrating: "When Cynthia and I were getting married, sometimes I wished I had made a recorded message that said, 'Hi, my name is Val. Yes, I'm a lesbian, and yes, I'm getting married to Cynthia. If you have any questions, comments, or suggestions, please leave them at the sound of the beep, and I'll get back to you. Thank you.'"

We call it Coming Out and Out and Out and Out. Because even though you might be having an all-gay ceremony (that is, one at which everyone, from your guests to the wait staff, is gay), you are—just by getting married in a nonlegal ceremony—making a political statement. No, you're not tying yourself to a building—just tying the knot. But in a sense, you're a pioneer. And that can be a pretty public thing, whether it's registering at the local department store or sending your engagement photo to the local paper.

So this chapter is about making decisions and declarations. And do you really want to deal with the straight world anyway? Our preference is Yes: walk it like you talk it. If you're getting married, you're entitled—it's your right as a dewy-eyed fiancée—to take advantage of the smorgasbord of wedding possibilities out there, from both the straight world and the gay

When Jane and I went to buy our wedding dresses, the woman who owned the dress shop appeared to be a bit confused and asked which one of us was getting married. "We both are," I replied. Then she asked who was getting married first. "It's the same date." Assuming it was to be a double wedding, she proceeded to help Jane try on a dress. In an effort to pick out the proper color for the dress sash, the owner asked her what color tuxedo her groom would be wearing. Jane looked at me, I looked at Jane, and we both looked at the owner. Jane took a beat, responded, "How liberal are you?" and went on to explain that she and I were, in fact, marrying each other.

—TESS

world, some from column A and some from column B. Our motto: Come Out, Come Out, Wherever You Are, However You Can. But this may not be right for you. Before you jump right in and rent that billboard in Times Square, read the following tales about the very different experiences of three same-sex couples.

Case History 1: Ruth and Jill

At first we thought, "Well, we're gay. We have sort of an *obligation* to patronize the gay community"—you know, politically correct and all that. Jill had this florist she always used to go to for work things—Mr. Jacobs—and we wanted to use Mr. Jacobs, but he isn't gay. (Right. We probably found the one florist who isn't.) And we thought it would be a whole thing to get into. But then we thought about it some more and decided, well, why not? I mean, he's part of our world; he should be part of our wedding. So Jill—who really has the relationship with him— talked to him about it, solo, just the two of them, and he couldn't have been lovelier. He was so touched that we had thought of him. And then we thought, "Well, why stop there?" And we ended up choosing all the businesses—the caterers, the stationers, the whole bit—based on people we liked who gave us the best value for our money. And each time we did it—telling people about us—it got easier and easier.

Case History 2: George and David

When we went to the store's bridal registry, it was clear that the woman behind the counter was uncomfortable. She didn't bat an eye, but we knew that she probably had never done this before. She could have taken care of us and just shrugged us off a bit—but we know what it feels like to be an outsider. So David really turned on the charm, and we made her feel comfortable by talking to her like she was one of our friends. And she was terrific. Our friends had more fun going into the store and pulling up our names on that computer screen.

Case History 3: Lisa and Kim

We had booked a private party room at a local restaurant for a prewedding shower; it was Sunday brunch. We arrived early with a few friends to get things in order, and, okay, I'll be the first to admit it: some of them look a little butch. As the waitress went to show us to our room, the owner pulled us aside and told us that there must be some mistake and we didn't have a reservation. He looked us right in the eye and lied. I asked him to check again and then I asked to speak to Nicole, who had taken the reservation from us. He told me that it was her day off. Meanwhile the restaurant became more and more crowded. Kim said that we should just go home. He said: "This is a family restaurant, and it would be better if you just left." I was really hurt and Kim was really angry, but in the end we were just happy that we didn't spend any money there. We waited out front, collected everybody, went back to our house, and put a little party together there. Maybe we should have cleared it all ahead of time.

Of course, telling everyone in the world is not a prerequisite for getting married. Some couples feel that it's nobody else's business. "Look," said Tony, "it was my wedding—well, mine and Randy's. And we didn't want anything to spoil it; we didn't want our special day tarnished by one bit of negativity. Which meant we were going to deal only with gay merchants. Oh, and not deal with Randy's mother."

Like Tony, many couples feel that the fact that they're gay and having a ceremony does not require them to come out to people. Plus, there are many people who, because of careers, living situations, or just personal preference, choose not to tell the outside world they're having a same-sex wedding. And *that's okay.* We think anything's okay, as long as it's what *you* want to do.

DEALING WITH THE STRAIGHT WORLD

If you do choose to tell people about your wedding, think about your *attitude.* How you deal with the outside world is a clear reflection of how you feel about who you are. So if you're going to tell the world, have a positive attitude, not a defensive one. If you're expecting the man from Abbey Rents to reject you, perhaps he'll get caught up in your emotions or vibes rather than your message—and you'll have created a self-fulfilling prophecy of rejection.

When dealing with the straight world, though, remember that same-sex coupling still pushes a lot of buttons for many people. If you encounter actual head-on prejudice, know in advance that it probably has nothing to do with you directly, but is the result of a million preconceived ideas mixed with ignorance.

On the other hand, don't be heterophobic; don't assume that just because someone is straight, he or she is going to be turned off by your ceremony. Nancy and Michele got married in the conservative, industrial New England town where Nancy grew up and where they now live. Nancy told us: "We decided that we wouldn't be reverse presumptuous about the local

A LITTLE ADVICE

Part of the fun of getting married is telling people, but you might not always get the reaction you're hoping for. Because of this, we suggest that, together, the two of you come up with a game plan to figure out—in advance—whom you are and aren't going to tell, how you're going to tell them, and what kinds of reactions you feel might be acceptable from *you* if you get any attitude. Be prepared for questions, and make sure you have some answers. For example, if you're coming out to your coworkers for the first time—*and* you explain that you have a lover, *and* you tell them that you're planning a wedding, *and* you invite them to attend—of course you should expect them to throw a few questions your way. (And not just straight friends; we've found that nonmarrying gays are also curious about our choices and the reasons for them.)

townspeople's possible prejudices. We wanted to support local businesses, and that's what we did. We went to the local photo lab with all of our slides; some of them were of us kissing. He didn't say a word. I think he was just thrilled to get the business."

If you do decide to open up your commitment ceremony to the straight world, know that you're acting as ambassadors for same-sex couples. It's very possible that whoever you're talking with has never met an engaged lesbian or gay man. Some people, dare we say, have never knowingly spoken with a homosexual. This isn't to put a burden on you (no, you don't represent every gay and lesbian in the world; you are not Everyqueer), but to make you aware that with each transaction, you could be opening a door for other couples. And it's your chance to shatter right-wing stereotypes. As we said, no pressure.

The good news is that in many ways you are expected to behave just as any run-of-the-mill heterosexual couple would. You'd better believe that the wedding industry isn't made up of a bunch of starry-eyed merchants whose only goal is to help lovers fulfill their dreams. They're in the business of business: to make money—your money, your gay money. Remember, you're plunking down your cash for goods and services; no one is doing you a favor because you're gay. So be prepared with the facts, and approach each of the vendors you deal with in a professional manner.

Now, what if you run up against some of those less open-minded individuals or businesses, and actually experience discrimination? We won't lie to you: it does happen. Maybe you tell the baker you want two men on the top of the cake, and you're suddenly shown the door. Perhaps the hotel has plenty of available rooms for the date you ask about—until you tell them it's for a same-sex wedding; then, oh gosh, they're now all booked up for that date. Or maybe someone takes your money but gives you inferior service. What do you do?

First of all, be absolutely certain that you're not being paranoid. Maybe they're not discriminating against you for being gay; there are a wealth of reasons why people get bad service, you know. But let's say that you are sure. Now what? Well, of course you can confront the person, but remember what it is you want to get out of this situation. If a hotel doesn't want you there, do you really want to try to talk them into it? It's your call.

You may have legal recourse—but it's a *very* big *may.* According to Washington, D.C., attorney Craig Dean, "Unless your locality, county, or state has a human rights act on the books that specifically prohibits discrimination based on sexual orientation, you don't have a case. Unfortunately, not that many places are covered."

GOING GAY ALL THE WAY

We decided to go all-gay because we didn't want any flak from anyone. So we only used gay merchants. And they were all so supportive. There were gay men and lesbians behind the counter saying how wonderful it is, and we got great feedback from them. We really felt like we were part of this great, loving community.   —MARY

Some couples feel that it's both politically correct and socially responsible to put their money into gay-owned businesses. Okay, but how do you find gay businesses? A good place to start is the gay yellow pages, a.k.a. the Community Yellow Pages—local non-telephone-company-issued phone books that list businesses that cater to a gay clientele. There is also the National Gayellow Pages, which gives numbers of services in areas ranging from Honolulu, Hawaii, to Dover, Delaware. Another possibility is to look through local gay periodicals (pay special attention to the classifieds) as well as night-life handouts. Call or write the gay and lesbian center nearest to where you live. Even if they're in a city a hundred miles away, they should be able to point you in the right direction. And, of course, don't forget word of mouth; ask around, because you never know what you might find.

 Consumer Alert

Although there are good reasons to support gay-owned businesses, let the buyer beware.

▼ The fact that a business is advertised in a gay publication or telephone book doesn't mean it's gay-owned or -operated. Some companies are merely "gay-friendly," which

OPTIONS, OPTIONS, OPTIONS

THE CATERER

Multiple choice:

❶ You can use a gay caterer.

❷ You can use a straight caterer and tell her or him it's for a gay wedding.

❸ You can use the caterer of your choice without giving a second thought to sexual preference.

---

means they welcome and acknowledge gay clients and really don't feel that sexual orientation is an issue. Other companies advertise in gay periodicals because it makes good business sense to cash in on gay and lesbian buying power.

▼ A business that is gay-owned or -operated won't necessarily give you more attention or offer a better price.

▼ As a consumer, you should always check out the quality of the service or the product. Again, the fact that a business advertises in gay publications doesn't necessarily mean it's good.

AMAZING TRUE STORIES

To inspire you, we herewith present some positive stories from the Experts, the Pioneers, the people who've actually done it: the gay and lesbian marrieds who went through the wars, fought in the trenches, and have these words of wisdom to impart.

I said to the printer, "Look, I need a good price, and I want you to know that this is an unorthodox alternate-lifestyle wedding. Will you handle something like that?" He said, "Why wouldn't I handle something like that?" I said, "Do you know what I'm talking about?" He said, "Yeah, you're gay and you're getting married. So what?"

—ROB

We went to an upscale mall to purchase the rings, and I wasn't sure if I would be comfortable there. What we found was that they were very supportive. The woman who ended up waiting on us was getting married the same exact day. She was excited for us and we were excited for her, so it ended up a very positive experience.

—SUSAN

We hired a restaurant we liked to handle the food, and they brought in a staff of six. We just said it was a wedding. I think I was afraid of running into discrimination. I really wanted this particular restaurant to cater it, and I guess I didn't feel that they needed to know.

When they got there, no one acted surprised, but I'm sure they were. All the waitresses were so professional and nice; I mean, at one point I was up there serving the cake and one of them came over to me and said, "Oh no. You just go on and have a good time. This is your special night."

—Jeff

My boss at work is one of my best friends, and she's gay. She told me that she'd really love to bring her girlfriend to the wedding. But she's not really out to the other people we work with, so I decided out of courtesy to her that I wouldn't invite anyone else from work even though I probably would have if it hadn't been for that circumstance. It was important to me that it be a special day for her too.

—Joe

We were shopping around for wedding locations and had to wait while a man in charge of a chapel ran through his spiel on the telephone with someone else, describing the size of the rooms and the sanctuary and checking dates. He finally turned to us and said, "So, who's the bride? Or is it a double wedding?" Then we explained that we were marrying each other. He took a moment to adjust and then was actually kind of entranced with the idea and showed us around with renewed enthusiasm. Before we left, he told us that he had once rented the chapel for a cross-dresser wedding but that no one there was gay.

—Beth and Patty

There was a country club where I had wanted my wedding ever since I can remember, but through the years I guess I figured it would never happen. Then Brit said, "Let's just call and see how they react." So when she called and made an appointment she said that there would be a lot of gay people in the wedding party. The person said that it wouldn't be a problem. But I'm thinking, "Sure, we told them we've got some gay friends, but that's not the same as two brides." So we called them back and told them that it was going to be a lesbian wedding, and was that a problem? They were fine with it. It just goes to show you, you just might get what you ask for.

—Pam

THE OTHER 90 PERCENT

Brian and I had a philosophy: if you were to put all the bigots behind a one-way mirror and they could see how Brian and I lived, they could not mistake what we had as anything less than a divine, inspired, special love that most people would compliment. We never hesitated to make an appearance at a place where, at the back of our minds, maybe we thought we weren't really wanted. We expected tolerance—maybe not acceptance, but tolerance.

—David

Jane made a cake top for us that had the two of us wearing wedding gowns and holding hands, with our two cats sitting on either side. We thought we'd put it on when we brought the cake home. But the bakery owner, who no doubt assumed that I was ordering a cake for myself and my groom, advised me to bring the top in so that they could decorate around it. When I brought the top in, I had it in a box. The owner was sitting having coffee with two older women, and told me to take it out so she could see it. I took a deep breath, removed it from the box, and set it on the table. The three of them examined it for what seemed like hours. Then one of the older women asked, "What kinds of cats are those?"

—TESS

Photo: Lynn Houston

▼

PART II

WEDDING LOGISTICS

AND AWAY WE GO!

TAKING ACTION

*C*ongratulations! You're getting married. Hey, that's great. You're flush with excitement, you have sweaty palms, your heart goes pitter-pat when your fiancé/fiancée walks into the room. Charming. Are you so much in love that the rest of the world just disappears? Are your penny loafers floating on air? Are you spending all your free time practicing your new hyphenated signature? Uh-oh . . .

Earth to reader!
Earth to reader!

It's time to snap out of it and get this show on the road. Or maybe you want to take a few hours this afternoon and rent *The Bride of Frankenstein* just to get in the mood? Okay, go ahead. But as soon as the end credits roll, you've got some mondo decisions to make.

 Communication Alert

The whole procedure of wedding planning can run the couple through a maze of overbearing florists, insistent relatives, and understaffed caterers, all with their own agendas. Everybody knows what's right for your wedding. You may find out how your future mother-in-law really feels about you taking her baby away from her. And you may discover yourselves bickering over whether or not to give out those Jordan almonds in little net bags tied with customized ribbons reading "Jonathan and Max, June 4, 1995." Emotions run high and everyone tends to get a bit crazy.

How to avoid Wedding Hell? Work hard to keep the lines of communication open. If you're not a very verbal person, this may be the one time in your life to make the effort to be more vocal. Dip into those old standbys—negotiation and compromise. Know that the bottom line is to decide what's in the best interest of both of you and that (sorry to break this to you) you can't have your own way all the time.

Try, whenever possible, to put your partner first; don't let your altar ego get in the way. If you have your heart set on saying your vows on a romantic cruise ship but your partner turns green just looking at a Jacuzzi, look for a more neutral setting. You're planning the celebration of your togetherness; you're a team, so act like one.

Cross our hearts, this is not a sexist remark: this whole thing may come easier to you if you're a lesbian couple than if you're two men. Let's face it, a girl is often more encouraged to look forward to her wedding day than a boy is; in fact, some females still train for it like the Olympics. Some girls dress like brides for Halloween, buy Bridal Barbie, and grow up to have ridiculous wedding expectations. Yes, even lesbians. Gay men, on the other hand, have suffered wedding deprivation on two levels: (1) as homosexuals, perhaps never contemplating the notion for themselves; and (2) as grooms, traditionally treated as little more than accessories at their own weddings. To this sexist, bigoted, homophobic, and narrow-minded view of coupling, we say, "Feh!" We know for a fact that men have planned weddings that are every bit as magical as those of their female counterparts. (Sometimes they border on spectacular.) Just because you didn't grow up reading *Bride's* magazine doesn't mean that you're not cut out for this. And that includes you gals.

So, where to begin?

Start the process by deciding what is really important to each of you. Don't be concerned yet with the practical; in fact, here we encourage you to let your imagination run wild. Pretend you're in a wedding movie, starring yourself. Are you wearing lace or are you wearing leather? Do you walk down an aisle? Whom do you kiss as they pass through the receiving line? Are you in a château in Paris or in your own living room? What are you eating? Do you hear music? Is it baroque or the Boss?

Do you make your exit in a taxi or a horse-drawn carriage? At this point, the possibilities are endless, so make mental notes about your fantasies. And don't cheat yourself, because in your fantasies, all of your dreams can come true.

Okay, let's say each of you has run your own movie through your head. Now it's time for a little editing; you need to splice together the two films and see if you're both on the same wedding wavelength. By homing in on the highlights of what each of you wants, you can begin to develop a practical approach to the celebration.

How big a deal do you want to make over this wedding stuff, anyhow? Do you want a private celebration, with just the two of you? If you want to keep it to a minimum and exchange sage-leaf rings in your backyard and go out to dinner, fine, live and be well. If, on the other hand, what you have in mind is a more public bash, you have a myriad of decisions to make. Choices, choices, choices.

THE BASICS

As you read through this section, try to do some prioritizing in your own mind. Begin by mulling over the dilemmas of when, what, who, and where.

THE SANDS OF TIME

Most couples give themselves between three and six months from the day they actually decide to get married until the day of the wedding. George proposed to David on David's birthday in February, and they planned on a May wedding. They didn't start finalizing their decisions until the end of March, and as David said, "It kept getting bigger and more complex, and the more I realized how far we wanted to go with this thing, the more certain I was we'd never pull it off in time." (They changed the date.) Allow yourself enough lead time to feel exhilarated rather than rushed. Open up those Filofaxes and consider the following questions.

Do you want this ceremony to take place on a date that already has significance in your lives? (We don't know why, but lots of gay couples choose to get married on an anniversary they already celebrate—the day when they met, the day they first kissed, the day of their first couples therapy session.) Maybe you've always wanted to be a June groom. Or perhaps you'd like to pick a holiday, like Valentine's Day or New Year's Eve; there's Arbor Day for you ecologists, and Susan B. Anthony's birthday for you feminists. Some couples have their astrological charts done to help them pick dates; others plan around a full moon or the winter solstice, which signifies a "returning of the light." June, August, and December are the most popular months and Saturday and Sunday the most popular days; be forewarned that you may have trouble clearing spaces and services during these periods, and even if you do manage to book them, you may end up paying a premium. Weekdays and nights generally have lower rates, and on weekends, days are cheaper than nights.

You might want to take some time off from work; when can you both do that? Do you have someone specific in mind to perform the ceremony whose availability you need to check on? How difficult will it be to book your church or synagogue? If you're planning on getting married outdoors, consult the *Old Farmer's Almanac* or a weather service so raindrops aren't likely to be falling on your head. And finally, take the lifestyles of your friends and families into consideration; check in advance with those whose presence is most important to you regarding the date.

Do you want to get married in the noonday sun (for mad dogs and Englishmen) or by moonlight? Are you a morning person or do you come to life at 8 P.M.? The time of day dictates to some extent the reception style as well as what people will expect to be fed.

THE CAST OF CHARACTERS

How many bodies do you envision yourself surrounded by on your wedding day? Your ten closest friends or everyone you've ever known in your life? Is it an intimate ceremony with a huge party afterward? Who, if anyone, will perform the ceremony? Will it be a clergyperson or the captain of a ship? Do you want attendants? Do you want lots of people to participate or do you want a two-woman show?

LOCATION SCOUTING

Where's the ceremony to be? In a church or synagogue or under your grandmother's fig tree? Will the reception be in the same place as the ceremony? Can you make quick friends with somebody who lives on an estate with hanging gardens, or do you want to rent the ballroom of a downtown hotel? Do you want to get married in the middle of Yellowstone Park or on an urban rooftop? Don't rule out unique places, from art galleries to the city zoo. Adventure may be as close as your own backyard.

PILES OF STYLES

The wedding-etiquette gurus all talk about the Wedding Style—which is kind of the gestalt, the big enchilada, the Zeitgeist of your wedding. But it is not something that ever needs to actually be articulated. When your Cousin Bernice planned her wedding, it was built into her genetic code that she would have a cocktail hour in the Rococo Room followed by a candlelight ceremony under the hotel's gazebo, followed by a sit-down dinner of prime rib and string beans almondine for four hundred of her most intimate friends. But if you had asked her what her wedding style was, she would have stared at you like a deer caught in the headlights. Yet the wedding style is nothing more than your individual tastes and personal priorities, which define the day. (For instance, you can assume from the rundown on Bernice's wedding that she didn't wear jeans.)

There are as many different wedding styles as there are couples. Here are the impressions of some of the people we spoke with who have been through it already.

👫 "It was right out of a thirties' movie."

👫 "We wanted to involve the people we care about, and by that I mean *all* the people we care about. Twenty-two people spoke at the wedding. No, we weren't bored; but then again, they were talking about *us.*"

👫 "Even though Jessica wasn't religious, I felt the need to have a ceremony in a house of worship and wear my grandmother's wedding gown. We had a beautiful candlelight ceremony at a Unitarian church."

👫 "Food is really important to us and our circle of friends. So we had a quickie ceremony followed by a sit-down dinner catered by our favorite restaurant."

👫 "All right, so we're a little theatrical . . . the ceremony lasted an hour and a half. People sang, people recited Shakespeare; there was even a skit. But there wasn't a person there who didn't have the theater experience of his or her life."

👫 "I don't think weddings should be a big deal, made into a three-ring circus. It's a solemn occasion where you're pledging your heart. We said our vows at sunrise and had twenty-five friends for a great breakfast."

👫 "I figured if I was going to do it I'd go ahead and invite some of my partners from the law firm. We had a private ceremony, then rented a midsize room at a downtown hotel and had hors d'oeuvres and dancing. It had a corporate feel, but then, we're corporate kind of women."

DON'T WORRY, BE HAPPY

It may be right about this time that you decide that the two of you will never reach an agreement (or, for that matter, the altar) and that maybe you should just have Chinese food delivered, watch *Rhoda* get married on Nick at Nite, and forget the whole thing. Don't panic: this is normal, this is universal. What Joe Average finds most overwhelming about planning one of these is that every decision hinges on a previous decision. We call it . . .

. . .THE SYNERGISTIC THEOREM OF WEDDING PLANNING

You won't know how many people you can invite until you know where you're having the reception; you can't really decide to have the reception until you know what's available and affordable; if you start looking for a place to have the reception, you have to decide on how large a space you need to hold all your guests; which brings you back to deciding how many people you're going to invite.

One reason you're probably feeling overwhelmed at this point is that you have too many options. The quickest way we know of to focus in on reality is to consider the almighty dollar. For example, if as part of your festivities you envision writing your names across the sky, you'll need to budget between $600 and $1,000 for your aerial announcement, leaving you no money to pay the minister. Eventually everybody needs to hammer out a budget. It may constrain your wants and desires, but it will keep you from getting carried away in areas that don't really matter to you, and it will help you figure out ways to get what you really want. If you have $2,000 to spend on your entire wedding, and your main priority is a reception at a four-star restaurant, take a dozen friends to the best dinner of their lives. If you wouldn't dream of getting married without your one hundred best friends, but your pockets are empty, go to a park and have a barbecue. We'll get more into budget specifics later, but for now try to think about how much money you can raise to put on this shindig. (Reflect on how much it can cost you to have friends over for a Superbowl party—and that's just Doritos, a few six-packs, and maybe a pizza.)

There are some other cold, hard realities, and these have to do with being gay. (You knew this would come up.) If you're Catholic and have always dreamed of a nuptial mass in Saint Patrick's, perhaps you should come back at a later date. If you've always wanted to have your parents walk you down the aisle and they deal with your sexual orientation by popping Prozac, you might have to make some adjustments. If the gang at the country club doesn't know that you and Brendan are more than tennis partners, having your ceremony there may bring you farther out of the closet than you're willing to go. Issues such as these can be daunting, even depressing, if you let them get out of perspective; but none of them need spoil your wedding if you keep in mind your original reasons for having this event.

The sad truth is that Mick Jagger was right: "You can't always get what you want." But don't forget the second part of that refrain: "You just might find . . . you get what you need."

By now the wedding wheels should be turning in your head. That can only mean one thing: you're ready for your first checklist. In the chapters to come we will deconstruct the following seemingly unanswerable questions:

FOR BRIDES- OR GROOMS-TO-BE: YOUR VERY FIRST CHECKLIST

INITIAL DECISIONS

You may not have made these decisions yet, but you need to make them almost immediately.

❑ Have you selected a wedding date and time?

❑ How many people do you want to invite?

❑ Where will you have the ceremony?

❑ Where will you have the reception?

❑ How much can you spend on the event?

❑ What style of celebration do you want?

FUTURE DECISIONS

These will be coming up before you know it; for now, just start a mental file on them.

❑ Will your religion(s) embrace your union?

❑ Who will perform the ceremony?

❑ Whom do you want to have participate in the ceremony?

❑ Will your family be involved?

❑ Will you have bridesmaids and/or attendants?

❑ Will there be music? At both the ceremony and the reception?

❑ Who will do the catering? What sort of food and drinks will you offer the hordes?

❑ What kind of wedding cake do you want?

❑ Who will photograph the event? Do you want a video record as well?

❑ What will you and your wedding party wear?

❑ What kinds of flowers and other decorations do you want?

❑ What do you want your invitations to look like?

❑ Will you exchange rings? If so, do you want them custom-designed?

❑ What sort of honeymoon would you like? Can you get enough time off from work?

▼ NUTS AND BOLTS

THE BUSINESS OF WEDDINGS

Beginning to feel overwhelmed? Do you already have little notes written on Post-Its and napkin scraps stuck in your appointment book, scattered on your desk at work, and sitting on your bedside table? Do the notes read: "Find baker," "Lose weight before buying new suit," and "fmp to Linfqr"? (No, we can't figure out what that last one means, either.)

One of the basic tenets of wedding planning is that this sort of thing either comes to you naturally or it doesn't. If it does, you know who you are; you're the person who's always asked to divide up the check when seven people meet at a restaurant. You never have trouble putting your finger on k.d. lang's *Shadowland* because all your CDs are alphabetized. You've been working toward an event like this all your life. On the other hand, if you're not one of those naturally organized people, do not despair. Throughout the book are lists designed to act as reminders; in this chapter you'll find a series of odds and ends with which to arm yourself as you go out into the cold, cruel world of wedding planning.

Stephanie Winston, in her best-selling book, *Getting Organized: The Easy Way to Put Your Life in Order,* explains that there is always an essential priority around which all other components group themselves. Once you determine what it is you want to achieve, Ms. Winston writes, practical solutions will flow fairly easily. Sounds easy enough. So, what is your essential priority?

Take some time right now to flesh out what it is you want and care most about in the wedding line-up. Sure, almost everyone plans on having flowers; but if you're a lover of flowers and going wild with blooms is of primary importance to you, by all means do it. Your priorities are just that—*yours*—and no one should be able to talk you out of them. These may include touches that would seem downright ridiculous to others, but for you the event won't spell *wedding* unless they're there. Provided your partner agrees, you should have them.

DIFFERENT
PRIORITIES FOR
DIFFERENT FOLKS

💰 elaborate wedding clothes

💰 a gourmet reception with free-flowing champagne

💰 flying in friends and family from around the country

💰 great dance band

💰 exchanging vows in an unexpected location

💰 state-of-the art invitations

No matter what you come up with in your designation of the highest and lowest priorities, the list will always lead you back to . . . money.

MONEY (CAN'T BUY YOU LOVE)

Can I have a great wedding that's an affordable event? *Yes.*

Is it possible to go over budget—but be able to pay for the little extras over a period of time? *Yup.*

Can I totally overdo it and end up with my savings account gone, my charge cards filled to the max, and my credit rating ruined forever? *Uh-huh.*

According to *Money* magazine, of the 2.4 million American couples who got married in 1990, at least half paid a portion of their own wedding costs. In other words, the days of mom and dad footing the bill are over, even for the straightest of couples.

Some couples we spoke with were reluctant to take money from their parents because they wanted this event to be their own special creation, without any interference. Plus, if you come from a family that would have kicked in some bucks for your wedding if you were marrying Samantha instead of Sam, chances are that back when they found out you were gay, they spent your wedding dowry on new wall-to-wall carpeting or patio furniture.

Still, funds for the wedding might come from parents, older "chosen family" members, aunts, uncles, or close friends who want to kick in some cash and lend a hand. Family members sometimes underwrite a specific portion of the costs, such as the flowers or the photographer.

Finances, as you must know by this point in your life, are a delicate subject, capable of toppling even the most solid relationship. Go easy as you and your partner figure out what each of you expects

and what you can afford. If it's just the two of you and this is the first financial planning you've ever done together, things might get a little more complex than you had anticipated. But look at it this way: you're getting good practice for your future years together. You may decide to pool your funds, or each of you may choose to be responsible for particular parts of the wedding; either way, it's important to determine where the cash is coming from and how the dollars will be allocated.

BASIC BUDGET SHEET

Deciding where to spend your money brings you back once again to priorities. When you look at the following items, think in terms of: (1) what you have your heart set on; (2) what you can do without; and (3) what you hadn't thought about previously but find, well . . . delightful.

THE CEREMONY

_____ Fee for site

_____ Fee or donation for officiant

STATIONERY

_____ Invitations and enclosures

_____ Postage

_____ Thank-you cards

_____ Printed matchbooks, ribbons, napkins

ATTIRE

_____ Gown or formalwear

_____ Shoes

_____ Accessories (veils, jewelry, etc.)

THE RECEPTION AND CATERING

_____ Fee for site

_____ Food (cost per person)

_____ Liquor

_____ Staff

_____ Rentals (linens, china, tables, sound equipment, etc.)

_____ Parking

_____ Favors and giveaways

_____ Gratuities

MUSIC AND ENTERTAINMENT

_____ Ceremony music

_____ Reception entertainment

_____ Band

_____ Disc jockey

WEDDING CAKE

_____ Baker's fees

_____ Cake top

PHOTOGRAPHY AND VIDEOS

_____ Reception and ceremony shots

_____ Formal portraits

_____ Wedding album

_____ Extra prints and videocassette copies

FLOWERS

_____ Ceremony and reception arrangements

_____ Bouquets

_____ Boutonnieres

RINGS

_____ Engagement rings

_____ Wedding bands

PREWEDDING ENTERTAINMENT

_____ Luncheons and other parties

_____ Entertaining out-of-town guests

_____ Rehearsal dinner

TRANSPORTATION

_____ Limousines

_____ Car rentals

_____ Airfares

THE HONEYMOON

_____ Transportation

_____ Lodging

_____ Meals

EXTRAS

_____ Gifts for those who helped

_____ Guest book

_____ Toasting glasses

_____ Cake knife

BUDGET

Okay, now it's time to sit down and compose, as you would a beautiful song, a realistic wedding budget that will give you some semblance of control in an area that could easily turn into quicksand. Making a budget is the easy part; the hard part is sticking to it. Be prepared: almost all of the couples we spoke with told us that they ended up spending more money than they had set out to when they first decided to get married. They didn't regret spending the extra money; in fact, almost everyone would do it again (and some couples would even do it bigger). But the unexpected costs threw everyone a curve.

Often what begins as a little gathering in the backyard with punch and cookies will mutate into a wedding resembling the one Charles and Diana threw in London a few years back. This happens to some extent with all weddings; for gays and lesbians, the excitement of having the opportunity to declare your affection publicly can quickly turn your thoughts away from an intimate ceremony and toward the Event of the Year.

As you begin to feel empowered or even entitled to all the wedding stuff that you once might have crossed off your list because you're gay, punch and cookies in the backyard begins to sound, well, not good enough. You find yourself asking questions like "Is it because we're gay that we're not planning a full-blown wedding?" It starts to hit you that this is not a birthday party for second-class citizens, by golly, it's . . . a wedding!

The more you use the phrase "This is a once-in-a-lifetime experience," the more the snowball builds. Mix that in with trying to please everyone, and the snowball begins to *roll. Rapidly.*

So go back to that previous list of priorities and start plugging in some figures. Realize that although they probably won't work in the real world, at least it's a start. You're likely saying, "But I don't have the faintest idea what that costs." Just fill in what you think you'd be willing to pay. (This will change; trust us.)

THE LESBIAN BRIDE OF FRANKENSTEIN: THE WEDDING INDUSTRY AND YOU

One day, you turn around and look in the mirror and—my God—you're like any straight bride or groom, steeped in wedding regalia. Your mind is crammed with price quotes and rules of etiquette. Sad to say, when you get right down to it, the wedding or bridal industry is exactly that: an industry—to the tune of about $32 billion a year in this country. (That's right, *billion.*) Awaiting you is a mob of florists, seamstresses, and photographers who make their living off weddings. Your wedding. They look at you and see a check with their name on it; having your best interests at heart is not necessarily at the top of their lists. As humorist Dave Barry once observed, the attitude of the wedding biz is, money can't buy you happiness, so you might as well give your money to us.

According to *Bride's* magazine (and they should know), the average formal wedding for about two hundred guests runs about $17,000. That figure can halve or double depending on where you live and how elaborate a celebration you envision.

Allow us to digress here a moment to talk about the mouthpiece of the wedding industry—the bridal magazines. Many same-sex couples we spoke with bought bridal magazines because they're there, they seem like fun, and for under $5 you get about 400 pages showing an overview of what's out there. The articles advise you on personal grooming, show you how to pick out the best vacuum cleaner for your new home, and offer chatty insights into eating dinner at your in-laws' (you should be so lucky). Some of them may work for you and some may not, but until there are gay wedding magazines available at your local Piggly Wiggly, these will have to do.

MOM AND POP QUIZ

Do these comments sound familiar? If any of them press your Guilt 'n' Spend buttons, rest assured that you're not alone.

✔ *"Do you want people to think you're skimping on your wedding?"*

✔ *"If you don't go the whole nine yards, well, you really aren't taking this very seriously, are you?"*

✔ *"Your Cousin Bernice had a six-piece combo— but then of course, that was a* real *wedding."*

However, the magazines (and the wedding industry) do one thing that is detrimental to *all* couples: they try to define what a wedding is supposed to be. Don't fall for this. In article after article, list after list, there is always a formula for the "perfect" wedding, and—big surprise—it usually involves putting money into somebody else's pocket. In reality, many of the customs that we associate with the wedding and the reception have been perpetuated by the Industry.

 Consumer Alert

No, not everyone involved with the wedding industry is an unscrupulous shyster, but you should be aware of some of the common pitfalls that lie gaping before all wedding consumers. Take the following precautions in all of your business dealings.

💰 Ask lots of questions and get written estimates as well as understandable contracts.

💰 Shop around and learn all you can about the wedding biz. Soon you will be spouting new vocabulary words like *thermography* and *tussy mussy.* The more you know, the better you will be at making decisions.

💰 We can't stress enough the importance of word of mouth and personal experience in terms of hiring help for the event.

💰 Be organized. Set goals and try and meet them, and make lists that present things in the order of what needs to be done first. (Weddings are list makers' dreams.)

💰 Keep in close touch with your vendors. Call to reconfirm and go over the details as many times as *you* feel is necessary. Don't be shy.

ORGANIZED LABOR

No matter which of the following methods you decide to employ, careful record keeping will make all the details fall into place more easily. You will not be able to do it all in your head. There are many wedding—okay, *bridal*—workbooks on the market that can be useful to help organize your to-do lists and keep planning charts straight. Some of the planners are quite ornate, with leather covers; on the other hand, a cheap spiral notebook can serve the same purpose.

THE NOTEBOOK METHOD

Buy a notebook with dividers, or make your own dividers by folding pages in at the corner. Loose-leaf binders come in handy if you feel that you want to be able to move information around, plus you can punch and insert papers you get from other sources—contracts, etc. Divide the notebook into separate sections for Overall Budget and Guest List, and then create sections for each major category such as Food, Entertainment, and Gifts. List and date all phone calls, referrals, and estimates, and record the names of people you talked to. Every time you spend money, record the expense.

THE INDEX-CARD SYSTEM

Stationery stores sell systems with preprinted index cards for keeping track of wedding guests so you know whom you've invited, their address, their phone number, and whom they're bringing. There's also room to jot down gifts that have been received and if/when you've written a thank-you note. Or buy a garden-variety file box and index cards, and put your own system together. You can also use cards to record estimates from vendors and so forth.

COMPUTER PROGRAMS

Whether you're a hacker or just use a home computer for playing Tetris, there are some terrific high-tech wedding-organizer programs on the market that will whip even the most unorganized brides and grooms into shape. For example, we found the Windows program "Wedding Workshop" to be clear and concise, providing not only easy fill-in-the-blank formats, but space to record several estimates for the same service, a budget that updates itself, a guest file, and a to-do list that alerts you as to what hasn't yet been done as your wedding day approaches.

CONTRACTS
(OR, IT DON'T MEAN A THING IF IT AIN'T IN WRITING)

Verbal agreements and handshakes are no way to conduct business. You should get every last promise and detail in writing from each service you engage. You will be given either a standard contract that has a ton of legal jargon, or a letter of agreement that looks more like—well—a letter. Both documents serve the same purpose.

And contracts shouldn't be scary; they're there to ensure that what you are expecting is what will be delivered. (Because what you see isn't always what you get.) If there's something you discussed with a vendor, and were told not to worry about because of course "it will be taken care of," it should be in the contract. Don't feel silly about reading the fine print.

All contracts or letters of agreement between you and each wedding vendor should spell out the following as they apply: (1) the exact length of time (including start and finish times) that the contractor will be working for you and what arrangements can be made if there is overtime required; (2) the breakdown of services and materials provided, including specifics such as colors and styles; (3) how the contractor and staff will be dressed; (4) who is liable for goofs (if

TIPPING TIPS

• A 10% to 20% gratuity may be added in advance to your catering bill.

• If a gratuity is not figured in, it's up to you to tip the servers as you see fit. Ask the catering manager about what is customary.

• If you're working closely with a caterer or wedding coordinator, it's really lovely (and unexpected) to acknowledge their contribution. This doesn't have to be money; we recommend a gift presented any time before the reception.

• At a large hotel or restaurant wedding, giving maître d's a gratuity up front will let them know that you value their work.

• Dianne Greenberg-Dilena, catering manager of the Hotel Bel-Air, told us that it's unusual for people to think of giving the chef a gratuity: "Here he's the one who really puts out and creates all these menus and wonderful foods, and no one ever acknowledges it. If you were to go back into the kitchen, introduce yourself, and give him a gratuity, it would make him happy as hell."

• In all cases, money should be presented in an envelope—preferably sealed, with the recipient's name written on the front.

the invitations end up reading, ". . . to the commitment ceremony of Susan Hernandez to Mr. Karen Reinhardt . . . ," who pays for the reprinting?); and (5) a list of delivery and return dates for rentals.

Once you're satisfied that all the information that needs to be there is there, and that it's correct, it's time to finalize the contract. Just a few must-do's:

✎ Make sure you get a signed copy of the contract with your signature, the vendor's signature, and the date each of you signed the contract. Technically, it isn't a valid contract unless it's signed and dated by both parties.

✎ On each finalized contract, list a contact person as well as phone numbers at the wedding site, the reception site, and your home. You may even include another set of numbers in case the contractor can't get in touch with you at the usual numbers.

✎ Double-check that the date and time specified on the contract match the date and time of your wedding. We know this sounds like a dumb mistake—so don't let it happen to you.

CREDIT WHERE CREDIT IS DUE

Over the next few months, you'll begin to feel like everyone you come into contact with wants a deposit. ("Yes, Dad, we're coming for dinner on Tuesday. Oh, you want a deposit?") You can do this in the form of cash, check, or credit card. Leave the least amount of money possible, and try to *put all deposits on credit cards* so that you will have recourse if need be. Not that there will be a problem; but if disaster does strike, the fact that you paid by credit card might be your only avenue to restitution.

But before you involve a credit card company in your battle over the total absence of seafood in the Neptune salad, you must attempt to rectify the problem with the caterer directly. So be sure to write lots of letters, and save copies of everything.

Fortunately, the couples we spoke with had no pending lawsuits or vendors from hell who had gone back on their word. But do take all precautions.

CANCEL THAT ORDER

"The wedding is canceled" are four words that no one wants to hear—not the chef, not the band, not no one. (As for dealing with your relationship, that's another book.) But just in case, know what your liabilities are. A big gay wedding, canceled at the last minute, could become a great TV movie-of-the-week—but the money the network gives you for the rights to your story will be spent paying off all the vendors standing in line.

When you look at a contract, be sure to note the cancellation policy and when (and if) the deposit will be refunded. Policies differ, ranging from "Full return of the deposit up to three weeks before the date," to "Return of deposit if the space or service gets rebooked," to "Sorry, Charlie, kiss your money good-bye" (although not necessarily in those exact words).

A HELPING HAND
(OR, IF YOU DON'T KNOW WHAT YOU'RE DOING, FIND SOMEBODY WHO DOES)

Bridal or wedding consultants, similar to the memorable Martin Short character in the remake of *Father of the Bride,* are coming back into fashion as brides and grooms lead busier lives and have less time to take care of wedding details on their own.

Working with a full-service wedding planner is like having a personal assistant or secretary at your disposal. The consultant will see that all of the elements of your event are in order and everyone remains in gear. If you're putting on an affair of grand proportions, and you really don't know how to pull this stuff off, a planner can lead you by the hand.

Yes, we know what you're thinking: "How much will *this* set me back?" Well, in the case of a large wedding, a good consultant will theoretically pay for him/herself by getting you better deals. A consultant who has been around the block a few times will be well connected, getting price breaks and negotiating contracts in ways that a virgin could never hope to. If you hire a wedding planner, protect yourself from a bill for swans in the fountain by telling her or him up front what your wedding budget is.

Some consultants charge by the hour; others a percentage of the total bill, typically 10% to 20%; others a flat fee. Still others charge you nothing, but instead get paid in kickback form from the services they engage for your wedding.

To find a good consultant, ask around at stationery stores, hotels, caterers, and houses of worship. Finding a gay or gay-friendly coordinator or party planner is best done through the grapevine of wedding vendors who will soon invade your life.

GAY AND GREEN

TIPS FOR ENVIRONMENTALLY FRIENDLY WEDDINGS

When it comes to planning a wedding that doesn't put too much strain on ol' Mother Earth, it doesn't matter what your sexual orientation is. We asked Pam Putch, co-owner of Earth Angels (an environmentally minded gift-basket company based in Los Angeles) for some wedding eco-tips.

• The best present you can give the earth on your wedding day is to use washable plates, glasses, and silverware. Another option is to purchase plastic dishes, glasses, and utensils that can be washed and reused again and again.

• Use recycled paper for your wedding invitations, programs, thank-you notes, and other paper goods. You can even go one step further and seek out a printer who will use soy ink. By using soy ink, you're lessening the amount of toxic residue that goes into our groundwater supply.

• If you want to be an environmental fashion trendsetter, use organic cotton fabric for wedding and bridesmaids gowns (and why not the grooms' suits too?).

• At the reception, instead of using cut flowers for centerpieces, substitute living tree seedlings or flowers and shrubs in pots. Encourage your guests to take these home; planting them is a great way to contribute to the betterment of the air quality in your city, and also plays a part in the slowing of global warming. If you do use cut flowers, make sure to compost them or dry them for use as decoration.

• If you register for wedding gifts, register with environmentally friendly companies such as Seventh Generation, Sundance, or Smith and Hawken.

• Insist that whatever stores you register with pack your wedding gifts in minimal, biodegradable packaging. Suggest they not use gift boxes or bubble wrap; encourage the use of wood shavings, raffia ribbon, and recycled natural wrapping paper.

• When gifts do come in boxes with lots of excess packing materials like those annoying Styrofoam peanuts, don't just toss these materials out. Save and reuse them, or take them down to your recycling center.

• Even precious metals can be recycled. Have your old gold jewelry and diamonds made into rings; you will be helping to preserve natural resources.

• Encourage people to carpool to the ceremony and/or reception. After all, since lots of people will know each other, why can't they ride four (or more) to a car? It will help reduce the smog emission levels, and if you're having valet parking, it might even save you a little money. If the celebration is some distance from where most of the people live, consider arranging for a bus to take everyone together.

• If you're having helium balloons as part of the decorations, please do not under any circumstances release them; just pop them. There are horror stories of balloons traveling unbelievable distances and ending up in oceans or lakes, where they become a hazard to marine life.

LEGAL, SHMEGAL

The best legal advice we can give you is this: see a lawyer.

Yes, at the time we are writing this, your wedding probably won't mean bupkus in a court of law. Believe it or not, this can actually be a reason for gays and lesbians to count their blessings. Think of it this way: there's no waiting period for a marriage license, no official agencies to notify in the event the bride chooses to keep her maiden name, and—God forbid there's a breakup—no divorce lawyers' fees to pay.

Even though you may have pledged your lives to each other, you are in most cases legal strangers. That doesn't mean you have to be left swaying in the wind. There are a number of steps you can take to give yourselves a leg up in the eyes of the law. But it will cost you. You'll have to go to a lawyer in order to approximate the legal protections that our nongay counterparts take for granted. It takes a patchwork approach of corporate, governmental, and legal steps to guarantee the same rights that would automatically be yours if the state recognized you as a couple when you say, "I do."

If possible, find a lawyer who deals in agreements between same-sex couples. You'll need to draw up separate documents for each of the areas of your togetherness. (And unfortunately, in case you come apart as well.) Some of the legal means by which you can try to cover yourself include power-of-attorney agreements, proxies, wills, insurance policies, and joint-tenancy agreements.

THE BAD NEWS

Odds are that not one scintilla of legal reinforcement will result from your wedding.

THE GOOD NEWS

You don't have to pay for a marriage license.

There are a number of books and pamphlets available that will guide you through the legal maze, and we've listed some of these in the Suggested References at the end of this book. But we repeat: even if you want to handle the bulk of the paperwork yourself, see a lawyer.

D-I-V-O-R-C-E

Tammy Wynette is sobbing, "Our d-i-v-o-r-c-e becomes final today."

This is certainly not a heading you'll find in any traditional bridal guide. But we feel that we need to at least mention what happens in this regard. After all, if the marriage isn't legal, what in the world constitutes a gay divorce, much less a gay divorcé or divorcée? Do they move to Fort Lee, New Jersey, buy a closetful of jogging suits, get a little nip and tuck, and join lots of clubs?

We're hoping you never have to deal with this issue, but just in case you do, it will be easier if you've laid some groundwork ahead of time. Discuss it before you make the big commitment. What are the deal breakers that would destroy your relationship, and how would the dissolution occur? You don't have to dwell on the negative, you don't have to go into details (unless you really enjoy it), but you *do* have to talk about the possibility. Once you get it out in the open, it won't be so scary.

While you will not have to be concerned with any state-generated documents, it's possible that your religious or spiritual organization will require some sort of dissolution papers—especially if you want to remarry. For example, MCC churches require that if a couple have had a union ceremony and they want to end the relationship, they both must sign off on it—an "uncommitment ceremony," if you will. Other individual pastors and rabbis have similar guidelines. Make sure you know what they are, because the last thing you want to become is a gay bigamist.

"I used to say, 'Why do we want to get married? It doesn't work for straight people,'" said Margaret M. Casella, a lawyer in Hartford who specializes in gay and lesbian issues. "But now I say we should care: They have the privilege of divorce, and we don't. We're left out there to twirl around in pain."

—"Gay Divorce: Few Markers in This Realm,"
The New York Times, August 11, 1994

The Countdown

Think of this as your Master List of things to do. The time frames are flexible, depending on how much lead time is available.

Phase 1 (6 to 12 months before)

- ❏ Set the date and time of day
- ❏ Establish priorities and set goals
- ❏ Discuss finances; make preliminary budget
- ❏ Set up organizational system
- ❏ Tell friends and family
- ❏ Draw up guest list
- ❏ Select and meet with officiant
- ❏ Figure out preliminary legal steps to take to formalize your relationship
- ❏ Think about what you'll be wearing
- ❏ Explore locations for ceremony and reception
- ❏ Shop around (get estimates and references, compare prices) for:
    - ❏ caterers
    - ❏ florists
    - ❏ photographers and videographers
    - ❏ musicians
    - ❏ invitations

Phase 2 (3 to 4 months before)

- ❏ Order invitations
- ❏ Shop for rings
- ❏ Determine attire
- ❏ Choose wedding-party members
- ❏ Register for gifts
- ❏ Decide on locations
- ❏ Contract caterer or make other food/drink arrangements
- ❏ Shop for wedding cake
- ❏ Think about the honeymoon
- ❏ Adjust budget

PHASE 3 (2 TO 3 MONTHS BEFORE)

- ❏ Mail invitations
- ❏ Finalize arrangements with:
    - ❏ caterer
    - ❏ florist
    - ❏ photographer/videographer
    - ❏ musicians
- ❏ Meet with officiant to work on ceremony
- ❏ Order wedding cake
- ❏ Think about all modes of transportation—limos, etc.
- ❏ Purchase or make rental arrangements for wedding attire
- ❏ Begin to record gifts as they're received; write thank-you notes
- ❏ Adjust budget

PHASE 4 (1 TO 2 MONTHS BEFORE)

- ❏ Decide on specific music selections; give to musicians and/or DJ
- ❏ Arrange for rehearsal dinner
- ❏ Finalize ceremony
- ❏ Work on ceremony announcement to be mailed to the press after the wedding
- ❏ Arrange accommodations for out-of-town guests

- ❏ Meet with travel agent and finalize honeymoon plans
- ❏ Do final attire fittings
- ❏ Buy gifts for attendants and each other
- ❏ Buy wedding-day accoutrements—guest book, birdseed to throw, etc.
- ❏ Go over list of shot requests with photographer
- ❏ Have final consultation with caterer concerning menu changes
- ❏ Talk through the day and list potential snags
- ❏ Adjust budget

PHASE 5 (THE FINAL TWO WEEKS)

- ❏ Reconfirm all services
- ❏ Make arrangements for final payments and gratuities
- ❏ Pick up wedding attire
- ❏ Get honeymoon gear in order
- ❏ Double-check all final counts with caterer
- ❏ Attend rehearsal and rehearsal dinner
- ❏ Get lots of sleep!

▼ # TELLING THE WORLD

GUESTS AND INVITATIONS

When your cousin Bernice planned her wedding, there were huge fights between her mother and the mother of the groom over the number of guests each could invite. The traditional guest list is divided between the bride's family and groom's family, and is often further broken down by parents' friends and business associates—not to mention the bride's friends, the groom's friends, and mutual friends. Tension is compounded if the bride's parents are footing the bill and feel entitled to a larger chunk of the guest list.

You may not have the same problems as Cousin Bernice, but in case we haven't mentioned it before, gay and lesbian weddings create unique circumstances that require some extra thought. For example, though you may really get along with the office manager at work, will *you* feel comfortable worrying about whether she will feel comfortable around your more—uh—colorful friends?

First of all, know that *there is no one you absolutely have to invite to your wedding.* This may be the only time you hear this rule, and at least for this one selfish moment know deep down inside that it's the truth. Your guest list should be made up purely of people who you feel will share in your joy and enhance the experience of a public declaration of your love. This is, of course, theory, and will occur only if you exist in a state of perfect grace, never feel any guilt, and cannot be influenced in any manner by friends or family.

So, keeping that ideal in mind, you can begin the process of putting together your guest list. First, each of you should sit down (together or separately; at the beginning it doesn't really matter) and compile a list of everyone, absolutely everyone, from your respective pasts and presents whom you would want to have at your wedding. If your parents are hosting the wedding, of course they'll have a list too. This first list is what we call the In a Perfect World List, and disregards budgetary concerns, space considerations, and social problems. Included on your In a Perfect World List might be:

THE BAD NEWS

Because homophobia still exists, not everyone you invite to your wedding will come.

THE GOOD NEWS

Because homophobia still exists, not everyone you invite to your wedding will come.

★ immediate family and relatives

★ people who are like family to you

★ people you work with

★ people from your old jobs

★ classmates and buddies from high school and/or college

★ the folks you go dancing with

★ fellow jocks from your weekend teams

★ people from your past who helped make you the person you are: your favorite teacher, doctor, musical instructor, football coach, spiritual adviser

★ friends from out of town

★ friends from your religious organization or support groups

Now put both of your lists together, and count. (Don't forget the clergyperson and everyone in your wedding party; see chapter 9, "Standing on Ceremony.") The refrain "Oh, my God! We'll never be able to fit them all in!" may be heard at this point. It's time for a dose of reality. Consider the following questions.

? Are you planning on having all guests attend both the ceremony and the reception? You don't have to invite everyone to both functions.

? What have you realistically budgeted for food and drink? This often ends up determining the fate of many "borderline" people.

? How big is the space that you will be using? (Sardines are not happy wedding guests.)

? How out are you to the people on your list? And are they supportive of your relationship? (Think about it this way: If you were invited to their wedding, would you feel comfortable bringing your mate?)

Remember that weddings are truly primal rituals and set off chains of chaos in even the most stable of family units.

IT'S A FAMILY AFFAIR

At the risk of sounding like pop psychologist Dr. David Viscott, know that even if you don't invite your family, they are still members of the wedding: in their absence, they are present. If there's one thing we've learned through our research on this subject, it's that there's just no predicting the reactions when the favorite son announces, "Mom, Dad . . . John and I are going to get married." (Remember, Mr. Gallup tells us that although 78% of all Americans approve of gays and lesbians receiving equal rights, only 35% believe in legally sanctioned gay marriages.) But what about the rest of your family of origin—siblings, aunts, uncles, cousins, and so on? We've formulated a few guidelines for you to ponder:

Rule 1: If You Invite Them, They May Come

Bill and Rick invited all their family members, because they just knew they'd refuse to show. Rick, however, made a slight miscalculation: two of his cousins from out of state decided the wedding was a great excuse to visit California. Rick was never that close to them to begin with. He ended up being very uncomfortable during the ceremony, which in turn made Bill uncomfortable. Although you'll probably find that many of those you invite from out of town will not be able to attend, don't invite them with that in mind, or you may be sorry.

Rule 2: Give Them an Out

Sometimes family members reluctantly agree to show up because they want to be supportive, but in truth they don't feel entirely comfortable. If you sense that this will be the case with your family, talk it over with them. Tell them that you appreciate their good wishes and vote of support, but give them an out: suggest that instead of attending, they may want to give a dinner party in your honor. If after your talk they say they wouldn't think of missing the ceremony, believe them, and count yourself blessed.

Rule 3: Don't Assume Anything

Tommy told us that he didn't invite his four brothers "because we've never really seen eye to eye on my sexuality, even though we do love each other. I assumed that they would be uncomfortable at the wedding. I invited my sister, and told her not to tell them. Well, she leaked it, and they still haven't forgiven me for not inviting them." Decide whether to invite someone based on whether *you* will be comfortable with them, but don't decide for them that *they'll* be uncomfortable.

I wasn't going to ask my parents, but I had just seen Torch Song Trilogy, *and in it Harvey Fierstein said to his mother, "You've never been a part of my life," and his mother said, "But you never invited me to; you've always made my decisions for me." So I sent my parents an invitation. My father said he'd come and my mother said she wouldn't; then she changed her mind. I think it was a very, very big step for them. They got to see my relationship and my interaction with Fran's family and with my friends. They were impressed by the fact that there were a lot of straight people there, and that people were dressed nicely. I think they expected a bunch of dykes in combat boots.*

—SANDY

Rule 4: Realize the Power of the Statement You're Making

Let's say your older brother is the Prince of Denial, and that although he knows you're gay, he refuses to acknowledge your partner. By sending him a wedding invitation, you are making a political statement. You're telling him that your committed relationship is not something you're ashamed of. Maybe, just maybe, this will help him to understand. And if he doesn't "get it" right away, your act may help him, over the coming years, to view your relationship with more legitimacy.

Rule 5: Don't Underestimate Their Love for You

If you really want Uncle Fred and Aunt Ethel to be there, invite them. What are you really worried about anyway? Do you think they'll giggle when you kiss? If they're open enough to the idea and love you enough to come, chances are they'll have the time of their lives. And Aunt Ethel will love dancing with your best man . . . or even with your maid of honor!

DOWNSIZING YOUR GUEST LIST

Okay, at this point you've made your lists, you've thought about your families, and you've made your first cut. But the lucky ones who remain are not finalists yet. You'll both probably have to give a little here and there. Remember that there are two of you, and that you may not both feel exactly the same way about every person you know. (If you do, you are inconceivably compatible and we envy how smooth

your lives are going to be.) You may have to lobby for certain people: "Okay, I'll let your two-step instructor come if you agree to having my old Marine Corps buddy there." Allow us to help you weave your way through some potential dilemmas:

New friends: An event like this can really cement a friendship; on the other hand, it may cause the relationship to become too personal too quickly.

Old lovers: Potential liabilities for obvious reasons. Will they attend to share in your happiness or to cast an evil spell over your union? Cindy told us, "If I had to eliminate everyone from the guest list who I had slept with, I wouldn't have had any friends there at all."

Ex-husbands and ex-wives: See "Old lovers."

Children: If you're gay or lesbian with grown children of your own, you can plug in the word *children* anyplace we have spoken of "parents" in this chapter. If you invite your son or daughter, and he or she chooses to come, just be happy about it.

The mix of people: If you have an eclectic group of friends, you may have a valid concern about whether they'll get along, or if they'll even talk. Randy and Joe told us, "We have an amazing assortment of friends, most of whom happen to be straight, ranging from their twenties to their seventies. You put all those people together, and it could be really awkward. So we made sure that every person we invited knew at least one other person who was coming." Similarly, you may at this point decide to completely exclude entire groups of friends. Do you really need to invite your entire UFO Abductee Support Group, or can you pare it down to just the people who went up with you?

With these new criteria in mind, how long is your list now? If you still have too many people, try counting a new way. Look at the single people on your list, and remember that you're under no obligation to let those people bring dates. (It's your wedding, not a square dance.) Then look at the families you've invited, and count the number of children. If you're really close to the kids, by all means invite them; but otherwise, do not feel it necessary to include them.

As a last resort, if you *still* have too many people on your list, consider having announcements printed to send to the overflow. A wedding announcement is merely a proclamation sent after the fact to let people know that you tied the knot.

So let's go back to where we started. Who should you invite to your wedding? When all is said and done and the rice is swept off the floor, the people make the party. Invite people whom you honestly, in your heart of hearts, want to be there.

GUESTS AND INVITATIONS

If you've decided to invite some people who may be shocked or confused when they open the envelope, why not enclose a personal note telling them that you're thinking about them and would love for them to be present at this important event in your life? This isn't a note of apology; it's a way of underlining how much they mean to you. You can also spell out what to expect: an exchange of rings and vows, readings, and so forth.

STOP THE PRESSES: CREATING THE INVITATION

We're about to take a trip through the Wonderful World of Wedding Invitations. We won't lie to you: there's a lot of scary stuff here. Designing or choosing your wedding invitation can be as intimidating as programming your VCR, but with proper guidance, it can actually be fun. We're going to give you all the information regarding the most traditional of the traditional, and then we'll give you a load of alternate ways you can go. Our philosophy in this chapter (and, indeed, in life) is that it's important to know what the rules are so you know what it is you're breaking.

The invitation may provide the very first knowledge some of your friends and relatives receive that you've decided to take this step. It may also actually introduce the entire concept of a same-sex union ceremony to some people. Naturally, it will provide essential information (who, what, when, where), but it's the look and sensibility, not just the printed words, that will tell your guests what to expect. If the invitation is on a piece of rawhide, your guests will probably figure out not to wear white tuxes and chiffon evening gowns.

Think of the invitation as your press release. Any invitation, by nature, sets the stage for the event to come; and a wedding invitation carries a special weight because it is heralding a once-in-a-lifetime event.

When you hear the words *wedding invitation,* a certain look and feel probably pops into your mind. There are too many envelopes; there is wording like "Request the honour of your presence," with *honour* spelled with a *u;* the date and time are written out in longhand; and what is that silly little piece of tissue paper doing in there anyway? It's called tradition.

Does this mean there is only one way to go? That you have to emulate the wedding invitations of the past? Some say yes. We say no, no, no! You can send a fax or send it E-mail; you can write an individual note or use a singing telegram. In short, you can draw from a long line of traditions or you can thumb your nose at them. But no matter what style you finally decide on, the invitation should be executed well. The care you take in the presentation, not the formality, will reflect your commitment to the ceremony and to the union itself.

Think about looking at this invitation in twenty years and try to imagine what your reaction will be. For example, if you insisted on having your high school graduation picture taken in a Nehru jacket, chances are that when you look at the picture now, you cringe. You don't want your wedding invitation to be like that. Also consider the possibility that one of your guests will end up giving you some sort of framed or decoupaged rendition of your invitation as a wedding present, and that you will be stuck having it on your mantel or wall for a long, long time. You'd better love it.

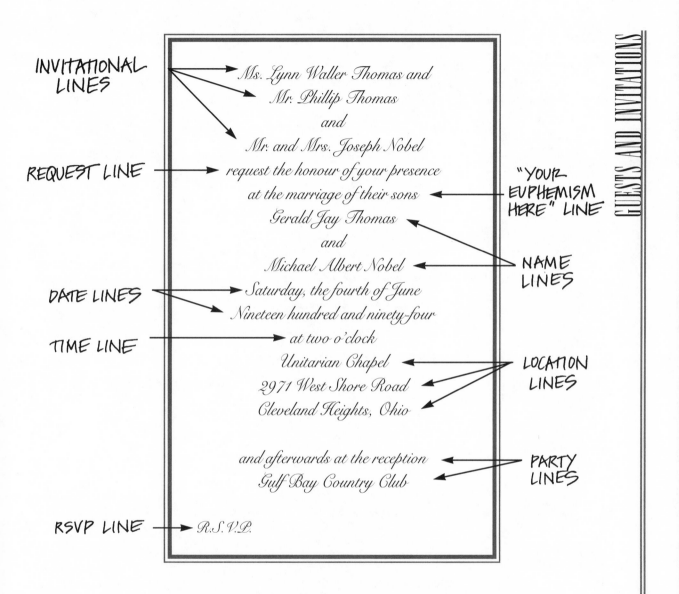

INVITATIONAL LINES

Ms. Lynn Waller Thomas and
Mr. Phillip Thomas
and
Mr. and Mrs. Joseph Nobel

REQUEST LINE

request the honour of your presence
at the marriage of their sons

"YOUR EUPHEMISM HERE" LINE

Gerald Jay Thomas
and
Michael Albert Nobel

NAME LINES

DATE LINES

Saturday, the fourth of June
Nineteen hundred and ninety-four

TIME LINE

at two o'clock
Unitarian Chapel
2971 West Shore Road
Cleveland Heights, Ohio

LOCATION LINES

and afterwards at the reception
Gulf Bay Country Club

PARTY LINES

RSVP LINE

R.S.V.P.

A WORD ABOUT WORDING

There are certain things that have to be stated on your invitation, and there is a formal way in which they are traditionally stated. But you can make this form into anything you want it to be. As long as your invitation is easy for guests to follow, you can adapt the guidelines as you see fit.

Let's take the basic form of a traditional invite and bounce off it. If you're obsessive and want more details, check your Emily Post or other book of etiquette, where you will find literally pages of rules concerning capitalization, punctuation, titles, military weddings, etc.

INVITATIONAL LINES

The invitational lines usually contain the names of the bride's parents—that is, those footing the bill, and therefore the "hosts" of the event. If one or both sets of parents are hosting your wedding, their names would come first. If you and your parents are in this together, you can use:

Diane and Andrea, along with their parents . . .

It's possible that even if your parents aren't paying for the wedding, they're supportive of your relationship and you would like to include their names on the invitation.

REQUEST LINES

Traditionally (and remember, we're talking *classic* here), there were only two acceptable request lines (although you were allowed to spell *honour* with or without a *u*):

The honour of your presence is requested . . .

or, along with the invitational line,

Mr. and Mrs. Paul Thomas Hernandez
request the honor of your presence . . .

But there is a vast array of contemporary wording possibilities for the request line that work for many gay and lesbian couples:

Please join us . . .

•

The pleasure of your company is requested . . .

•

Our happiness will be more complete if you will share in . . .

•

With joy Randy and Joe invite you to join them in their celebration of . . .

THE "YOUR EUPHEMISM HERE" LINE

This line is in all the etiquette books, but it's really a part of the request line; traditionally, it says "marriage." You may decide on using one of the many other phrases for what you're about to do: Holy Union, Wedding, Commitment Ceremony, Affirmation, and so forth. (See "Other Things You Can Call This Event," in chapter 1.) Place your euphemism on this line.

THE NAME LINES

Whose name is going to come first? Tradition says that the woman's name comes first. Big help, huh? You're going to have to fight this one out between yourselves. The best suggestion we can offer is to list them alphabetically.

THE DATE LINES

These lines include both the day of the week and the date of the month, with the numbers spelled out, such as:

Saturday, the sixth of June

Believe it or not, the year is not required, but if you're going to include it, it looks better spelled out. For example:

Nineteen hundred and ninety-five

THE TIME LINES

This gives the hour of the day, spelled out without numerals, such as:

at two o'clock

and may or may not include the period of the day, such as:

in the morning or *in the afternoon*

It's assumed that people can figure out whether you're going to be married at ten in the morning or ten at night, but if it's an offbeat time, it doesn't hurt to bang them over the head with it. If you're having a night wedding on the beach, you'd better say so.

THE LOCATION LINES

Obviously, these specify the church, temple, club, or home . . . but don't forget the street address and the city and state.

THE PARTY LINES

If all guests are invited to both the ceremony and a reception that takes place right after, a combined invitation may be sent without separate enclosure cards. The copy might read something like this:

Reception to follow

or

and afterwards in the church parlor

or even

then party, dudes

You can also tip them off as to what they might expect . . .

Dessert and champagne to follow

If the reception is at a different location, think about using a separate reception card.

RSVP LINE

If you decide not to enclose a reply card (which we'll get to in a moment), you should include:

RSVP or *the favour of a reply is requested*

This goes at the bottom left corner of the invitation. In this case you are assuming that the recipient has your address or will save the envelope with your return address. If you'd like the RSVP called in, make sure you print your phone number on the invitation.

PARTS OF THE INVITATION PACKAGE

In the most general of terms, an invitation to a wedding ceremony comprises the invitation itself and an envelope. Period. Life would be so simple if that's where we could end this chapter. However, society has had centuries to develop a myriad of confusing options and protocol. Here's the breakdown of everything that can conceivably be shoved into an envelope. (Purists call it the *wedding ensemble,* not to be confused with the musicians you hire for the reception.)

THE WEDDING ENSEMBLE

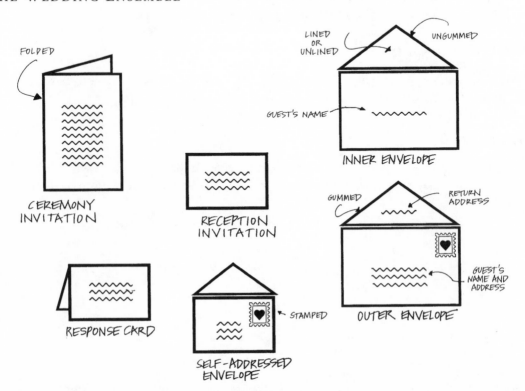

GUESTS AND INVITATIONS

CEREMONY INVITATION

This invites the guest to the wedding itself. Traditionally, it is engraved on the front of a piece of white or ecru 100% cotton rag stock and folded. It is the main course of the invitation package.

INNER ENVELOPE

Ungummed and unsealed, with or without lining, this encloses the invitation itself and bears the name of the guest on the outside. It may also contain reception and response cards and any other enclosures. The inner envelope is certainly not mandatory, especially if you're ecologically minded—in which case everything goes into a single (outer) envelope.

OUTER ENVELOPE

This contains the inner envelope, bears the guest's name and address and your return address, and is stamped.

RECEPTION CARD

If the reception is to be held anywhere other than where the ceremony is held, it's suggested that there be a separate card for it—the reception card, which announces to the guests the location, time, date, and any other specific info regarding the reception. This is not just one of those Emily Postian rules with no reason behind it. With the reception information on a separate card, the invitation to the ceremony becomes easier to read.

RESPONSE CARD AND STAMPED SELF-ADDRESSED RETURN ENVELOPE

Some cards simply request that you respond but are otherwise blank, allowing the guest to write a personal note:

The card may also state:

So, guys, guess no more late
nights at Suds 'n Duds.
We'll be there! Can't wait.
Love, Mike & Kip

The favour of a reply is requested.

---

*Please respond on or before
the twenty-eighth of June*

M._____

*will*_____ *attend*

Because my own wedding invitation was very formal, Jane and I wanted to let our friends know that we were still going to have a little fun with the occasion, and decided to do that via the response card.　　　　　　　　　　　　　　　　　　　**—Tess**

Make your response deadline about two weeks before the wedding. This will give you time to hunt people down and still be able to give the caterer a count one week before the event. Remember, you are the Supreme Master of your guest list. If Clive hasn't responded by your deadline, phone him and ask him if he's coming. If he says, "Yeah, I'll be there; and is it okay if I bring my cousin from Cedar Rapids who's going to be in town?" tell Clive that you look forward to seeing him but that there's just not room for his cousin. Be firm.

Dear Tess & Jane,

_____ Yes! I'd love to see 2 women get married

_____ No . . . I'm liberal, but not *that* liberal

_____ Sorry . . . I know I'm missing the party of the year, but I can't make it.

Love, _____

_____

Please respond on or before May 30th, 1992

The Great Response-Card Debate

In her 1956 book, Wedding Etiquette Complete, *Marguerite Bentley states, "In my contact with brides' families, I find that they are aghast at the number of persons who have not replied to their invitations up to a few days before the wedding. This situation makes it difficult to compute the numbers of guests for which preparations must be made and is a thoughtless and rude gesture to a gracious invitation." We say, Right on, Ms. Bentley!*

Old-time etiquette regarding a wedding invitation required a personal response on one's own stationery, and most etiquette gurus are appalled at the death of this custom. In fact, some treat it as the end of civilization as we know it. We, on the other hand, are big fans of the response-card method because (1) it's easiest on the guest, (2) it's the most practical way of keeping track of who's coming, (3) it's fun to check the mail every day, and (4) your friends will make witty comments on the cards, which you'll save in a shoe box and take out and read on your anniversary.

If you don't have much lead time, phone RSVPs are definitely the quickest way to go. However, it can get you in trouble if you're inviting more than fifty people. You'll invariably lose count and end up spending more on the catering overage than you saved by not paying for response cards. Or one of you will hang up the phone and not be able to find the list that's supposed to be kept right next to it, and a fight will ensue and then the whole wedding will be called off anyway. So do yourself a . . . favour. Send reply cards.

In addition, the following cards may accompany the ceremony invitation:

- MAP CARD: Gives directions to the locations of the ceremony and/or reception. You can have someone draw maps or have them done on computer, or the directions can be written out.

- TRAVEL CARD: Gives special directions or information such as where to meet the chartered bus or find the right beach.

- ADMISSION CARD: Used as a pass to get into a wedding held at a popular public location such as the Cleveland Museum of Art or Saint Patrick's Cathedral.

- ACCOMMODATION CARD: For people coming from out of town. This specifies the hotel where you have made arrangements, and may include a mention of discount rates and a contact person.

- RAIN CARD: Tells where to go in case of rain. (Best used when the ceremony or reception is to be held out of doors.)

- "WITHIN THE RIBBON" CARD OR PEW CARD: Sometimes a specific section of the ceremony site is reserved for wedding party members or other special guests, who would give one of these cards to the usher. (Try not to assign these seats based on the generosity of the wedding present.)

- AT-HOME CARD: Small card that lets your guests know your new address and the date you will be ready to receive mail—and visitors—there.

- NAME CARD: Lets everyone know whether there is to be a name change. Gay and lesbian couples can add just one more twist here with the option of including changes in both names. (See chapter 22, "The Aftermath.")

By now your eyes are no doubt spinning over the different components of a wedding invitation. But don't despair: here's where the real fun begins. If you've decided that the standard invitation forms appeal to you, you can either (1) seek the help of a professional, (2) produce them yourself, or (3) decide to skip the wedding and put the money into home improvements instead.

GUESTS AND INVITATIONS

THAT SILLY PIECE OF TISSUE PAPER

Pieces of tissue paper were originally used to keep the oil-based ink on an engraved invitation from smearing as it slowly dried. Even if you don't order them, don't be surprised if a stack of them is sitting there when you open your box of invitations. You can use them in the invitations, or you can use them to blow your nose; the choice is yours.

SEEKING PROFESSIONAL HELP

If you've chosen option one in the preceding paragraph, here's your rundown of who the pros are:

STATIONER: A store that specializes in personal and social stationery. They have those voluminous wedding catalogs, but more importantly, they employ people who are up on everything from wording to trends in ink colors. They may have their own sources for paper, designs, and all the trimmings. This category also includes the more tony jewelry stores such as Tiffany and Cartier.

PRINTER: A place you'd go to get something reproduced, usually by the offset method— a type of lithography. They too will have those voluminous wedding catalogs, but you may not get as much help here as you would from a stationer.

COPY SHOP: A new option, with services such as high-tech photocopying, computer type, color copies, etc. Forget having anybody help you with much of anything here; know what you want when you walk in.

DEPARTMENT STORE: More voluminous wedding catalogs, and a trained bridal consultant who may have advised Eleanor Roosevelt on her invitations. They sometimes have good prices and sales promotions.

MAIL ORDER: If there's any way that you can find an alternative to mail order, we suggest that you do so. One of the main problems is that you may find the companies "correcting" your copy so that, for instance, "Sally and Michelle" becomes "Sally and Mitchell." However, if the idea of going in person to someone in your own town really makes you uncomfortable, and you have your heart set on that invitation with the embossed doves, we have included a mail-order source for you in the Resource Directory at the end of this book.

OTHER OPTIONS: You can go to your local Hallmark shop, look at the sample books, and note the names and style numbers of the ones you like. Then go to the National Gayellow Pages, call one of the print shops listed, and give them the name and style number.

If you choose to use a straight printer, the initial response you get will tell you whether you want to use them or keep on looking. For the most part, we found very little evidence of attitudinal problems. However, if you have the bad luck to call the same print shop that just took the *Friends of Pat Robertson Newsletter* off their press, they will probably be a little hostile to you. So what? Hang up and call the next place on your list. As we said in chapter 3, *your* attitude is everything.

Don't be afraid to shop around, and don't feel that you have to come out to every single cashier. You don't have to say, "I'm gay and going to marry my homosexual lover, what's it to you?" in order to get a price quote. And one other thing: don't expect this decision to be taken care of in fifteen minutes; in fact, be prepared to make at least two trips before you finalize everything.

Okay, now that you're ready to make your way to the stationer, printer, or whatever, here's what you need to take with you:

Be sure you have (in writing) the date, times, locations, and addresses. Try to have some idea as to the wording you prefer. You should know the approximate number of guests you're planning to invite. And, as silly as it may seem, make sure you know the correct spellings of the names and places that will appear on the invitation.

Once you arrive, the salesperson will show you those voluminous wedding catalogs of invitations that range from the simple to the bizarre. (Some designs, of course, will be totally inappropriate—a bride and groom walking over a footbridge, for example.)

THE MONEY PIT

We haven't mentioned money yet, but now it's time for a reality check. You can't buy a greeting card for fifty cents, so don't expect to get your custom invitations for that. Plan on spending at least $2 per set (which includes invitation, inner and outer envelopes, reply card, and reply envelope); there's a chance that by the time you've left the store you may even have spent as much as $5 per set. It could be worse: invitation "specialists" charge between $35 and $95 per invitation. (If you can afford that, you're probably having somebody read this book for you.) One printer we spoke with told us that the rule of thumb she passes along to couples is to plan on spending about a dollar per item; the ceremony invitation and envelope would be a dollar, the reception card would be a dollar, the response card and envelope would be another dollar, and so on. She says you'll probably end up paying less than that, but that this is a good way to ballpark the cost. And don't forget to add on the cost of stamps—including extra postage if the invitation is heavy or oversize, plus stamps for the response-card return envelope. (Yes, you have to pay the return postage; it's tacky not to.)

How many invitations will you need? Take a count of your final guest list and add at least 25 to that; this will cover you for last-minute invites and souvenirs. Then add at least 50 extra envelopes so that whoever is addressing them can make mistakes and not feel suicidal. Surprisingly, an extra 25 or 50 invitations will not raise the cost of the order much, and can help you avoid spending lots more on a second run.

Invitation prices will rise and fall based on the following:

PAPER

The heavier the paper, the higher the grade. The paper is probably the most important place to put your money, because a change from typing paper to rag bond, for instance, gives you an entirely different look. Other options include parchment, vellum, rice paper, handmade paper, and recycled paper.

PRINTING METHOD

Hand letterpress is the most expensive printing method, because, as the name suggests, it's all set by hand—you know, like the Gutenberg Bible. Next comes *engraving,* which involves a copper steel plate that is etched with the type; it's extremely classy looking, the Rolls-Royce of printing. *Thermography* is probably the most popular choice, because it simulates the raised lettering of engraving at a more affordable price. *Offset printing* has a flat surface and can be effective depending on the image to be reproduced. Last but not least, there's *photocopying.* If engraving is the Rolls-Royce of printing, a photocopy may well be the Hyundai. If you're part Picasso, part Hockney, you can make a real statement with color photocopies; otherwise this method will probably not provide the look you want for your wedding.

INK

Black is standard; other colors may cost more. Some printing companies also have what they consider to be extraordinarily special colors of ink that they'll charge extra for. (Of course they'll charge extra, because they hired a creative team to come up with color names like "elderberry," "oatmeal," and "moss.") Also, if you choose more than one color, expect to pay extra.

TYPEFACE

Most companies offer a variety of type styles. Some also give you a large range of type sizes, allowing greater flexibility in fitting your wording into the space available. Computer-generated typefaces open up a whole world of possibilities, including Hebrew and Chinese characters.

ENVELOPES

You may want the outer envelope to have a lining, which of course will cost you extra.

ADDITIONAL PRINTING

This includes printing the return address on the back flap of the outer envelope, printing your address on the response-card envelope, and printing extra lines on the invitations themselves.

You may also opt for *blind embossing* (that bumpy raised printing without ink) for the return address (especially if you don't want anyone to know where you live; we find *blind embossing* hard to see).

If you're anything like us, you've done all of your home work . . . but when you go to the printers, you're going to forget that list of questions you had to ask. We've done you a favor here—photocopy this page and take it with you.

PRINTING PRIMER: QUESTIONS TO ASK

? *Will I get to see a proof?* Some printers offer this service for a small fee. You might want to consider looking at proofs, because you'll be better off paying for any changes ahead of time than ending up with a finished product that's less stunning than you expected.

? *Who takes the fall for any errors that occur?* A good printer will make corrections of typographical errors for free.

? *How long will it take for my order to come in?* It could take anywhere from 2 to 8 weeks.

? *Can I see some samples of actual invitations?* You may want to make sure that what you're seeing in the book is what the finished product will look like.

? *I like this design but can't afford it; can I get a similar look for less money?*

? *Do I have to leave a deposit? How much?* 50% is standard; anything more than that is a little unusual.

I DID IT MY WAY

This section encompasses the parallel universe—the Bizarro World—version of the formal wedding invitation. You may decide not to have the invitation done in the standard way for one or more of the following reasons:

GUESTS AND INVITATIONS

THOSE VOLUMINOUS WEDDING CATALOGS

If you go into a store or print shop for your invitations, or if you get your invitations through the mail, you're going to be inundated with options to purchase other things that have your names on them. These include, but are not limited to: personalized napkins, matches and ashtrays, ribbons, wedding programs, scrolls, informal personal notes, thank-you notes, place cards, keepsake boxes, balloons, bookmarks, notepads, cake boxes or bags, and videocassette holders. Then there are engraved items such as cake cutters, toasting glasses, picture frames, charms, key rings, pen holders, and Christmas ornaments. You can even order those personalized swizzle sticks you've always longed for.

- "Bob and Butch's wedding invitation looked like it came from Charles and Di."

- "It's a lot more fun to sit at my word processor in my underwear than it would be to get dressed to go see a printer."

- "I'll bet with the money we save by printing the invitations ourselves, we can go to Aruba for our honeymoon."

- "The owner of the only print shop in town has an incredible collection of Nazi memorabilia."

Smashing results can be achieved with a little creativity and footwork. (Extra credit will be given for originality.) Be forewarned that you may or may not save money using alternative methods of production.

You can use calligraphy, rubber stamps, stickers, collage, or even potato printing to make your own statement. But try to make sure that the finished product looks handcrafted, not homemade. (What's the difference? How good it is.) If you're not quite so artsy-craftsy but still want to put it together yourself, try one of the following on for size:

PERSONAL COMPUTER

Be P.C. with your PC or Mac: compose your own invitations using a program that has a selection of typefaces and sizes. You can do the whole thing at home if you have access to a state-of-the-art printer, preferably a laser printer. Warning: experiment first with various sizes and weights of paper stock to see what your printer will do. Make sure you're happy with the results before you spend your week's paycheck on two thousand sheets of rice paper that end up jamming the printer and plunging you into Computer Hell. If you're not happy with your printer, you can still use your computer to compose camera-ready art that you can pass on to an offset printer. (Let *their* machine jam up with the rice paper.) And finally, if your computer doesn't have the type-program flexibility you'd like, you may be able to find one of those computer places that rents time on terminals.

BORDER CARDS

A border card is not what helps you to cross from Italy into France. It's a standard-size card that has a preprinted border with anything from bows and flows of angel's hair to ice cream castles in the air. The center is blank, for you to fill in as you see fit. Border cards often come with matching envelopes and smaller cards for inserts. You can fill them in by hand, run them through your PC printer at home (see: "jam up," above), or take them to a print shop.

ART CARDS

Decorative postcards or greeting cards can make great invitations, either hand-printed, run through a computer printer, or offset. Do you and your partner both love gardens? Find a Monet water-lilies postcard. Are you fans of folk art? Buy a box of American quilt cards. Passionate about film? Choose an appropriate Hollywood portrait. Art cards are everywhere (try your local museum or museum catalogs) and only as limited as your imagination. And as long as we're rewriting the rules, why not use a standard postcard, preprinted on the back, for your response card?

Alternative LIFESTYLES, *Alternative* Invitations

We've mentioned that the invitation tells the guest what to expect from the wedding ceremony and/or reception, either in its formality or in its eccentricity. An unconventional invitation sends up a flag that the celebration will be, oh, let's say, *different*. The more individual the circumstances, the more fun and specialized you can make your wedding invitation. The following are some ideas we've come up with.

SEND A WEDDING INVITATION "KIT"

- You've been together for twenty years and have finally decided to have a commitment ceremony? Send time capsules of what the world was like when you met: a peace symbol, a copy of a 1970s *Advocate* cover, a string of love beads—all inviting the guest to your wedding party at a Grateful Dead concert.

- Send a kite along with the invitation to a relaxing "Sunday in the Park" reception.

- Print your invitation on a beach ball and mail it (preferably deflated) to announce your beach-party wedding.

- Get copies of an appropriate 45 rpm record (yes, they still exist), such as Bette Midler's "Chapel of Love," and print bogus labels for the B side, telling all about the who, what, when, where, etc.

- Do a short home video of one of your mothers inviting guests to the wedding. Have it copied and send it on out. Later, submit this to *America's Funniest Home Videos* and win lots of money.

• Instead of envelopes for mailing the invitations, consider boxes, tubes, or cans.

REFLECT YOUR PROFESSION OR HOBBIES

• Lawyers: Send a "summons to wedding" or a notice of legal partnership.

• Trivia lovers: Create a crossword puzzle or pop quiz about yourselves and the event. (Don't forget to enclose an answer sheet or no one may figure out how to get there.)

• Gourmands: Go to a cookie company and have your invitation printed on large cookies or slabs of chocolate. But don't order too many extras or you'll never get the cummerbund around your waist.

PHOTO FINISHES

• Go through the drawer that's filled with loose old photos; enclose one in each invitation, asking people to join you in creating new memories. You may even find a picture from a keg party to send to your old sorority sister.

• Have a photo taken together that reflects the theme of the party. A couple we know whose house looks like pages 24 to 36 in the Sundance catalog got dressed up in full cowgirl regalia and had their portrait done atop a stallion. The caption asked the guests to join them at the roundup.

• Go into a photo booth at the mall and get strips of funky two-shots to enclose in each invitation.

• Have a photo taken of the two of you holding hands in a trendy public place. Before you have the copies made, put those little black bars over your eyes so that you look like something from the *National Enquirer.* Have the caption read: "Strange but True: Woman to Wed Woman!"

In short, the sky's the limit. Dare to be different. If you have the chutzpah (and money) to hire an organ grinder and have the monkey hand-deliver each invitation, you have our blessing. (And please include us on the guest list.)

TIMING IS EVERYTHING

Here's a rough schedule of what kind of lead time you'll need for the invitations and related possible emergencies. This time line is designed to place the least possible amount of stress on the couple in terms of getting the word out. (Notice we said, "least possible amount," because frankly there's not a chance in hell you'll get through this without any stress at all.)

SIX MONTHS BEFORE THE WEDDING

❏ Begin to determine your guest list.

❏ Look at other cards and invitations.

THREE OR MORE MONTHS BEFORE THE WEDDING

❏ Think about wording and style.

❏ Shop around for your invitations (which can actually take a couple of weeks if you're one of those people who have trouble deciding on white or wheat toast for breakfast), and order them from the printer or stationer.

❏ Collect names and addresses of your guests, check accuracy of spellings and zip codes, and make sure addresses are current.

WHILE YOU'RE WAITING FOR THE INVITATIONS TO ARRIVE

❏ Finalize the guest list, check it twice, and decide who's naughty, who's nice, and who can be eliminated.

❏ Devise a method of keeping track of everyone on your guest list. In your tracking system you can list—in addition to RSVPs—the gift given, the correct name of the guest's significant other, and the name of the hotel your out-of-town guest has chosen.

❏ Investigate how you are going to get your invitations addressed. Options include hiring a calligrapher, using computer-generated script, and doing it yourself.

TWO MONTHS BEFORE THE WEDDING

❏ You get the invitations back from the printer and boy, aren't they wonderful! *Or:* the invitations come back from the printer, and—ohmygod—they've misspelled your middle name. All is not lost. We've built in a two-week buffer zone; you have plenty of time to get hysterical, deal with the printer, and have them rush you the replacements. (Keep a few of the misprints just for posterity.)

❏ If you're lucky, the typo is not on the outer envelope, which is the one that gets addressed—which is what you'll be doing while waiting for the redone invitations.

I always advise my clients to address the envelopes as soon as they possibly can; then stick them in a conspicuous place with a big sign on them saying, "Mail on September 21." I can't tell you how many dizzy clients did all the addressing and stamping two months in advance, and then three weeks before the wedding realized that they forgot to put them in the mail.

—SANDY PINNEY,
of Sandy's Printing in
Glendale, California

❑ Get your envelopes addressed. If you hire a calligrapher, allow one to three weeks. If you're using a computer, you can produce a diskette of your guest list from which you or a stationer can print up the envelopes.

FOUR TO SIX WEEKS BEFORE THE WEDDING

❑ Leave yourselves plenty of slop time when it comes to mailing your invitations. For out-of-towners, six weeks is not really unreasonable; for those in town, four weeks is probably sufficient. On the other hand, you don't want to send the invitations so early that your guests fall into the Scarlett O'Hara "I'll think about it tomorrow" syndrome and forget about the response card altogether.

❑ Take a completely stuffed invitation packet to the post office for weighing (and measuring if it's oversize) to make sure that one first-class stamp will do the trick. You don't want your invitations arriving stamped "Postage Due." While at the post office, pick out a special stamp. The Postal Service usually has something current with "love" printed on it, but go ahead and use that Elvis stamp if that's your passion.

Instant-wedding alert: What's the absolute bare-bones minimum amount of lead time you can get away with to have a professionally printed invitation? Let's say you've just decided that you want to have your ceremony on the anniversary of the night you met at the Gertrude Stein Democratic Club meeting, but that's next month. And you have your heart set on a classic Crane's engraved wedding invitation. *C'est possible?*

Mr. Huckleberry Finn
Mr. Tom Sawyer
1000 Riverview Terrace
Hannibal, Missouri 00000

Mr. Finn and Mr. Sawyer

OUTER ENVELOPE   INNER ENVELOPE

Yes; after all, we do live in the Electronics Age, and with fax machines, overnight shipping, etc., you can probably pull it off three weeks before the ceremony. You'll need to pay the stationer extra for rush service, you may have to pay your little brother to address envelopes, and you won't be giving your guests much advance warning—but yes, it is do-able.

ADDRESSING THE SITUATION

THE ENVELOPE, PLEASE

Here are a few hints to keep in mind as you hit the home stretch in the Wonderful World of Wedding Invitations.

✎ The address on a wedding invitation is always handwritten, never typed.

✎ If you're using two sets of envelopes, the inner ones are the ones that are un-gum-med; they'll even come from the printer wrapped in a warning strip that says, "Do Not Address These Envelopes!"

✎ In the ultratraditional world, the terms "and Guest" and "and Escort" are never used. You're supposed to ask for the date's name and address and send him or her a separate invitation. If you ask us, "and Guest" is perfectly acceptable, but remember that you're under no obligation to have everyone come in pairs.

✎ If a lot of your friends have children, and you decide not to include the kids, simply make no mention of them on the invitation. If you want them to come, add each individual name, because if you use the phrase "and family," people may show up with their third cousin once removed. Also think about hiring a baby-sitter to watch all kids during the reception so that the parents can celebrate while the kids play or nap.

THE RIGHT STUFF

Stuffing an invitation packet is as simple as stuffing a turkey. Here's how it's done:

❶ Make sure you've addressed the envelopes before you begin assembling the packets.

❷ Place the tissue over the printed portion of the invitation.

❸ Put all inserts within the fold of the invitation or in front of the tissue.

❹ Put the invitation folded edge first into the unsealed inner envelope with the printed side facing the flap.

❺ Put the inner envelope into the outer envelope with the guest's name facing the flap side of the outer envelope.

❻ Finally, if you still have the strength, seal the outer envelope.

✎ If you're especially close to a friend's preteen or teenage children, thrill them with their very own invitations.

✎ One of Letitia Baldrige's rules of etiquette that we're very pleased with: If two people are living together, they receive one invitation and their names are listed alphabetically—that is, not necessarily with the woman's name first.

✎ For your guests involved in long-term but non live-in relationships, it's nice to send separate invitations. But before you mail them out, call the one you're closer to and make sure they're still speaking.

✎ For a straight married couple where the woman has not changed her name, put her name first, on a separate line from her husband's.

✎ We also feel that if "Mr. and Mrs." doesn't suit the couple you're inviting, giving the woman equal billing is nice; for example:

> Ms. Roz Wolpert
> Mr. Jay Wolpert

Jane and I heard that if you send a wedding invitation to "The President of the United States, 1600 Pennsylvania Avenue, Washington, D.C. 20500," you receive a beautiful response blessing your marriage and signed by the president and first lady. So we sent one to George and Barbara Bush, and—big surprise—got no answer whatsoever. Then we decided to see if we'd have better luck with the Clintons and sent another invitation off to them, with a note explaining why it was four months late. Several months later, we received this in the mail:

*—*TESS

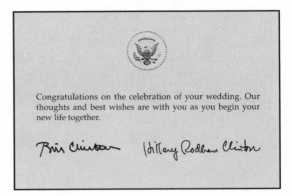

Congratulations on the celebration of your wedding. Our thoughts and best wishes are with you as you begin your new life together.

HERE, THERE, AND EVERYWHERE

LOCATIONS

*I*n the world of real estate, the answer to the question "What are the three most important things to consider when buying a house?" is "Location, location, location." The same thing can be said for a wedding. Here the practical greets the razzle-dazzle. The ideal location must be all things to many different people. It must convey the ambiance you've always dreamed of. It must be accessible to your guests. It must have outlets for the hot plates.

You are now ready to embark on the execution phase of the wedding adventure, during which you may well schlepp from houses of worship to the House of Fabrics. Figuring out where to hold the whole shebang will affect everything about your wedding day. But once you've got a handle on this one facet, other things will begin to fall into place. At this point, it will help if you think of your wedding as two separate events—the ceremony and the reception—that meet in the middle. Some quick examples follow.

> *Every couple wants their wedding in a mansion with a view.*
>
> —HANNELORE HAHN,
> **editor of** *Places*

☛ John and Rick had a religious ceremony in their synagogue followed by a party in the temple's reception room.

☛ Tina and Joanne opted for a full package deal at a small hotel in Kansas City, where they had a short ceremony in the hotel's garden followed by a champagne brunch.

☛ Mary Jo and Keesha booked the Unitarian Chapel they wanted and rented the rec room of a nearby school for a country square-dance reception.

☛ Raul and Mark had a private exchange of rings atop the Eiffel Tower, then went home to Boise and, a month later, had a huge party to celebrate.

SOME PRELIMINARY QUESTIONS

Ultimately, you'll need to answer the question "One site or two?" But first, take a minute to look at some of the broad questions you'll need to ponder as you pursue your final destination(s).

WHAT'S MOST IMPORTANT TO YOU?

There is no single "correct" place to hold your wedding. Some people feel that the ceremony itself is the paramount moment of the day and that partying, if any, should be low-key and sedate. Others want to go all out, and think of their union ceremony as a bang-up, blowout, once-in-a-lifetime, pull-out-all-the-stops kind of a party. Your choice of emphasis will be key in determining where the wedding is to take place.

CAN YOU DEAL WITH A PUBLIC LOCATION?

At some point, even nongay brides and grooms grapple with the issue of private ceremonies in public places. There are people who love being the center of attention and having the rest of the world press its nose to the window to see what they're doing. Then there are people who are innately more shy and private, who really don't want any strangers to intrude on their space. A wedding almost by definition will make you the center of attention—in your own circle, anyway. Before you decide to hold it in a public arena, make sure you know how you'll feel about total strangers becoming a part of the event, and decide if it matters to you whether that public arena is specifically gay. Brian and John had their ceremony on the grounds of city-owned Greystone Mansion in Beverly Hills, and they told us afterward that "people kept walking by, looking in on a wedding and then trying to figure out where the bride was. We thought it was great!"

WHAT ABOUT COMMUNITY AND ACCESSIBILITY?

Now think about geography. Which city will you have your wedding in? (Or even which part of the world, if you have a bad case of wanderlust.) Traditional straight couples often end up getting married in the bride's hometown because her family is footing the bill. This never really seemed entirely fair to us, and many families would no doubt agree. This is one of those areas where we can work toward making a positive change. We've found that most same-sex couples opt to have their wedding in the town or city where they currently live, rather than in either of their hometowns. After all, aren't most of your friends in the city where you live now? And if either or both sets of parents are into it, they can always honor you with a postnuptial party back in the town where they live.

Still, you may be thinking about gathering up the gang and going to another city—say, the one where you vacation. We know of two women who took over Provincetown in the off-season and had their ceremony on the lawn of an inn that was the scene of their previous summer's escapades. After the vows were said, they had a procession right through the middle of town, culminating with festivities at their favorite restaurant. The votes were unanimous that it was a once-in-a-lifetime gathering. A "wedding weekend" can be a real adventure and provide an unsurpassed memory.

One word about distant locations: give some thought to how your guests will get there. Is the city within driving distance of where most of them live? If not, can they afford to fly? Will you put them up for the weekend? And if you want your grandma to be there, will she have trouble boarding the plane with her walker?

HOW MUCH GUIDANCE AND HELP DO YOU NEED?

The amount of built-in help available to you in coordinating and planning your event will greatly depend on where you finally decide to have it. If you go to a hotel, you may in essence be hiring a wedding planner in the guise of the hotel's director of catering. If you go to a restaurant, you might have a wonderful chef who knows everything about food but nothing about pacing a reception. If you have your wedding in a public park you may have to talk your best friend into being in charge of crowd control. There's also the possibility of first hiring a caterer who will know the great party sites in your area and lead you to them. So before you book the hall, think about how much of this you want to do yourself.

There are both practical and romantic sides to finding the *where* or the *wheres*. Before you start your research, you need to get clear in your own mind the following items: number of people you want to invite; how much you can spend; first and second choice of dates; and how you envision the event in general (formal, informal).

Now you're ready to do some window-shopping to see what's out there.

GET ME TO THE CHURCH ... OR NOT: FINDING A LOCATION FOR THE CEREMONY

We don't care who you are or what your sexual orientation is; when you get right down to it, there are basically only two choices of ceremony: civil and religious.

Many people, whether they consider themselves religious or not, want to have their weddings sanctified by the blessings of clergy. (Maybe because it's a time-honored fashion, or maybe because they want to be close to somebody who they feel is closer to God than they are.) Some gay couples feel that it isn't a "legal" union unless the ceremony is performed in a house of worship. Perhaps some gays seek out religious blessings because we are denied legal blessings.

We exchanged vows in a private ceremony—just the two of us—in the church where I had been confirmed thirty years before. No one but the two of us knew about it, but it didn't matter. We really wanted to be in a church, and I really wanted to be in that particular church, which officially wasn't going to have any part of us. But it was an unbelievably special moment that could only have taken place there. The next week we had a huge party at the Holiday Inn.

*—*MADELINE

If you have a specific religious or spiritual affiliation, you'll likely want to hold your ceremony at your house of worship. Chances are you know your church's policy on same-sex ceremonies; if such ceremonies are common, sign up! If you don't know that your church has ever sponsored a same-sex ceremony, remember that there's a first time for everything; make an appointment with the appropriate person from your congregation to get the ball rolling. If you're successful, you'll have cemented the ceremony site; if you're not, you can begin to look elsewhere. It's also possible that you adore your pastor but for one reason or another aren't interested in using your actual church building. In that case, the pastor, rabbi, minister, or whatever can come to you. (Once you decide where you will be, that is.)

If you're not a member of a congregation, it'll probably cost you more to have your ceremony there (that's right, expect to pay a fee for the use of any religious building; more on that later), and they may also have certain dates and times reserved for their own congregation.

You may be interested in a particular church or spiritual center in your area for a number of reasons: you get a good sense from people you know in the congregation, you've always been intrigued by the quotes they post on their signboard outside, or you're simply a fool for the building's architecture. You've got nothing to lose by making a phone call. Tell them that you're not a member of the congregation and that you're curious about their policy; then, if it looks like there's a chance of the rental happening, get into the specifics. They may have never done a same-sex union ceremony, but hey, maybe no one ever asked.

There are numerous chapels that are nondenominational, and we've found that they can be very receptive to nontraditional ceremonies (yep, that sounds like a same-sex wedding to us, all right) because their bread and butter is weddings. The spaces themselves can be quite charming. You know: "wood-and-glass structures in perfect harmony with the blue sky and pines overhead"—those kinds of places. Sometimes they come complete with a minister, and sometimes you can bus one in yourself. Other services might include taped music, an on-site wedding planner, and party facilities.

Before you make a final decision and commit to having your ceremony in a specific place, ask the following questions. Not all of them may be applicable, but make sure you get answers to those that affect you.

DOWN-TO-EARTH QUESTIONS FOR SPIRITUAL LOCATIONS

? How much are the fees for the space? Is a deposit required? At what point can I cancel and still get my money back?

? Must we use clergy affiliated with the location, or is a visiting minister allowed to assist or preside over the ceremony? How is the clergyperson's fee determined?

? During which hours can I use the actual space for rehearsal? For the ceremony?

? How many people does the space hold? (It should be large enough to accommodate all of your guests but not so big that you feel the need to drag strangers in off the street to fill it.)

? Are there facilities for the wedding party to dress in (or pace back and forth in) ahead of time? Are there two separate spaces in case we decide not to see each other until the wedding begins?

? Is there a dress code? (No tube tops or gauchos?)

? What about throwing rice, birdseed, or rose petals inside? Outside?

? What are the cleanup requirements?

? Are there any limitations as far as candles, flowers, or decorations?

? Are there any rules about what our ceremony and vows can be like?

? Will there be any problem with photographers or videographers being inside the church or temple?

? Are there any restrictions on songs or the type of music to be played?

? What is available in terms of music? Is there a piano? An organ? A sound system? How about a boys' choir? Are there extra fees for this?

? Does this location have facilities for a reception?

? Is the site affiliated with a specific catering company that we must use, or can we use our own catering source?

"'SAME-SEX, DIFFERENT-FAITH MARRIAGES' . . . TODAY ON *OPRAH!*"

What if you're one of those couples who are of the same sex but of different faiths? You've no doubt discussed your religious differences; you'll need to arrive at a compromise for your union ceremony. Interfaith weddings are less complex when they take place on neutral ground—for example, a club, hotel, or historic site—because it's easier to mix symbols and customs outside of a religious building. It was important for Melissa to get married in a church, and Rachel and her rabbi agreed to it; but Rachel ultimately realized that she'd be uncomfortable saying her vows beneath a cross, and they moved the ceremony to a friend's home.

What if you choose not to have your ceremony within the walls of a traditional religious center? Read on, and consider all the options we suggest for reception sites.

The reception . . . is the gay part of the wedding where your friends come to greet you and to wish you happiness.

—MARGUERITE BENTLEY,
Wedding Etiquette Complete (1956)

SITES UNSEEN:
FINDING A LOCATION FOR THE RECEPTION

If you have decided to use a church, temple, or spiritual site for the ceremony, you may also want to have your reception on the premises. If you're not the churchgoing kind, you're probably looking for a nonreligious location for both your ceremony and reception. You can choose from a wide variety of sites—

gardens, hotels, private homes, amusement parks; the list is endless. Just as a church provides a specific atmosphere, so too will any nonreligious space. Do a little flashback to that imaginary home movie of your wedding we had you run in chapter 4, and think again about how you can turn your fantasy into a practical reality.

When picking a spot for the reception, you must be sure to do the "We're a same-sex couple" bit. Even if you feel it's nobody's business and your reception will be taking place behind closed doors, think about the fact that there will undoubtedly be interaction between the people running the location and your party. The person you're booking with is not the same person who will be serving food, tending bar, or checking coats the day of the wedding, and his or her unspoken acceptance of you as a lesbian or gay couple is not necessarily a guarantee of a happy party. Discuss it: tell them the truth, the whole truth, and nothing but the truth ahead of time.

Josie and I found a garden room in a really nice hotel, and we loved everything about it. The catering manager was really hip, and when we told him why we were interested in renting the space, he seemed cool about it and said that he'd get back to us. When he called the next day, he seemed a little embarrassed but told us that he didn't think the staff could handle it, and that we might enjoy ourselves more someplace else. Off the record, he recommended another place that turned out to be ideal.

—Luisa

Now, when you're booking a space for your wedding, you might be renting just that—the space. Period. No chairs, no tables, no nothing. (*Nada. Niente.* Zilch. Zippo.) Certainly a park or a pier might fall into this category. Other spaces such as a hotel may be able to provide everything from a four-course sit-down meal to place cards with your names on them, and may come with program coordinators who will work with you to make sure every detail is taken care of.

When sizing up locations, be sure to examine the whole range of what is provided. Your guiding principle should be to find out exactly what is or is not included in the price, because unexpected extras can add up quickly.

A package deal can be tempting because it makes things feel more manageable. However, beware the packages! With them you may find yourselves sacrificing some of the things you truly madly deeply wanted because the package didn't offer them. (You may not even be allowed to bring in an outside cake, or if you are, they may charge you a "cutting and serving" fee.) With locations that provide nothing but the space, you can have it all your way—the flip side being that this may of course mean much more careful planning, and many more potential headaches.

Oh, we can hear you now: "What are they talking about? We want to get married in the park. What could be so difficult about that?" Maybe nothing; but you should make sure you understand what is ahead of you. The list of things you may have to supply is extensive and may include: food, beverages, tables, chairs, dishware, utensils, staff

DREAM A LITTLE DREAM

Spend some time investigating your first choices; a swank hotel or a private yacht may be more attainable than you imagined. There are ways to trim costs and still get the wedding of your dreams.

★ If you have your heart set on a certain hotel, go to the catering director and see if you can strike a deal for an off night.

★ Brunch, lunch, and dessert receptions can be done much more inexpensively than a sit-down dinner in the same setting.

★ If you want that restaurant with the revolving bar that gives a 360-degree view of the city, you can book it for two hours, have cocktails and nibbles, and be done with it.

★ Stay away from June!

. . . maybe even electricity for the sound system. We're not saying it's not do-able, because it happens all the time. Just be prepared to be detail oriented.

With this fun factoid placed firmly under your belts, let's take a look at some location categories you might want to consider.

HOTELS AND CATERING HALLS

Hotels do a huge business in arranging banquets, bar mitzvahs, conventions, proms, and of course, weddings. There are also large buildings called catering halls that have a number of separate party rooms along with a few non-sectarian chapels. Hotels and catering halls are pros when it comes to handling large affairs, and they'll try to grant your every request. They'll have experience with and suggestions for just about everything, from menus to seating arrangements.

Each operation is run differently, but most places require a minimum number of guests, at least for their main ballroom. If your guest list isn't lengthy, ask to see other spaces in the hotel, such as breakfast rooms, meeting halls, and side lobbies.

Some hotels and halls can sell you a package that includes food, drink, decorations, flowers, a cake, and maybe even a house band—everything from soup to nuts. (And some will insist on it.) Some can furnish altars, aisles, tents, and canopies. Some hotels have gorgeous garden settings, maybe with a gazebo thrown in, where you can hold the ceremony; afterward, guests move to another part of the hotel for food and fun.

One big downside to these places is that they can be very busy, without a great deal of privacy. Catering halls often have several weddings on the same day, and stories run rampant about grandparents wandering into the wrong wedding, unruly children running from room to room, and guests being able to hear strains of "The Bunny Hop" from the party next door while *their* party is doing the hora. And if you add to this mix the fact that you are a wedding couple of two men or two women, the possibilities for confusion are endless. (On second thought, a schmaltzy gay wedding at a catering hall sounds like it might be a lot of fun!)

The decor in hotels can also be—dare we say it?—tacky. (There, we said it.) Make sure that when you take a look at the room you're considering, you do so at the same time of day that you'll be celebrating in it. One couple we know checked out their hall one weeknight after work and it seemed fine; they were somewhat dismayed when at their afternoon reception, the daylight revealed large water stains all over the wall-to-wall carpeting. On the other hand, some hotels have stunning decor—you'd move in in a second—but their food is less than inspired. If you end up booking a hotel for the big day, you'll have to do the ambiance/food balancing act here, and try to come up with an acceptable level for both.

Also be sure to follow up your initial visits with one last scouting trip about a week before the event to make sure the antique furniture you loved has not been replaced with chrome and high-tech.

A hotel lends itself to a formal or semiformal reception. It's also something to think about for receptions where guests may be traveling long distances, as the hotel may offer special room rates for group bookings. (They may even throw in a free honeymoon suite for good measure.)

RESTAURANTS AND NIGHTCLUBS

Did you ever try to take your Aunt Bessie from out of town to your favorite French bistro, only to find a Closed for Private Party sign on the front door? Just think, that could be you inside! Restaurants can be ideal for informal receptions. Larger restaurants often have a special room they will rent out for parties; others will make arrangements to let a private reception take over the entire place on an off night or during off hours. If there's a restaurant that you frequent and you sort of know the folks who run the place, see what they can do for you. Restaurant owners like loyal patrons, and in their eyes everyone who attends the party is a potential customer.

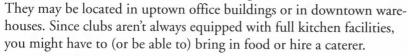

Nightclubs and dance bars can work out nicely for a reception in the morning (brunch and break-dancing after the ceremony, anyone?) or early afternoon or on a weeknight. They may be located in uptown office buildings or in downtown warehouses. Since clubs aren't always equipped with full kitchen facilities, you might have to (or be able to) bring in food or hire a caterer.

PRIVATE CLUBS

If you're a member of a country club or a private club (anyplace that has membership requirements or restrictions), you can consider having your wedding or reception there. Because we know that some clubs are quite conservative, you should consider the "public" aspect of holding your wedding there. We think it's great if you're comfortable dealing with the reactions you may get from the other members—another one of those golden opportunities to educate!

You might be eligible for club privileges without even knowing it. Check out alumni clubs, especially if you live in New York, where there's a Harvard Club, a Princeton Club, a Yale Club, and so on, each with its own uptown facility. And throughout the United States there's

An Italian restaurant where we sometimes go for dinner closed down for our Thursday-night wedding reception. There was a funky juke box that entertained the crowd with hits from the '60s and '70s— perfect for our age group— and the owner gave us a deal on wine and beer, and only charged us for what we drank. He made minipizzas for hors d'oeuvres, and for dinner he served his house antipasto and a couple of pasta dishes. We ended up singing "That's Amore" until the wee hours of the morning.

—JONATHAN

an organization called the University Club, whose facilities are open to the graduate of any accredited college who is sponsored by a current member. Call the alumni office of your alma mater to see if you qualify for membership and if there is a club location near you.

Depending on where you live, there may be places having club affiliations with sororities, fraternities, professional guilds, unions, charity organizations, etc. In many downtown offices there are business clubs with restaurants that serve lunch each day and are then used to host receptions and meetings. Ask around to see if anyone you know has access to these spots.

Some private clubs can be in choice locations and beautifully appointed; they're really exclusive restaurants in disguise. Others might simply be meeting halls, providing you with the basic space and few amenities. You'll have to ask the same questions you would with any other location, and find out about the particulars of services offered.

PRIVATE HOMES

Home weddings have always been popular with the general population, and in our travels we've found that they're often the first choice of gays and lesbians. (See chapter 8, "Try This at Home, Kids.")

Having the wedding at home happens to be the easiest situation in terms of not having to deal with hassles from the outside world, because you're bringing everyone into *your* world.

A home wedding ceremony and/or reception has other advantages: you know the location well, it's always available, there's no charge for the facilities, it allows for flexibility, you don't have to worry about going overtime, and it's the most personal of all places. If you have a beautiful yard or garden, it can be the ideal place for the vows. (And gardens help keep the cost of flowers down.) You can have the food catered, or you can make it a covered-dish affair.

OUTTA SITES! (UNEXPECTED LOCATIONS)

Did ya hear the one about Ginger and Patty?

Ginger O'Connor and Patty Johnson wanted to have the most unusual wedding ever, and agonized over the location for months. Finally they agreed that they would exchange vows in the remote jungles of Africa. They chartered a plane for the wedding party, and arranged to have a herd of elephants carry them to the ceremony site, a recently discovered altar dating back to the second century B.C. As they neared the destination, Ginger and Patty turned to each other with congratulating smiles at having pulled off the unique wedding of the decade. At that moment there was the roar of a trumpet, the elephants stopped, and the guide announced to the crowd, "All make way for the Marenthal/Smith wedding!"

This story is of course apocryphal, but it illustrates the futility of trying to create your entire wedding celebration around being the first at something or using your celebration as a

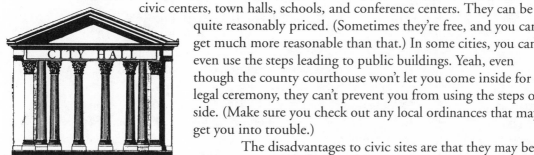

platform for being entirely different. Let's face it: you're two women, you're two men, you're getting married—that's pretty adventurous. By all means, if you're dying to exchange vows on a carousel at the amusement park because that's where you met, go for it. But don't do it simply because you think it's unique; we're here to tell you that almost everything has been done before. We've all read the wacky wedding letters sent to "Dear Abby"; we know that people have been married during the Rose Parade, in hot-air balloons, surfing, bungee-jumping off a bridge, scuba diving, during a marathon, and 200 feet underground in a cave. Question why you might need to make an outrageous statement, and ask yourself if you want your wedding to be truly memorable to *you* or if you want it to be the answer to a future Trivial Pursuit question.

But these are the extreme cases of stunt weddings. We're not saying that if you don't have your ceremony in a church and your reception in a hotel, you're bizarre beyond belief. There are a number of fascinating and unusual places for you to have your ceremony, your reception, or both.

As you go through your average day, look at every place you see as a potential wedding site. We've heard of some spectacular weddings taking place in office buildings. Yes, you heard correctly—office buildings. Take a good look at your lobby and try to picture it without the delivery men and security guards. Commercial-building lobbies have been called the cathedrals of the twentieth century, designed by the finest architects and built using the best and most unusual materials. Throw out your preconceptions and look at every space you enter with a new eye.

Consider civic sites, which include parks, gardens, amphitheaters, recreation centers, civic centers, town halls, schools, and conference centers. They can be quite reasonably priced. (Sometimes they're free, and you can't get much more reasonable than that.) In some cities, you can even use the steps leading to public buildings. Yeah, even though the county courthouse won't let you come inside for a legal ceremony, they can't prevent you from using the steps outside. (Make sure you check out any local ordinances that may get you into trouble.)

The disadvantages to civic sites are that they may be booked up months, even years, in advance; they can be real hellholes; and your locality may or may not have a liberal attitude when it comes to renting to you. You'll also have to check into the catering rules governing the places you're considering—can you bring in anyone you choose, or do you have to go with someone from a preapproved list? If the site is outdoors, make sure you have a plan B in case of inclement weather.

To find out what is available, contact your local parks and recreation department, visitors/tourism bureau, or chamber of commerce.

An excellent source is your nearest historical society; contact them to see if they rent out sites for private functions. Historical societies will have a roster of designated buildings ranging

Lambda's Marriage Resolution

"Because:
Marriage is a basic human right and an individual personal choice.
Resolved:
The State should not interfere with same-gendered couples who choose to marry and share fully and equally in the rights, responsibilities, and commitment of civil marriage."

Signers of this resolution include everyone from the usual suspects (Martina Navratilova, RuPaul, and Madonna) to the not-exactly sur-prising (Kathy Najimy, Gloria Steinem, Whoopi Goldberg, Ted Danson, and Mary Steenburgen) to the "Gee, I had no idea they were that lib-eral" (Helen Hunt, Laura Dern, David Duchovny, and Coretta Scott King).

from deco mansions to vintage diners. In addition, think about not-for-profit institutions such as aquariums, museums, theaters, botanical gardens, and colleges. Renting party spaces is a source of revenue for many of these organizations, and they'll have at their fingertips all the pertinent information on costs and availability of some fabulous spaces.

Another great source is a book called *Places: A Directory of Pub-lic Places for Private Events and Private Places for Public Functions* (see the Suggested References at the end of this book). In addition to a list-ing of some of the country's prime civic sites, the book also includes privately owned buildings that rent out to the general public and gives contact phone numbers for all listings. *Places* focuses on major cities, listing sites by their maximum capacity. (If you're in New York and planning on having a large reception, it's good to know that Roseland Ballroom holds 3,450.) Typical listings include galleries, piers, race-ways, rinks, aquariums, museums, and schools. It lists pages and pages of amazing suburban and rural sites such as former estates, villas that are now community centers, opera houses, manor houses, fairgrounds, rustic mills, dairy farms, and wineries. If you're baseball fans, go to Maryland and get married at Babe Ruth's birthplace. If you've never been one for the kindness of strangers but adore the drama of Ten-nessee Williams, you can be married in the New Orleans house where he lived in the forties and got the inspiration for his Garden District plays. In Boston, rent Faneuil Hall Marketplace for the day.

THE SEA OF LOVE: WATER WEDDINGS

We don't know why this is, but we've found that a number of gay and lesbian weddings are held at sea. (Maybe it's because we don't feel a part of the mainstream or the mainland.) Thomas and Michael held their Los Angeles union ceremony on a boat in international wa-ters to symbolize that same-sex marriage is not recognized legally in any state. Their invitations were printed on art-deco steamship posters carrying the words "Recognized by No Nation, Married in International Waters."

A wedding on the water offers you a number of options, from barges to riverboats. A few gentle warnings about steering this course: first of all, realize that there's no leaving the party early, so you'd better make sure that everyone is having a damn good time; and unless you're just cruising around the marina, rough seas can potentially put quite a damper on the entire affair. (And traditionally, champagne and Dramamine do not mix well.)

Then there's a full-fledged cruise—you know, the ones that sail the Caribbean or take you down the coast of Mexico? Several companies have cruises exclusively for women or exclusively for men, and they all offer wedding ceremonies as part of the amenities included in the price of your ticket. Babs Daitch, the publicity director of Olivia Cruises, told us that on every one of their sailings, the ship's captain performs two or three weddings. They provide cake and champagne, flowers, and certificates.

THE LOCATION LITMUS TEST

QUESTIONS TO ASK WHEN VISITING A SITE FOR RECEPTIONS AND/OR CEREMONIES

❑ Is the ambiance of this location what you had in mind for your wedding? Is it so formal that you'll be uncomfortable, or is it just a little too loose? Make sure you visit the site at the time of day you're planning on having the wedding.

❑ Is this the actual room where the event will be held? Don't be fooled by the phrase "Your room looks just like this one," because each space will have small peculiarities that make it unique.

❑ How many guests will be drinking, schmoozing, dining, and dancing in this space? What is the maximum number allowed by law, seated and unseated? Will it seem like the room is empty, or will it be so crowded that the guests won't be able to lift their glasses for the toast?

❑ How are the auxiliary facilities such as kitchens, bars, and bathrooms?

❑ Do you have access to adjacent spaces such as foyers, anterooms, gardens, etc.?

❑ How will the space handle the flow of the event? If both ceremony and reception are to be held in the same space, can it handle both?

❑ Will there be anyone else using that particular space on the same day? Will there be any other weddings in the building at the same time? Are there any provisions for privacy?

❑ What about handicap access?

❑ Is there a place for you to primp before the ceremony? A changing room for you to use before you take off on your honeymoon?

❑ Can you decorate in any way you want?

❑ Is there adequate parking? If there is valet parking, what is the fee?

❏ What about climate control? Is there air conditioning in the summer? Heating in the winter? Can the windows be opened?

❏ Is there someone on the premises who provides catering? Is it okay to bring in outside liquor and food services? Is there a penalty for doing that?

❏ Is there staff to assist you on the day of the wedding? (This can range from servers to the catering director.)

❏ Is there security in the building? Will there be support staff there on the day of the wedding in case of electrical or plumbing problems?

❏ Who is responsible for cleanup?

❏ Will music be effective in this space? Will dance music be loud enough, and is there an area for people to talk if they don't want to dance? Is the sound system provided, and is it appropriate for both live music and a DJ? Is there a piano available?

❏ Are there any restrictions as to kinds of music, loudness, hours when music can be played, and so forth?

❏ What are the exact hours that you can use the facility? What are the added charges for overtime? Are setup times and cleanup times included?

❏ How are the charges broken down? Is there a flat fee or an hourly rate? Is it less expensive if you are a member? What about a deposit?

❏ If you have to cancel, can you get your deposit back?

Try This at Home, Kids

Home Weddings

Undoubtedly the most personal and intimate place to have your wedding is right in your own backyard or, if you don't have a backyard, right in your very own living room. (Or if you don't have a living room, right in your very own—uh—whatever. You pick. You might want to draw the line at the laundry room, but hey, we're loose.) When you invite guests into your home, you are bringing them into your private world, lending a special poignancy to the celebration; after all, this is the physical space where you as a couple have set up the foundation for your lives together. Entertaining at home is an invitation for guests to participate in your individual tastes, styles, and—yes, your eccentricities. (We *know* you have them.)

At-home weddings are also, hands down, the most private of all weddings. Depending on where you live, there is a safety associated with being in a house or apartment that works out well for same-sex couples. Some of your friends—or indeed, you yourself—may feel that it's easier to loosen up and let your hair down in a home than it is in a hotel or restaurant.

And depending on whom you invite, a home wedding can even be seen as a political act, an act of literally opening doors. We've heard stories of coworkers being invited to the festivities who for the first time in their lives are walking into the house of a gay or lesbian person. Any doubts they may have had to begin with disappear when they see that your shared home is just like any other couple's—maybe even warmer or happier or more comfortable.

CLICK YOUR HEELS THREE TIMES AND
REPEAT AFTER ME, "THERE'S NO PLACE LIKE HOME . . ."

Remember when we talked about the wedding style? Well, in a home wedding, your home becomes part of the style. Your uniqueness, your *you*-ness, is presented in the details that are automatically there. The backdrop for the gathering is the piano top full of photos that tell the history of the two of you together; it's the collection of your favorite "Doonesbury" comic strips and art postcards that you have attached by magnets to your refrigerator; it's your framed doctorate that hangs in the guest bathroom. Your individual and combined personalities are immediately reflected as guests find themselves surrounded by the things you treasure.

At this point you might be saying, "Yeah, I'd love to have our wedding at home, but we don't live in a very impressive place and we don't really have a huge area that would be appropriate and that back room is kind of junky and . . . " Hold it right there, pardner. You may be feeling that you're not set up for a large gathering because you're so used to seeing your habitats as just that—your habitats. The kitchen is for cooking, the den is for reading, the bedroom is for . . . sleeping. Try instead to look at everything with new eyes. Wander through the various parts of your home and think about using any and all of the spaces you have. It will help if you begin to de-clutter the house a little, even mentally, as you take this initial tour. You'd be surprised at how inviting a side porch can become when you remove those big bags filled with recyclables.

Don't be too hard on your place. We've heard of absolutely great weddings taking place in small apartments and modest backyards. But if after much examination you decide that your home just isn't appropriate, don't forget the possibility of using somebody else's digs—maybe those of a member of your family or a close friend.

HOME WEDDINGS

TIPS FOR HAPPY HOME-WEDDING HOSTS AND HOSTESSES

Carefully consider the number of guests you're inviting. Look at the space with a critical eye, and try to imagine how many people could stand there with elbow room. (Think of all of them lifting glasses to their mouths to drink; now you know why they call it elbow room.) Depending on what sort of vittles you'll be serving, think about where all the folks will perch in order to eat. Unless you live in a large home or have spacious grounds, you may have to limit your guest list.

Take over all of the space that you have. Leave no stone unturned in your quest to maximize your usable space. The dead space at the end of the hall is perfect for a small card table that you can turn into a self-service bar. The dining-room table can be pushed against the wall to open up the room for mingling. The utility room can house tubs of ice that hold chilled soda and champagne. Can the basement be cleaned up a bit and its lights turned down low for dancing?

Let the character of your home help establish the character of the celebration. If you have a balcony or a room with a view, use it as a natural backdrop for the ceremony. Invite your guests an hour before nightfall and exchange vows as the sun begins to set. If you have wide-open spaces and you love dancing, hire a DJ and get down, get funky.

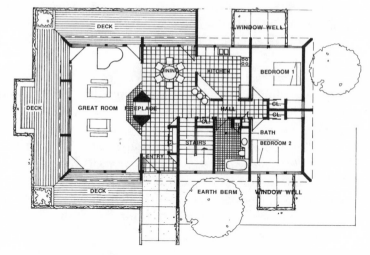

Design your day in a way that suits you. Whether you're hiring a caterer to do the food and a florist to do the decor or doing it all yourselves, remember that this is your celebration, in your home, and that it should reflect your tastes, not the tastes of the people you're paying. (Unless you don't have any taste yourself and that's what you're paying for.)

Consider an open house reception. An open house is perfect for smaller homes where you want to invite fifty people for the reception but are afraid they won't all fit at the same time.

Are you thinking of using your home for both the ceremony and the reception, or merely for the festivities following a church wedding or vows exchanged on the steps of city hall? If you're doing everything at home, you may want to think in terms of creating separate spaces for the two parts of your event. Prearrange to have certain people move furniture; you can quickly turn a romantic wedding-vow area into a party room. (If the move is at all complicated, you might even want to have a rehearsal of this the day before or the week before.) Anyway, the home ceremony and the home reception each have special needs. Let's tackle the ceremony first.

SETTING THE SCENE FOR THE CEREMONY

As you search for the perfect place to say "I do," keep the following suggestions in mind.

Look for a background with some drama. This is not as hard as you think. Favorite spots include in front of a fireplace, on a balcony, at the foot of a staircase (you can make an entrance!), under a tree, and on a back lawn. Spaces that informally frame the ceremony—between two columns, for instance, or in a doorway—work very nicely, thank you. The archway between a living room and a dining room creates both an architectural framework and a large space in which guests can gather. You can even rent a wood or brass arch for under $50.

Don't feel obligated to create a formal audience seating area. Guests don't have to sit on chairs separated by a middle aisle as they would in a chapel or synagogue. They don't even have to be separated in a formal way from the "stage." Think of them as being a part of the action, like Sensurround.

All of your chairs don't have to match. You can rent or borrow folding chairs if you wish, but don't rule out a mixture of sofas, stairs, ottomans, and rocking chairs, with pillowed floor space for the kids and the agile.

Guests can stand. But in all fairness, don't expect them to be comfortable on their feet for more than about fifteen minutes.

Don't rule out minor cosmetic surgery. Although you shouldn't have to redo your house for the wedding, you can certainly minimize its flaws by covering them up with something beautiful. Oh honey, they do it in Hollywood all the time! Drape fabric over a blank wall, surround your ceremony area with potted flowers, or if it's an evening affair, use candlelight. Splurge on an entire bank of flowering plants to line the hall.

Take a long look at your front porch. If you have a modicum of privacy there, or if you don't give a damn what the neighbors think, have the ceremony on your front porch. This is really wonderful because immediately after you've said your vows you can lead your guests over the threshold and through the front door to the first party you have in your home as a married couple.

WHERE'S THE PARTY?

Do the same space analysis that you did when sniffing out your ceremony area, only now consider the other activities you're planning—eating, dancing, entertainment. You don't want to have a reception that isn't appropriate for the space. Don't expect to hire a rock-and-roll band and then have people just sit around and listen; they're going to want to dance. Make sure they won't be doing it on the tabletops. If you're serving "complex" food, there should be a place where people can sit down and actually put their plates on something other than their laps. Can you seat people outdoors on quilts spread on the lawn? If you've hired a psychic to read palms, is there a separate room where that can happen—and take some of the burden off the main party area? You get the picture.

FOR A HASSLE-FREE HOME CEREMONY

🏠 Have a rehearsal at home just as you would in a church. Set up and check the sound system, the movement you've planned for the ceremony, the musicians for the reception, etc.

🏠 Post a mother or mother substitute at the front door before show time. He or she will greet the guests, tell them where they can leave their coats, and direct them toward the ceremony site.

🏠 Assign some friends to act as ersatz ushers and help people with seating. Early arrivers will probably rush to reserve good seats; those who intend to stand will find a spot with good sight lines.

🏠 If you have a minister or rabbi, ask if you need to set aside a private area for him or her to change. (People really are curious about what clerics wear under those robes, you know.)

🏠 Assign someone to deal with guests who arrive late. Decide whether latecomers will be allowed to sneak in, or whether they will be asked to remain in the hall until an appropriate break in the service.

🏠 Ceremony music should be provided by a single musician, or a CD or tape player. Don't get too complex unless you have professional sound facilities.

THE TECHNOLOGY OF TENTING

Let's say you've got a great backyard area, only it's not very private, or the lawn is in atrocious shape, or you're afraid that it's going to rain or that the sun will be so hot that your guests will be dropping like flies. A tent just might be the answer to your prayers; it's like putting a reception hall right in your backyard.

Tenting is the perfect solution for weddings at homes or historical sites. Tents are completely flexible, allowing you to create anything you want inside: you can make them look like parks with trees and archways, or you can make them into elegant rooms with chandeliers, parquet floors, and stained-glass paneling. You can have air-conditioning or heating, depending on your needs. Some tents come with their own generators for cooking, heating, cooling, and electricity for musicians or a DJ. The cost of a tented affair can be about the same as that of a similar function in an established location— a state-of-the-art tent for 150 people might rent for about $1,500—but the upside is that you're celebrating on your own turf.

ANTICIPATING PROBLEMS BEFORE THEY HAPPEN

Extraordinary circumstances (inviting fifty people into your home would qualify) require extraordinary preparation. You'll have to plan your crowd control carefully or risk confusion or even chaos. It's important to anticipate possible problems. Here are some things to keep in mind:

✔ Check with the police department for local ordinances regarding traffic and parking. Are there regulations about parking on the street? Is there enough room? If there's a large crowd coming, check into valet parking. If traffic congestion is an issue, you may want to have a certified person directing traffic and parking. You certainly don't want your guests to be taking home traffic tickets as mementos of your wedding day. The police department can also give advice on security. It might be a good move to get a rent-a-cop to watch cars during the shindig.

✔ Speak with or send a note to your neighbors, explaining to them that a party will be taking place (especially if you're thinking of hiring Megadeth as the band).

✔ Consider the size of the kitchen and bathrooms. Are the facilities appropriate for the number of people expected?

✔ Critically analyze your refrigerator. Is it going to be able to handle the stress?

✔ What about power? If you're having band amplifiers, microphones, strings of lights, etc., your normal house current may not be able to handle the extra load. For about $50 a day, you can rent a generator that will eliminate these worries.

HELP! I NEED SOMEBODY

The good news is that professionals can help out in areas where you are deficient; they can also do the things that you hate to do when throwing a party. Even if you've never hired any party help, this is the one occasion where you really should give the idea serious consideration. Can't cook worth a damn? The food can be brought in. Don't want to lift a finger? Call an employment agency and hire servers and bartenders for the day. Or maybe you and your friends want to do everything yourselves. You can still hire a cleaning service to make sure that the house is in pristine shape before the guests arrive—or after they leave.

If you hire a caterer, they'll work with you to determine the setup of your space and tell you what you need to rent or borrow in order to pull it off. A truly professional caterer, and one well worth the money, will actually function as a wedding planner for you, coordinating with the florist, the bakery, even the entertainment. (See chapter 11, "Eat, Drink, and Be Married," for everything you need to know about a caterer.)

If you're doing most or all of this without professional help, ask yourself the same questions you would ask of an outside caterer. You must be concerned not just with the cooking, but also with the storing and presentation of the food. Some guidelines:

🔑 Enlist the help of family and friends to assist with cooking and baking a few weeks before the wedding; use recipes for dishes that can be frozen immediately and defrosted before the wedding.

🔑 If you're a great cook and want to do most of the food yourself, you might still hire a caterer to handle finishing touches and to prepare any on-the-spot dishes.

🔑 Check out your kitchen equipment and your serving pieces. Count your own dishes, flatware, and glassware. Pull out all of the platters and utensils, and make thorough lists of what you have. Include those old pitchers and bowls you never thought you'd use.

☞   See what you can borrow. Friends may be able to loan you most of everything you don't have. (And make a list of everything you borrow.)

☞   Make sure you have adequate refrigeration; you can resort to ice chests for most items on the day of the wedding.

☞   If you can't afford full catering but are not into cooking, consider takeout for one hundred. (Drive-through windows not recommended.)

☞   Use food as decoration. Browse through cookbooks for serving suggestions and food-planning ideas. We've seen towers of colorful food in canning jars behind the buffet, raw veggies spilling from hollowed-out cabbages, and fruits and vegetables becoming still-life sculptures.

☞   In the bar area, display a sample bottle of each of the beverages you're serving. Keep drinks iced in large galvanized tin tubs, which can be bought quite cheaply at hardware centers.

WITH A LITTLE HELP FROM YOUR FRIENDS (OR MAYBE EVEN A WHOLE LOT)

When word of an impending wedding gets out, friends and family are often so happy that everyone wants to get into the act. They'll be calling you and asking, "Is there anything I can do to help?" This is great; it means you have been blessed with a warm, supportive, and generous circle of friends.

However, remember that old adage about too many cooks and what they do to the broth? Let it be a mild warning to you; don't let control of the planning and running of your wedding

HOME WEDDINGS

slip through your fingers, unless of course you choose to gratefully bow out and have others take over. Be on the lookout for folks who are well intentioned but won't fulfill their end of the bargain as promised. Otherwise, as you prepare to walk down the aisle, you'll find yourselves holding slips of paper that say "I.O.U. one bouquet" instead of the floral arrangements your (until now) best friend promised to make for you.

Be careful about who gets what assignment. The first person who says, "I just got a new camera. I can be the photographer!" may not be the one best qualified for the job, and you'll find your wedding album filled with blurry pictures, mostly of the food table and the husband of one of your coworkers, whom you had never met until that day.

DAMAGE CONTROL: SELF-HELP HELP

Be absolutely clear with friends as to exactly what you expect them to do. Go over their duties with them as much in advance as you can; then call to double-check as the ceremony gets closer.

If they're doing something that you would have paid someone else to do anyway, offer to pay them for their services (though they'll probably refuse).

If you initially approach them for the favor, say something along the lines of "We'd love it if you'd consider making some of that incredible guacamole dip of yours as a wedding present. You will? Great, can you make it for fifty?"

If the job requires professional expertise, make sure you are familiar with the person's work before you commit.

Practice and use the sentences, "No thank you. We really appreciate your offer, but it's already taken care of. We want you to just come and enjoy yourselves."

If you're going away immediately afterward, put one person in charge of organizing cleanup.

Don't ask people to double up on jobs; appoint a different person to each specific task if possible.

It's best if you don't enlist a friend to tend bar. If he or she is not a drinker, chances are your friend won't be very good at pouring drinks; and if he or she *is* a drinker, your bartender might just have a few too many and wander off to socialize, leaving the bar unattended.

▼ # STANDING ON CEREMONY

THE WEDDING CEREMONY

*A*lthough we like to think of everything in this book as vital and fascinating, what's coming up here is probably the most important chapter. That's because the ceremony is the cornerstone of a wedding celebration; without it, there would be no reception, no registering, no tuxedos, no showers, no flowers . . . well, you get the drift. Straight couples with similar religious and cultural backgrounds have fewer big decisions here. (Are we going to quote from *The Prophet*? Who can we get to sing "Wind Beneath My Wings"?) For lesbians and gays, the ceremony has more wrinkles, more texture to it than you can possibly imagine.

That's because you are on the cutting edge here, kids. How fortunate you are that there are no rules, no scripts, no long lists of "Have to's" that your mothers will wave under your noses. It's *your* wedding ceremony, and anytime you choose to draw on established traditions, you will be doing so with an acute awareness of why you're doing it, not just because "that's what you do in a wedding."

If you want a more or less traditional wedding ceremony, substituting two brides or two grooms for the heretofore customary bride and groom, that's great. And if you want to combine traditions and customs from different cultures that you find meaningful, well, that's great too. With gay weddings, there is not yet any true "tradition." (Although someday there will be, and you're making it right now.) So you get to create your own symbols that are new and appropriate— symbols that reflect your own personal realities, as well as the reality of you as a couple.

One thing we can guarantee is that no matter what your ceremony is like, there will not be many dry eyes in the house. Because not only are you two people joining your lives together, you are also performing an act of bravery in the face of a society that in general has not embraced the magic of your love. Every couple we interviewed responded with some variation on what Bob said: "We were bawling, and everyone in the church was bawling. It looked like they were all surrendering, there were so many white handkerchiefs." Oh sure, *any* wedding is emotional . . . but gay weddings arrive without a sense of inevitability. At this point in our history, rarely does a guest sit through the ceremony thinking, "Ah, I always knew they'd get married someday."

Long after the party is over, the essence of your ceremony—the words, the atmosphere, the love and joy generated—lives on.

MEMBERS OF THE WEDDING

A traditional wedding party is also sometimes referred to as a "bridal party" (*ugh*). It consists of some or all of the following: a maid or matron of honor, bridesmaids, a flower girl, a best man, ushers, a ring bearer, the mother of the bride, the father of the bride, and the groom's parents. Throughout history they have each had their designated job descriptions, but the etiquette of this too has evolved; in modern weddings you're apt to find the bride walking down the aisle unescorted or the couple's golden retriever appearing as the ring bearer. The best man can be a woman, and the maid of honor can be a man. Geez, if the straight world is gender-bending like this, just think of what *you* can do.

We've heard of the participants in a same-sex wedding referred to as guardian angels, the good folks at the altar, honor attendants, our best people, and the inner circle. Call them what you will, they are the people you want close by on one of the most important days of your life.

Selecting the people you would like to participate in your wedding is in some ways like walking through a mine field. If somebody who thought all these years he was your best friend doesn't make the final cut to be an usher, his feelings are going to be hurt. Ask one sibling to participate but leave the other six out and some of them will be angry.

When scanning the available pool from which you will eventually pick your wedding party (and we'll get to those job descriptions in a sec), there are certain characteristics you should look for in all of your choices. Some of the adjectives that seem to pop up with regularity in the bride magazines are: *cooperative, friendly, cheerful,* and *perky.* The people you choose should also be calm and reliable, because you're going to be so nervous that you want them to be like the Rock of Gibraltar. Here, then, is a rundown on the various bodies you might need.

SOMEONE TO GIVE YOU AWAY

Some people blanch when the concept of giving a person away comes up, because they associate it with women as property. It all depends on how you look at it. We like to think of it as someone accompanying you to the border you're going to cross as you begin the next part of life's journey. It's like the moment in *The Wizard of Oz* when the Munchkins have led Dorothy to the border of Munchkinland; as soon as she puts that ruby slipper on the Yellow Brick Road, it becomes her own ball game.

If you're particularly close to one or both sets of parents, consider including them in the processional. Beth and Patti told us that when they started planning their wedding, the idea of being given away struck them as "kind of an awful custom. . . . But we've come to think that maybe both of our parents should escort us down the aisle. More attractive to this part of the ritual is rite of passage, the acknowledgment that we are now at a new place in our lives, one of creating family."

If your parents won't be participating in the ceremony in this fashion, don't despair. Most of us make our friends into our extended family, or our chosen family, and there are probably a number of people that you can consider for the honor of escorting each of you down the aisle. Why not choose your best friend? Or have your *two* closest friends flanking you? A son or daughter from a previous marriage? Jane chose her literary agent, Martin.

PEOPLE TO TAKE GOOD CARE OF YOU (A.K.A. YOUR BEST PEOPLE)

The best man is historically the guy you'd want at your side in time of war or conflict; the maid/matron of honor, your closest confidant.

We've come to look at these two roles, no matter what gender you choose to fill them with, as involving people who can help you out ahead of time if need be (so they should probably live in your area) and, most important, those who know you the best—friends who know your tricks, know when you need support, and know when to nail you to the wall if you're being unreasonable.

PEOPLE TO TAKE CARE OF YOUR GUESTS

In days of yore people who looked after the guests were known as ushers, attendants, and so on—your "good people." Fill these slots with men or women who are friendly and have stamina. Conventionally, ushers arrive at the wedding site early to make sure everything is in order, accompany people to their seats while partaking in some light banter, and help elderly or out-of-town guests get from the ceremony to the reception. If you're having formal seating, you should think about having at least one usher for every fifty guests.

PEOPLE TO CARRY THINGS FOR YOU

You may need someone to carry the train of your dress, or people to hold up a *chuppah,* as well as ring bearers and flower children (who typically are four to eight years old; conventional wisdom says that if they're too young, they cannot be counted on to perform predictably in front of a crowd). The ring bearer often carries symbolic (read: "fake") rings on the cushion just in case his footing is a little unsteady. The real rings can be carried by you, your best people, one of your parents, or your officiant. We've found that in gay weddings these spots are often filled by people who may not be the couple's very closest friends but who hold a special place in their hearts. P.S.: If a close friend is coming in from out of town and you want him or her to be part of the ceremony, this role is a simple one to jump into.

PEOPLE TO PERFORM

There's nothing more touching than having good friends lend their performance talents to the ceremony. But do yourselves a favor and ask only accomplished singers or musicians; the only thing worse than no music is bad music. Performers also include people who will recite or read, tell stories, or reminisce. (They can also come from your supply of "good people.")

PEOPLE TO TEND TO THE DETAILS

There should be one or two designated gofers or "helper bees" to tend to the details—one for the ceremony site and one for the reception site. They need to be responsible, organized, and good at communicating. Their main responsibilities are to coordinate the ceremony rehearsal, whip the wedding party into shape and get them moving down the aisle, do last-minute repair jobs on your hem or straighten your tie, and keep an eye on the caterer. (If you've decided to hire a wedding coordinator or planner, he or she might handle some of the helper bee's work load.)

SOMEONE TO PERFORM THE CEREMONY

A priest, a minister, a rabbi, or a combination usually performs the ceremony. Another option is to eschew religious institutions altogether and go with a layperson—for example, a judge who, although not able to make the proceedings legal, can in a sense sanction your union just by his or her presence. We've also heard of ceremonies being conducted by "the woman in whose house we first met," "our professor of philosophy," "our medicine man," or "my guru." And Beth and Patti told us that their "mutual contemporary spiritual path has been to spend thousands of dollars on psychotherapy. In light of this we asked each of our therapists to preside at our wedding. We feel that these are the true contemporary ministers, those who have helped us heal and create this kind of committed relationship. Both were highly honored, and one even cried."

The important thing to remember is this: your ceremony should be conducted by someone who has—or who represents an institution that has—some meaning in your life.

Aside from being a calming captain for the voyage, as experienced professional can give you the basic outline for the ceremony; then all you have to do is fill in the blanks. Randy told us that when he and Joe sat down with their good friend (who also happens to be a Jesuit priest) to talk about the ceremony, "he helped us structure it. I remember him telling us, 'This is my job; think of me as the emcee of this event.' He also asked us to tell him about some of the guests who would be there, and our relationship to them—because he wanted to write for his audience."

There are varying degrees to which officiants will become involved in planning the ceremony. Some will give you input on every last line and will work with you to choose and interpret symbols and scripture. You may trust your officiant to the point where you may not feel the need to approve the ceremony in advance. Aletha and Janette spent a great deal of time with their minister to let her know what kinds of things they'd like to have included, but chose to be surprised by the specifics on the wedding day.

Some officiants will require you to attend counseling sessions before they commit to presiding over the union. The sessions often deal with potential road bumps that you may face as a couple. Or you might not spend much time at all with your officiant before the ceremony; sometimes all it takes is a phone call or two to iron out the details. If at all possible, though, try to get a little quality time with your officiant: invite her or him over to dinner, and tell the story of your lives together. (Don't you just love telling it? And doesn't it seem that you're just not asked often enough?) Whether any of that information makes it into the ceremony is irrelevant; it will provide great background material for your officiant's sense of what makes your relationship work.

There's also the option of having no officiant, of running the show yourselves. This is being done with some frequency in same-sex ceremonies. It actually is in line with the attitudes of the many religious denominations that maintain that the church doesn't marry you, you marry each other, and the officiant and congregation are your witnesses.

On a practical note, there is almost always a fee involved when a professional performs your ceremony; sometimes it's called a donation, but it is rarely optional. Fees can range anywhere from $50 to $300 and up, and some people charge mileage in addition. Ask about the fee in advance.

(GIMME THAT OLD-TIME) RELIGION

Since many commitment ceremonies are religious or spiritual in nature, we're going to give you a rundown on where some religions stand concerning gay marriages.

Although many religions simply refuse to be associated with commitment ceremonies, others are beginning to affirm same-sex unions in varying degrees. One thing is for certain: lesbians and gays who opt for religious ceremonies are having an easier go of it all the time in finding

ministers, rabbis, and other mainstream religious leaders to officiate. Don't get us wrong; this is not happening without widespread debate and well-publicized con-frontations. But it *is* hap-pening.

Before we launch into the stances of vari-ous religions, there is one important note to be made: many mainstream religions today have gay/lesbian offshoots. For example, there are gay synagogues in many cities, not to mention numerous gay and gay-friendly Christian con-gregations and gay "sub-divisions" of many denominations. You are always welcome there, and can be assured that the representative clergyperson will be happy to perform a union ceremony. Still, in any traditional religion, you cannot totally divorce yourself from centuries-old practices and policies about homosexuality. So here's a reading on some of the world's religions—and how they feel about you (so you can figure out how you feel about them).

JUDAISM

No individual synagogue is required to sanction a same-sex wedding; it is the individual rabbi's call. However, the Reform and Re-constructionist branches of Judaism are the most tolerant and welcom-ing of same-sex unions. (Although Conservative congregations are beginning to deal with homophobia, it is unlikely that an Orthodox rabbi will ever perform a same-sex wedding.) The Reform movement tends to make a distinction between the ethical and religious teachings of Judaism, interpreting Jewish practices and beliefs according to West-ern standards (which may or may not be good news for gays and les-bians). "Reconstructionist Judaism believes that in each generation there is a mandate upon Jews to figure out how to make Judaism work for us today," says Rabbi Julie Greenburgh of the Jewish Renewal Life Center in Philadelphia. "The logic behind this is that you can't just 'in-herit' a four-thousand-year-old tradition; you have to shape a future."

The Jewish wedding service is a blend of religious and cultural practices that are often interpreted by each individual couple. At the end of the ceremony, there is the reciting of the Seven Blessings, offered as a means of praising and thanking God for the occasion. Sometimes seven different friends/family members bestow the Seven Blessings on the couple. Lastly, a glass is smashed, and everyone says, "*Mazel tov,*" or "good fortune."

MCC

A special note has to be made of the MCC congregations, which have been religious pioneers in serving the lesbian and gay communities around the country. The Universal Fellowship of Metropolitan Community Churches was the first church to recognize the sanctity of a same-sex union, and is believed to have generated the phrase *Holy Union.* MCC has basically no denominational requirements, usually asking only that at least one of you be a believer in the Christian message. The church actually has a few tiers of ceremonies you can choose from. The *Rite of Blessing* involves a simple prayer that acknowledges the relationship and offers it to God. The *Holy Union* is a contract or agreement, a covenant between two people, and is usually reached after the couple have spent a significant period of time together. (MCC also performs a *Rite of Holy Matrimony,* but at this point, we're sad to report, that ceremony is reserved for couples of the opposite sex and involves legal responsibilities.) There are over 250 MCC churches across the United States.

Most MCC churches require that the couple have lived together for at least six months before they make the public commitment of Holy Union, that both partners be at least eighteen years old, and that they attend counseling sessions. The number and length of the sessions are decided by each MCC minister; usually two or three sessions of an hour or two each are required. The Reverend Dusty Pruitt, of MCC Long Beach, says, "Counseling is the time for the couple to work things out and make sure that this is what they want to do. At the end of it, I still might think they're not right for each other, but if they want to do it, I'll marry them anyway. Who am I to say they're not going to make it? And I've been wrong before."

MCC ministers have performed holy unions in churches, in private homes, and in discos. The ceremony is closely based on a traditional nondenominational Christian one, but special language has been added that addresses the same-sex issue.

QUAKER

The Society of Friends—usually referred to as the Quakers—has arrived at sundry decisions regarding sexual diversity, union ceremonies, and celebrations of commitment.

There is a movement among "unprogrammed" Friends (one of the Quaker branches) to extend recognition of marriage to lesbian and gay couples. The couple applies to be married "under the care of the Meeting"; then every member must reach consensus, or what Quakers call "clearness," before the marriage can take place. Often, Quaker meetings are willing to recognize same-sex unions, but some Friends are reluctant to call such unions "marriage." The clearness process can take months, and appearing before the clearness committee can be compared with undergoing counseling in other religions.

At a monthly meeting in January 1993, Central Philadelphia Friends approved the following statement:

> *From our belief that there is that of God in everyone flows our testimony on the equality of all persons. Thus, Central Philadelphia Monthly Meeting affirms our willingness to celebrate marriages of all couples, including lesbian and gay, who have a substantial relationship with our Meeting. In each case we will follow the same careful procedure of arriving at clearness in accordance with our traditional procedures. At every stage we intend to treat all couples with respect, care and love.*

In a wedding ceremony under the care of a Quaker meeting, the Friends sit in a circle around the couple, who sit on a "facing bench." One at a time, people share their thoughts about the occasion. During the service the couple rise, join hands, and make their promises to each other. After the ceremony, the couple get a marriage certificate that has been signed by everyone present.

UNITARIAN UNIVERSALIST

In 1970, this religion of free faith called for an end to gay and lesbian discrimination; in 1984, it officially recognized gay and lesbian weddings, which are called "services of union." Its official literature says, "Human loving and human sexuality are not less sacred and good when shared between members of the same sex. The culture and history of gay and lesbian people is important to all society." This embracing of our culture is why many spiritually minded lesbians and gays turn to the Unitarian Church to get the religious sanction they want for their ceremony, with a dash of freethinking thrown in.

Though Unitarian roots are in the Judeo-Christian tradition, Unitarianism is not a Christian faith; rather, it is a pluralistic religion in which each congregation determines its own affairs.

A Unitarian ceremony can be quite traditionally Christian, or it can incorporate a number of rituals from other religions and philosophies; the important thing is that it is collaborative. Couples spend time with their officiant to decide together what the service will consist of, and are encouraged to build a service that is meaningful to them and that draws from whatever spiritual, religious, or humanistic traditions they share.

OTHER RELIGIONS

Clergy within the *United Methodist Church* will often perform same-sex ceremonies, which can be religious or not, according to the wishes of the individual couple. How long they must have been together depends on both the minister and the couple.

Some *Episcopalian* ministers will also bless unions in commitment ceremonies, making the unions sacred in the eyes of the church, of God, and of the community.

Presbyterians from the More Light Congregation perform holy unions, which they see as a blessing of an already existing commitment.

There are seldom weddings of any sort in *Buddhist* temples or shrines in America, since there is no prescribed Buddhist wedding ceremony. A Buddhist priest may be asked to bless a union, in which case the ceremony is written to the couple's specifications. The people who are marrying are also marrying all of those present. These folks are known as the *sangha,* or community, who commit their full support to the marriage. The ceremony stresses love and deep compassion for self, others, and all sentient beings, and makes the point that marriage takes time to ripen.

You may also be interested in knowing about two "renegade" religious organizations of lesbians and gays that have broken off from the mother churches while still maintaining the essence of the religion:

The *Roman Catholic Church* reserves the sacrament of marriage for man and woman. While the church now says that it's okay to be gay or lesbian, it also says that it's not okay to live that way. *Dignity U.S.A.* is a nationwide organization for lesbian and gay Catholics, with one of its goals being to someday reunite with the Catholic Church. Father James Mallon of Dignity confirms that priests will perform blessings of commitment or blessings of love, but warns that these ceremonies are not sacraments and are not meant to be the equivalent of marriage. If you wish to declare vows during a service, you must write them yourself, but you will not be pronounced life mates, helpmates, partners, or anything else by the priest.

Gay and lesbian *Mormons,* turned away from their own ministries, have formed the *Restoration Church of Jesus Christ.* The traditional Mormon marriage ceremony is called a "temple sealing," and the Restoration movement expanded its services to offer three basic ceremonies: sealing, betrothal, and union. A sealing is a covenant to each other and to God to work at the relationship, and is expected to last forever; you must have been together for a year, go through counseling, and vow sexual exclusivity. A betrothal means you're not quite ready to make a covenant to God, but want to affirm your relationship in a public way. A holy union is a way for couples to stand before friends, family, and community and declare feelings for each other without committing to anything as serious as a sealing.

ALTERNATIVE CLERGY

We have heard of couples asking clergy to officiate at their ceremony knowing full well that their religious denomination does not sanction same-sex unions. This leads us to a whole new type of religious officiant that we call the "off-duty cleric"—a gay-friendly priest, minister, or rabbi who, unofficially and not connected with her or his congregation (but ostensibly connected with God), will bless your union. Usually these people have a personal relationship to the couple.

There is yet another option, and that is to go with members of the "alternative clergy," who may or may not have their own congregations and, in fact, may work out of their homes and hearts. One example is the clergy of the Universal Life Church, a mail-order ministry that pretty much leaves beliefs up to the individual clergyperson. Don't be put off by the word *mail-*

order; these are often deeply religious people who become ministers because of their profound spiritual feelings. You can probably find these ministers through the yellow pages (gay and otherwise) and, as ever, by word of mouth.

VARIATIONS ON A THEME

A lot of couples feel that their wedding is the perfect time to integrate rituals from different cultures, culling elements from Western and Eastern traditions, folklore, and a variety of religions, ethnic backgrounds, and spiritual outlooks. We're just skimming the surface with this sampling of what some of them have done.

HANDFASTING

Tying the knot did not start out being an abstract term; the lover's knot, or handfast, that binds two hands together represents an indissoluble union, and the tying of a knot is still practiced in various ways by different peoples as a symbol of love, affection, faith, friendship, and duty. Handfasting once symbolized betrothal, and later came to mean "marriage."

For the Wiccan (pagans who follow religious traditions from pre-Christian Europe), handfasting originally involved a spell that two people cast on each other. In the ritual, the couple is joined together hand in hand, using a colored ribbon. But care must be taken in how the ribbon is tied, because after the ceremony it must be removed without untying it, as its untying would constitute divorce.

In the Russian and Greek Orthodox religions, a wedding ceremony closes with the couple, hands bound together, being led around a ceremonial table three times while the congregation, singing, asks God to "grant them many years."

Some cultures such as the Portuguese drape a stole over the couple's hands as a symbol of union.

JUMPING THE BROOM

Jumping the broom is an honored tradition in the African American community. This ancient custom once involved jumping over a branch or tree trunk; later, the branch was replaced by a broom. First, a circle is swept clean with the ritual broom, which is then laid out before the couple as they state their vows. Then, holding hands, they jump over the broom toward the east, the direction of beginnings.

WATER RITUALS

Water rituals symbolize purification. You can use plain old tap water, but we've heard of using rose water, and one couple had sea water from both the Atlantic and Pacific. Using water that is set at the altar, you can wash your hands to cleanse yourselves of past commitments and affiliations, pour hot and cold water over the rings as a blessing of them, or rinse each other's faces.

FIRE RITUALS

One Native American tradition calls for everybody present to gather up something old that they want to let go of and throw it into a large communal fire. These things can be either tangible, like photos or old mementos, or symbolic, such as illness. You as a couple can burn any insecurities or jealousies. Also sacred in Native American cultures is "smudging the temple," or walking around with smoking, burning sweetgrass, sage, or cedar to cleanse the area.

Candles can symbolize many things—a divine light, the light of inspiration, and the flame of unconditional love. Candle-lighting ceremonies have become extremely popular, even mainstream. Often, partners hold lighted candles and use these to light a third candle together, symbolizing the combining of two into one. You can also pass out candles to all of the guests, to be lighted during the ceremony. (Be sure to check with church authorities about any fire regulations.)

FOOD RITUALS

Some couples use food in their ceremony as a symbol of spiritual and emotional nourishment, as well as an act of sharing. Foods can signify various things: bread is a symbol of life; fruits and vegetables suggest the harvest and a time for renewed hope and fresh beginnings.

In the Wiccan tradition, the couple prepare a tray of various foods: something green, some roots, some stems, some leaves, some flowers and fruits. (Don't panic; these can be as harmless as carrots, celery, cauliflower, dates, almonds, and oranges.) Then they feed each other, saying, "May you never hunger."

Many religions practice "the sharing of the cup," where the couple drink something (often wine) from the same cup, symbolizing commitment to share all that the future may bring. The cup itself can have a significance that will enhance the ritual: you can drink from a Navajo wedding vase, which has two spouts; from a special goblet; or from a *kikombe,* a unity cup from the African tradition.

מזל טוב

MAZEL TOV!

The Jewish tradition of drinking blessed wine from a glass, then wrapping the glass in a napkin and breaking it, has a multitude of interpretations. We found that many lesbian and gay couples, Jewish and non-Jewish alike, incorporated this ritual into their ceremonies.

We have chosen a joyous, metaphysical theme. The idea is that this glass represents a vessel of God's light. By breaking it, we allow this light to enter our lives and yours to provide greater understanding and foster divine love.

—BRIAN AND DAVID

To us, the breaking of the glass is a statement: 'For anyone who wants to come between us and our love, you must first put the glass together.'

—LUANA AND YAEL

We broke two glasses while holding hands, to symbolize that we were going forward together.

—FRAN AND SANDY

Before our ceremony actually began, Nancy and I stood outside while our guests watched a slide show. It was a chronicle of our lives, showing us as kids, at high school proms with our boyfriends, all the way up to the two of us as a couple. I know it sounds strange, but it was the perfect thing to do. We live in a small town, and the guests who were there were very diverse—everyone from childhood friends to local merchants to friends from the lesbian community—and the slide show kind of broke the ice. Then the ceremony itself was really funny and sentimental and unique, so by the time the eating and the touching and the dancing was taking place, everyone had leapt through the barrier of "Isn't this a little strange?"

—MICHELE

THE MOMENT OF TRUTH: CREATING YOUR CEREMONY

It doesn't matter if your approach to your wedding is New Testament or New Age; writing your own ceremony or choosing it from existing ones can be the most rewarding process you go through in getting married. Your ceremony is being held so that you can tell the world, or your world anyway, about what your love means to you and where you want it to take you. What do you want to say about your relationship in this public forum? And since a wedding ceremony is like a blueprint for your relationship, what are your hopes for the two of you? And because your wedding can also be an opportunity to teach, what do you want people to learn?

You can use any existing ceremony in its entirety, add personal touches, or combine selections from several different services. This is a team effort; the two of you must combine your visions for the ceremony. In this chapter we have included a variety of things you can do and say, but don't let this be your definitive list. Brainstorm, gathering material from a wide range of sources; then photocopy your favorites, go through the copies, highlight anything that grabs you, and add to it. Think of it as ordering from a Chinese restaurant; you know—one from column A, one from column B.

Let's deconstruct your basic wedding ceremony and take it from there. We've seen it broken down into as many as a dozen parts, but for sanity's sake let's simplify it a bit:

The introduction includes anything before the ceremony that leads up to it: the processional (how you get there), a convocation (welcoming the gathering), an invocation (calling on God's presence), a remembrance of those not present, and any opening remarks that the officiant or anyone else wants to make.

The main body of the ceremony is, well, just what it says. It may include songs, selected readings, the address by the officiant, a consecration, and prayers.

The vows are the "I do's" or the "I will's" (also known as the "expression of intent") as well as the "I, so-and-so, take you, so-and so . . . ." They often include a personal sentiment, such as: "Rick, I have always looked for someone like you without knowing it." The vows can be read, recited from memory, or repeated a line at a time after the officiant.

The exchanging of the rings is the principal symbolic gesture; but other rituals of this nature may include the blessing of rings, the lighting of a unity candle, and a flower ceremony.

The pronouncement is the "I now pronounce you—whatever" part, the public proclamation that you now are united in the eyes of your community, a higher power, etc. If you're changing your names, you get introduced for the first time using the new ones.

The closing of the ceremony covers the kiss, the benediction (blessing your union), and the recessional (your exit).

Something else to think about is doing an emotional dry run of the proceedings. Many couples counselors, therapists, and ministers can provide a framework in which to do this. The process developed by Dr. Lois Sprague and Dr. Gwynne Guibord of Los Angeles, which they call an "emotional rehearsal," can include as many significant members of the wedding party as you'd like. Dr. Guibord told us that "at an event with this emotional impact, often people are not really 'present' due to the anxiety and excitement. People look back on the day and say, 'I don't remember that.'" In an emotional rehearsal you physically walk through the ceremony and answer questions such as: Who is sitting in the audience and what do they mean to you? Who isn't in the audience that you wish was there, and why are they missing—death, estrangement? Who are the people standing up for you and what part have they played in your lives? Why did you choose that particular song and what does it mean? Going through this process ahead of time can allow you to experience the moment to the fullest when it finally arrives.

YOU CAN'T TELL THE PLAYERS WITHOUT A PROGRAM

It's becoming more common in nongay weddings for brides and grooms to prepare a program that's distributed at the ceremony. This explains the meaning of various traditions and practices that take place during the ceremony, helping to make it more meaningful for those who have not yet been to, say, a Greek Orthodox wedding. Since your ceremony may well be the first same-sex wedding some of your guests have attended, a program seems to be in order.

THE WEDDING CEREMONY

I find it difficult to believe that a church that blesses dogs in a Virginia fox hunt can't find a way to bless life-giving, lasting relationships between human beings.

—JOHN SPONG,
Episcopal bishop of
Newark, New Jersey

I've performed a number of ceremonies for same-sex couples, and there's nothing more beautiful than seeing those couples in love. But once I attended but didn't officiate at a perfectly awful lesbian ceremony that was all about politics and "We have this right" and "We have to seize the power" and all of that. It was an angry celebration. I felt like saying, "Get over it! Look at the beauty of your love!"

—THE REVEREND
ROSALIND RUSSELL

If you're not coming from a very specific tradition, you have to make sure that the words you're using are going to be helpful for you as a couple. The ceremony needs to really reflect who you are. And it needs to say the things that you need to say to each other and the things you need to hear.

—THE REVEREND
MARY GRIGOLIA

The program can also contain the names of your attendants and who they are or even how you met them; a poem; a special note to your guests; and your vows. Have them handed out by some of your "good people."

MAKING A STATEMENT

One of the first things you need to think about is whether you want the ceremony to deal directly with your being gay. This isn't as odd a concern as you might at first think. We spoke with many couples who didn't feel it necessary to draw attention to their sexuality. Randy told us: "There was nothing at all in our ceremony about us being gay. It wasn't really a conscious decision, but neither one of us wanted the day to be about being gay. Later on, in the toast, it was dealt with, and I guess it was kind of a relief. It did seem that at some point, somebody should at least mention the fact that it was two guys!"

For others, a vital part of the ceremony has to do with the very fact that a same-sex wedding is not yet commonplace. Rabbi Julie Greenburgh told us: "As a clergyperson, I think it is important to say the words *gay* and *lesbian* from the pulpit during a ceremony. Because it is a very powerful contradiction to people's shame and fear and sense that gays and lesbians don't 'deserve' to have the same privileges of society and of long-term relationships. So I think it's important to stand up there in my robes and to say that we're celebrating the creation of a new lesbian or gay family."

FIRST THERE WERE THE WORDS

What kind of source material can you use? Anything you love, really. This is one time that plagiarism is okay. Use famous and/or obscure poetry or literature. Quote your favorite songwriter or use lines from *Casablanca.* Borrow a saying from a Hallmark card if it speaks to you.

Some couples sit down with their minister or rabbi months ahead of time to structure the ceremony; others procrastinate until the night before the wedding. Whether you're using an officiant or going it alone, we suggest you leave yourselves plenty of time.

We found that just about everyone either writes their own vows, or changes some traditional wording around to make the ceremony more personal. Andrea told us: "Once we figured out what we wanted to say to each other, the rest of the process flowed along more

Photo: Donna Binder, Impact Visuals

easily. By dealing with our vows, we had created the essence of our ceremony: what we felt it would be about and the values we wished to express."

TAKE A VOW

The heart and soul of the ceremony is the wedding vows.

A vow is just that: a vow. A promise. Or many promises. It's that simple—which makes it that complicated. Your vows are your contract, the pact between you and your partner that becomes the basis of your marriage. Your vows are the ground rules for the rest of your relationship.

You may be comfortable expressing yourself on paper, or you may feel, as Tommy did, that "it's really hard for me to say what's in my heart since I'm not good at putting words together. So I found words that other people had written."

One minister we spoke with has a routine that she does with couples at the end of pre-marital counseling: "I have them sit there for an hour. I tell them that they have to write their vows here and now, and to just write from their hearts. I instruct them to write a covenant of love. It can be just one paragraph but it can't be longer than one page, and they must finish it in that hour. It works every time, because instead of worrying about it, you just *do it*. It's really the primary gift that you're giving your mate; if at any time you ever have trouble, it's impossible to reread it and not believe you're in love."

You may want to share your vows with your mate ahead of time, or you may opt to keep them a secret until the ceremony. On the one hand, it's nice to read your vows ahead of time so that you can *really* hear the words when the time comes; on the other hand, it sure makes a great surprise.

When Brian and I had our ceremony, only our families and the members of our inner circle knew that Brian was HIV-positive. So different people interpreted our vows in different ways.

Brian vowed to remember the moments we share, the ones we have shared; this is what will last forever, not just until tomorrow or till death do us part.

Vows usually present an idealized romantic rose-colored vision, as if you knew what lies ahead. We had that over many people, a kind of 20/20 view of the world.

—DAVID

Okay, we know you're feeling a lot of pressure about this. So just to get you started, we've put together some . . .

HINTS FOR VOW WRITERS

✍ *Make sure your vows are like you.* They can be humorous, they can be flowery, they can be serious; but whether they're your own words or someone else's, they should reflect *your* sensibilities and personality.

✍ *Go easy on the metaphors.* Try to avoid lines like "You found me adrift on the sea of love and threw me a life preserver," unless of course you always talk that way.

✍ *Be specific.* There's nothing more real or more touching than a groom saying, "I promise to love you even when you snore."

✍ *Less is more.* Watch the length of what you write; try to keep it under three minutes. Remember that you're going to have to say all those words with a dry mouth.

✍ *Stay on the subject.* It's easy to meander when you want to get everything in. Do a little judicious editing-out of anything that isn't truly vital.

✍ *Know your limits.* If you want to memorize your vows, go ahead, but be aware that it's easy to forget your lines in the emotion of the moment. Give a copy to the officiant ahead of time, just in case you choke up and the audience is treated to a series of Pinteresque pauses.

✍ Oh, and one more thing: "Obey" is out; "cherish" is in.

SAMPLE VOWS

In a typical Protestant ceremony (like the ones you've seen in dozens of old movies), the minister says to the groom: "Stanley, wilt thou have this woman to be thy wedded wife; wilt thou love her, comfort her, honor and keep her, in sickness and in health, for better and for worse, for richer and for poorer, so long as you both shall live?" Stanley responds, "I will," and then the whole thing is repeated with Stanley's bride. Certainly no one is going to stop you if these are the vows you want to use (with the genders cleared up, we hope), but there are plenty of other ways to go. The following are some examples of vows.

The vows of Jane and Tess:

Minister: Jane, will you love Tess when you are together and when you are apart; when life is peaceful and when it is disordered; when you are proud of her and when you are disappointed in her; in times of leisure and in times of work; will you honor Tess's goals and dreams and help her fulfill them?

Jane: I will.

Minister: Jane, repeat after me: "I Jane, take you, Tess, to be my partner, to love and to cherish you, to honor and to comfort you, to stand by you in sorrow or in joy, in hardship or in ease, to be both your lover and your closest friend."
As you place this ring, symbol of your commitment in marriage, on Tess's finger, repeat after me: "With this ring, I wed you and pledge my faithful love."

The vows of Ricardo and William:

I, William, take you, Ricardo, to be my beloved partner, to love and to cherish all my days.

Vida, si tuviera quatro vidas, quatro vidas serian para ti. (My love, if I had four lives to live, I'd live them all with you.)

The vows of Susan and Mary:

These vows come from my heart. I pledge to love you forever. To be open, honest, and faithful to you. I promise to be your best friend—to laugh, cry, sing, and dance with you. To nurture your spiritual growth and to support your dreams. To allow you freedom and room for personal growth to become the person you are yet to be. I promise to help create a home filled with reverence for learning, loving, generosity, and serenity. To bring gentleness to the relationship. I promise to listen—and honor your words and feelings. To work through the conflicts and to resolve our problems. I promise to comfort and to challenge you. And to nurture your sexual being and to be your romantic lover.

The vows of Joe and Randy:

And now . . . with this ring, and before our friends and God, I promise to stay by your side, sharing our tomorrows and all that they hold; to be with you in good times and bad; through sickness and health, and through times of happiness and despair. I will always be faithful to our love and to you . . . my lover, my spouse, and most of all . . . my best friend.

The vows from David to Norman:

Norman,
This is my commitment to you:
To always be here for you,
In comfort and in joy
For good, for better, and for best;
To always value your thoughts and feelings,
Even when they may differ from my own;
To always be honest with you,
Even when that honesty may be hurtful;
To always respect you as my best friend,
My one and only love,
And my soul mate,
In this life and hereafter;
And to never let any man, woman, animal, or object
Become more important to me
Than this, our mutual bond.
To seal these solemn commitments,
I call as my witnesses
Oscar Wilde,
Andy Warhol,
Tennessee Williams,
Gertrude Stein,
and Alice B. Toklas.

SAMPLE READINGS

Readings can be scattered throughout the service and recited at appropriate times by clergy and others. Select your material from scripture, poems, plays, song lyrics, or children's stories. Incorporate the use of quotes, citing meaningful words from anyone—from Proust to your grandfather.

"Love is something you and I must have. We must have it because our spirit feeds upon it. We must have it because without it we become weak and faint. Without love our self-esteem weakens. Without it our courage fails. Without love we can no longer look out confidently at the world. We turn inward and begin to feed upon our own personalities, and little by little we destroy ourselves.

"With it we are creative. With it we march tirelessly. With it, and with it alone, we are able to sacrifice for others."

—Chief Dan George

"The family unit is two or more persons who share resources, share responsibility for decisions, share values and goals, and have a commitment to one another over time. The family is that climate that one 'comes home to,' and it is this network of sharing and commitments that most accurately describes the family unit, regardless of blood, legal ties, adoption, or marriage."

—*A Force for Families,*
a pamphlet published by the
American Home Economics Association

The Book of Ruth (1:16–17), in the Old Testament, is often cited in lesbian ceremonies. Naomi loses all her sons and her husband, and is left with only Ruth, her daughter-in-law. Ruth pledges undying devotion to Naomi:

"And Ruth said, Entreat me not to leave thee, or to return from following after thee; for whither thou goest, I will go; and where thou lodgest, I will lodge. Thy people will be my people, and thy God my God.

"Where thou diest, will I die, and there also will I be buried: All this the Lord do unto me and more, if aught but death part me and thee."

The following reading from the Book of Samuel (18:1–5; 20:16–17) is often used in gay ceremonies:

"Now it came about, that the soul of Jonathan was knit to the soul of David, and Jonathan loved him as himself. And Saul took David that day and did not let him return to his father's house. Then Jonathan made a covenant with David because he loved him as himself.

And Jonathan stripped himself of the robe that was on him and gave it to David, with his armor, including his sword and his bow and his belt. So David went out wherever Saul sent him and prospered: and Saul sent over men of war. And it was pleasing in the sight of all the people and also in the sight of Saul's servants. . . . So Jonathan made a covenant with the house of David, saying, 'May the Lord require it at the hands of David's enemies.' And Jonathan made David vow again because of his love for him, because he loved him as he loved his own soul."

And, below, is only one (Sonnet 116) of 154 Shakespeare sonnets you have to choose from.

Let me not to the marriage of true minds
Admit impediments. Love is not love
Which alters when it alteration finds,
Or bends with the remover to remove:
Oh, no! it is an ever-fixéd mark,
That looks on tempests and is never shaken;
It is the star to every wandering bark,
Whose worth's unknown, although his height be taken.
Love's not Time's fool, though rosy lips and cheeks
Within his bending sickle's compass come;
Love alters not with his brief hours and weeks,
But bears it out even to the edge of doom.
   If this be error and upon me proved,
   I never writ, nor no man ever loved.

OTHER SUGGESTED READINGS

"Song of Songs" from Song of Solomon (4:1–5:1)

"Two Sticks" from *Women Who Run with the Wolves* by Clarissa Pinkola Estes, Ph.D.

Dancing the Shout to the True Gospel; or, the Song Movement Sisters Don't Want Me to Sing by Rita Mae Brown

Leaves of Grass by Walt Whitman

Sonnets from the Portuguese by Elizabeth Barrett Browning

The Velveteen Rabbit by Margery Williams

Come, and Be My Baby by Maya Angelou

"Whether or Not to Marry" from *The Riverhouse Stories* by Andrea Carlisle

Still stuck? Take a look at *The Oxford Dictionary of Quotations,* a very comprehensive source that has listings according to subject matter.

SAMPLE PRONOUNCEMENTS

Think of the pronouncement as the first time you are formally recognized as a married couple. How do you want to be introduced??

In the presence of this good company,
By the power of your love,
Because you have exchanged vows of commitment,
We recognize you as married.

Since you have consented to join together in the bond of matrimony, and have pledged yourselves to each other in the presence of these loving friends, I now pronounce you partners in life.

With the sense of incomparable joy that you have found emotional sanctuary for your heart, that you have discovered your life's true love, I now pronounce you married.

By the power vested in me by the church and in the name of the Spirit of Love, which performs every true union, I hereby present to you George and David.

SAMPLE BENEDICTIONS

The benediction closes the ceremony; parting words are said both to the couple and to all who witnessed the ceremony.

Those whom God has joined together may she [or: he] generously bless forever.

May the wings of angels uphold you through all the life of your love, may you live forever in happiness with one another. May your hearts be full; may your lips stay sweet. May your love grow strong; may you love long and happily in one another's arms.

An Apache blessing:

Now you are two people with one shared life before you. Go now into your dwelling place to enter into the days of your lives together. And may your days be good and long upon the earth.

PRELUDE TO A KISS

A few words of wisdom from those who have been there:

Out of the entire wedding, the thing that made us most nervous was the kiss. We had never kissed in front of our parents before. So we were quite chaste—no tongue action.

—FRAN AND SANDY

A Jewish blessing:

The Mother's Sabbath Prayer (adapted)

May the Lord protect and defend you.
May He always shield you from shame.
May you come to be in paradise a shining name.
May you be like Ruth and like Esther.
May you be deserving of praise.
Strengthen them, O Lord, and keep them from
    all dangerous ways.
May God bless you and grant you long life.
May God make you good partners for life.
May the Lord protect and defend you.
May the Lord preserve you from pain.
Favor them, O Lord, with happiness and peace.
Oh hear our prayer. Amen.

An Irish blessing:

May the wind be always at your back.
May the road rise up to meet you.
May the sun shine warm on your face,
The rains fall soft on your fields.
Until we meet again, may the Lord
Hold you in the hollow of His hand.

HOW TO INVOLVE YOUR GUESTS IN YOUR CEREMONY

❧ Hand out flowers to each guest as they arrive. During the ceremony, instead of asking if anyone objects to the union, ask that anyone who wants to affirm the union come forward to a bouquet stand and place their flower in it.

❧ At some point during the ceremony, personally greet all your guests. (Not recommended for weddings of over fifty.)

❧ Involve any children who are a part of your family through special readings or what is known as the "circle of acceptance" ceremony: the child is called to the altar, where the family joins hands to form a circle; then the couple ask the child for his or her blessing and support.

❧ When the officiant asks, "Who blesses this union?" have all the guests join in saying, "We do."

❧ Have friends share stories and memories about you and your lives with them.

❧ Have members of the wedding party dance around a maypole or something equally theatrical.

❧ Have your pet participate by carrying the rings or sitting by you during the ceremony.

❧ Have everybody sing.

❧ Acknowledge people who could not be there that day.

❧ Have people throw rose petals as you exit.

❧ In the Quaker tradition, have your guests sign a marriage certificate, as witnesses to your commitment to each other.

IF MUSIC BE THE SOUND OF LOVE . . .

Music is one of the most important elements contributing to a memorable wedding ceremony. Because it speaks directly to our souls (and let's face it, for most of us, the list of things that do that just ain't very long), it helps set the mood before the ceremony begins as well as providing a meditative punctuation after words spoken during the ceremony. While we're not going to try to tell you that music is absolutely crucial, we will say all the couples we interviewed told us that their ceremonies had music of some sort.

So, if you do want your ceremony to include some tunes, there are several ways to go about it and a world of music to choose from. You can hire professional musicians, or you can ask friends who are good enough to be professional. You can have instrumental music only: the traditional organ; violins, guitars, or harps; flute and piano—anything you want, really. (Tess even had a harmonica player in her ceremony.) You can add vocalists—soloists or an entire choir. You can use prerecorded music, either purchased or recorded by you and your elves ahead of time.

If you're having a formal or semiformal ceremony in a church or synagogue, you'll want to make an appointment with the organist or other musicians well ahead of time to discuss what you have in mind. (And remember to consult your clergyperson about any restrictions; some ministers just wouldn't appreciate your use of "Love to Love You

IN SECLUSION

There is a lovely Jewish tradition known as *yichud,* or "seclusion." As soon as the ceremony is over, instead of rushing into the reception, the two of you go off to a private room for a few minutes. (Sometimes guards are even posted at the door to keep other people out!) This gives you a chance to be alone before you lose each other in the turmoil of the rest of the day. It can be a sort of emotional consummation of the ceremony, and is also symbolic of the couple's right to privacy. Tradition says that during *yichud* you are also to share your first meal together as spouses, so have a friend or the caterer fix you a plate of your favorite things (even if it's Hershey bars and potato chips) to eat while you catch your breath.

Baby," even though it *was* playing on the jukebox the night you met.) Give the musicians a list of selections and specify the version as well. (If you like a particular rendition, you can even supply sheet music or cassettes.) Then, if you have any doubts as to their abilities, meet with the musicians later on and listen to everything. This is the time to try to make it exactly what you want; don't wait till the rehearsal the day before the wedding.

And aren't you relieved that you don't have to enter to the strains of Wagner's Bridal Chorus (also known as "Here Comes the Bride")? (And now that *The Newlywed Game* has used Mendelssohn's Wedding Recessional as its theme song, that tune is pretty much ruined for everybody.) As far as selections go, there's just no limit. Throughout the ceremony, you can use everything from hymns to show tunes, as long as they're meaningful to you. Tess and Jane made their entrances to saxophonist Dave Koz playing "Amazing Grace"; Michele and Nancy, to Native American flute music. Couples have used Sufi songs and Hawaiian wedding chants, the Hallelujah Chorus and Kenny Rogers compositions, Gershwin and gospel; so search your collective memories for those songs that hold a special place in your hearts.

A FEW MORE MUSICAL NOTES

♫ For a formal wedding you should time each musical selection so you have some idea as to pacing. (As much as you'd like to include your personal Top Ten songs, there isn't time for them all.)

♫ Start the warm-up music (also called the prelude) about a half hour before the ceremony to set the mood. This is usually something instrumental, but you can also compile a tape of your favorite pop songs or whatever. (Randy's lineup peaked with Bette Midler's rendition of "Chapel of Love.")

♫ The recessional (your exit music) should be more upbeat and of a slightly quicker tempo than the rest of your selections.

♫ Because Michele and Nancy had a very untraditional ceremony, they wanted to make sure people knew when it was over, so they played a recording of Bonnie Raitt's "(Let's Give Them) Something to Talk About."

♫ If you're giving your guests a program of the ceremony, it's a nice idea to list the prelude and other musical selections along with the names of the composers and the performing artists.

For more musical information, see chapter 17, "That's Entertainment!"

♫ 50 GREAT WEDDING SONGS ♫

"In My Life" (Lennon/McCartney)

"Here, There and Everywhere"
(Lennon/McCartney)

"All of My Life" (Irving Berlin)

"Keep It Precious" (Melissa Etheridge)

"The Rose" (Amanda McBroom)

"Amazing Grace" (traditional)

"For Me and My Gal" (Leslie/Goetz/Meyer)

"Come Rain or Come Shine"
(Mercer and Arlen)

"Zing Went the Strings of My Heart" (H. Arlen)

"Our Time" (Stephen Sondheim)

"Can't Help Falling in Love"
(Weiss/Peretti/Creatore)

"There But for You Go I" (Lerner and Loewe)

"My Heart Is So Full of You" (Frank Loesser)

"There Is Nothing Like a Dame" (Rodgers and
Hammerstein)

"Love Me Like a Man"
(Chris Smither)

"It Had to Be You" (Jones/Kahn)

"Always" (Irving Berlin)

"Have I Told You Lately" (Van Morrison)

"If I Ever Needed Someone" (Van Morrison)

"Something to Talk About"
(Shirley Eikhard)

"Book of Dreams" (Bruce Springsteen)

"If I Should Fall Behind" (Bruce Springsteen)

"For You" (Tracy Chapman)

"A Song for You" (Leon Russell)

"My Funny Valentine" (Rodgers and Hart)

"Love Don't Need a Reason"
(Allen/Callen/Malamet)

"You Are So Beautiful to Me" (Billy Preston)

"Our Love Is Here to Stay" (George and Ira
Gershwin)

"If We Only Have Love" (Jacques Brel)

"Hawaiian Wedding Song" (Charles King)

"A Simple Song" (Schwartz and Bernstein)

"Still Thrives This Love" (k. d. lang and Ben
Mink)

"If Not for You" (Bob Dylan)

"When You Wish upon a Star"
(Harline and Washington)

"Stand by Your Man" (Wynette and Sherrill)

"Try a Little Tenderness"
(Woods/Campbell/Connelly)

"The Last of the Romantics" (Rupert Holmes)

"Stand by Me" (King and Glick)

"Your Song" (Elton John)

"Many Rivers to Cross" (Jimmy Cliff)

"True Companion" (Marc Cohn)

"Crazy for You" (George and Ira Gershwin)

"I Live for Your Love" (Allan Rich)

"Just in Time" (Comden/Green/Styne)

"Simple Song" (Bernstein and Schwartz)

"Anyone Would Love You" (Harold Rome)

"Girls Just Wanna Have Fun"
(Lauper and Hyman)

"True Love Ways" (Buddy Holly)

"One Hand, One Heart" (Leonard Bernstein)

"As Long As I Have a Heart" (Kathy Mattea)

WHO'S ON FIRST

At this point we're sure that you understand why we can't give you any precise advice on who stands where and next to whom and when—because *you're* picking from so many individual options that all the rules go out the window. However, in an effort to give some definition to how you're staging the ceremony, we've compiled some tips from the etiquette gurus. Use 'em or lose 'em.

❦ The standard order of the wedding party in the processional and recessional is different for Christian and Jewish weddings. We think the most striking feature they share is that the groom comes in early and the bride is the last one to enter. This will never do for you. No matter who you have preceding you ("good people," flower children, etc.), the two of you should be the last ones to arrive and the first to leave.

❦ If you come from a divorced family, and your natural parents loathe one another or their spouses are jealous about the whole affair and your parents' part in it, think through the seating for them. You don't want any hurt feelings to ruin the day for you.

❦ Your ushers won't have to worry about this, but if you're standing at the back of a Christian church looking toward the altar, the left side is traditionally the bride's and the right side the groom's; in a Jewish ceremony it's just the opposite. Expect those ushers with a sense of humor to say to each person they escort, "Are you a friend of the groom's, or a friend of the groom's?"

❦ If you're going to walk down an aisle, you can rent or buy a runner that will add a little magic to the look, as well as prevent those new high heels from slipping out from underneath you. This runner is rolled out by the ushers just before the processional starts; that way, your guests' shoe prints won't ruin it ahead of time.

❦ Think of a wedding in a chapel and you probably envision the officiant facing the congregation. What's wrong with this picture? Your backs, the backs of the guests of honor, are to the audience. No director worth her or his salt would ever stage something this way. Why should you? Change places with the officiant and let your guests look at *his* or *her* back. Or stand in a "V", with the two of you looking at the officiant but "cheating" toward the audience.

Brian and I kept our vows secret until the moment we read them during the ceremony. We decided whoever read their vows second would have to march down the aisle first. It was a good compromise.

—DAVID

MAKING YOUR CEREMONY YOUR OWN

To get your imaginations working, look over this list of what others have done to customize their ceremonies.

If you have access to a flagpole at the ceremony site, have a special flag made to fly over the festivities. It can be a solid color, a rainbow flag, or one that you've designed yourselves. Later, take it down and have everyone sign it.

Trinity and Desiree and twenty-six friends made a thousand gold paper cranes, origami style. (They started early; they figured it took them 150 hours altogether.) The cranes were strung up at the ceremony, assuring the couple of good luck always.

If you're not getting married in a church or temple, make an altar anyway. It can be like the ones in many homes in Latin America—covered with colorful cloth, flowers, and a tree-of-life candelabra. Or go for an Eastern look, with crystals, Tibetan chimes, and a bowl of fruit.

At their union ceremony, Joanne and Jodie had a table set up with paper hearts on which people could write messages; the hearts were then hung from a nearby apple tree, to blow about in the afternoon breeze.

In Jewish ceremonies, the couple stand under a *chuppah* (a canopy made of flowers or richly decorated cloth), which is held up by members of the wedding party and symbolizes the home. Rosanne and Judy had a *chuppah* that was made entirely from pieces of fabric given to them by friends and family members. They received cloth ranging from baby blankets to old wedding dresses to pieces of fabric designed especially for the *chuppah*.

Some people arrange to have doves released at the end of the ceremony. Done properly, it can be a beautiful thing; just be respectful of the animals. Along with the birds, hire a trainer who knows what he's doing. Doves should be used indoors only; for an outdoor wedding, the bird of choice is a homing pigeon.

THE WEDDING CEREMONY

Photo: Michael Arden

Photo: Michael Arden

RING ME UP

WEDDING RINGS

The ring is one of humankind's oldest forms of jewelry, worn as far back as the time of the pharaohs in Egypt. Made of straw, leather, bone, stone, or even plaited rushes (which seem to have dipped ever so slightly in popularity in the 20th century), rings symbolized eternity—a sign that life, happiness, and love have no beginning and no end. Later, the early Romans chose durable iron to make their wedding rings, representing the strength of the union. As different metals became more accessible, people used silver, copper, or brass, with gold becoming numero uno in wedding-ring materials just as soon as it was readily available to the masses.

Although in the last decade of this millennium you're likely to find a ring encircling or piercing almost every conceivable part of some person's body, the third finger of the left hand remains the primo location for a wedding ring today. Why? Well, sometime after the Middle Ages, folks began to believe that a vein ran from that finger directly to the heart. That's the romantic interpretation, anyway; the more pragmatic one goes like this: the third finger is the least active finger of the hand (no snickering please; we mean that it's hard to lift independently) and is therefore the best place for a ring to be displayed and not get worn out.

> The circle is the symbol of the sun and the earth and the universe. It is the symbol of wholeness and of perfection and of peace. The ring is a symbol of unity into which your two lives are now joined in an unbroken circle, in which, wherever you go, you will return unto one another.
>
> —FROM *Handbook for Commitment Ceremonies,* UNITARIAN UNIVERSALIST CHURCH OF CANTON, NEW YORK

A RING OF TRUTH

There are two things about wedding rings that are or can be highly political: buying them, and wearing them. Let's start with the wearing part.

Maybe you're thinking that you won't want to wear rings after you're married. After all, didn't the Puritans believe that a ring was "a diabolic circle for the devil to dance in"? And didn't a ring on a woman's

Joe and I began to wear wedding rings after being together only a few months; I guess that's because we treated our relationship as a marriage almost from the beginning. When we decided to have a wedding on our five-year anniversary, we took the rings off just before the ceremony, put each other's in our pockets, then placed them on each other's fingers during the vows. And that was the last time they ever came off.

—RANDY

finger once symbolize that she was the property of her husband? The answer to the first question is yes, to the second, no.

Throughout history, rings have actually indicated a positive side of relationships. Egyptians used rings as a monetary unit, and when the Egyptian husband placed one on his wife's finger, it was a demonstration that he trusted her with his property. And what was attached to the wedding ring of an Anglo-Saxon wife? The keys to all the couple's worldly goods.

Rings are one part of the straight relationship world that many gays adopted from the get-go. It isn't uncommon for lesbian and gay couples who live together in monogamous relationships to wear wedding rings, even if they've never had any kind of a formal ceremony. This shouldn't come as any surprise, because for a long time wearing a wedding ring was seen as one of the few ways for gays to "get married." Many chose to exchange rings to symbolize their commitment to each other—just the same as any married heterosexual couple would.

Rings are a way for anyone, gay or straight, to make a public statement proclaiming love and devotion. When you wear a band on your ring finger, you're saying, "Hey, I share a life with someone, so if you're interested in me, tough luck. I'm not available."

Because wearing a wedding ring says to the world that you are in a committed relationship, at some point someone—it may be the hardware store cashier or it may be the mailroom boy at your office—will notice your ring and make a reference to your spouse. It is at that moment that you get to make a choice as to whether to avoid using gender in your response or just throw caution to the wind and let 'er rip. For example, Victoria told us that she loves it when somebody admires her engagement diamond and wedding ring set and asks about her husband: "I say, 'No, it's a woman,' and then I sit back and watch them process it."

You may or may not be up to the challenge of this kind of unabashed honesty, and in fact, it isn't always necessary to tell your entire story to each person you encounter. (Mark Twain said, "Only tell the truth to people who deserve it.") But we're here to tell you that wearing a wedding ring will put you in a position of having to decide. Joe told us that his mother is trying to accept his being gay, but asked him not to wear his wedding ring around relatives who don't know. "It's a big conflict between us. I told her she'd never take *her* wedding ring off, and neither will I."

Make no mistake about it: a wedding ring makes you visible.

FINDING/CHOOSING/BUYING RINGS

You have a lot of choices when it comes to buying wedding rings through the mail; you'll see ads in gay magazines, the Gayellow pages, and your local gay rags: "a full line of contemporary commitment ring designs for when you've met the man of your dreams . . . ." You can also order some beautiful designs—14-karat gold union bands encircled with twelve interlocking triangles, and gold "pride" rings— from the gay catalogs.

But take a deep breath and think seriously about the two of you walking into your favorite jewelry store, in person, and picking out your wedding rings together. Based on the couples we interviewed, we can almost guarantee you an Experience, because we got more great ring stories than stories on any other subject. And we didn't hear of a single case where a couple were treated disrespectfully or rudely by a jeweler or shop owner.

Going into a jewelry store, standing in front of the display cases, and looking at the dazzling array of rings is almost a *rite de passage* in and of itself. You can stand there and think of the unbroken line of other couples—probably all heterosexuals, but that's okay, you're changing that—who stood in the same spot, flushed with excitement, thinking of their futures together. Well, you can have it, too. *Carpe diem*, kids, and don't let anybody stop you.

One of the other great things about doing this in person is that you can make all of those classic comments as you try the rings on— you know, things like, "I want it to be one size too big so I can get it off in a hurry." Think of how impressed the salesperson will be that you can be just as silly and juvenile as any heterosexual couple.

Six months after we started dating, we were in Switzerland on a job and found a ring maker who worked in platinum, and we decided to go for it. They were very expensive and we were very poor. We spent every penny we had on them. And we had them engraved on the inside. Mine says, 'Forever, Bob,' and his says, 'Forever, Rod.' A younger woman with limited English was helping us with the ordering. We told her they were wedding bands and she wanted to know when the wife would be coming in. We said, 'There is no wife, it's the two of us.' She was confused and thought she was losing something in the translation. So she went and got the store manager, an older woman who understood immediately, and she was totally gracious about the whole thing. Then when we went back to pick them up, it kind of felt like the whole store was there waiting for us, to see who these big queer Americans were.

—Rod Jackson-Paris

GOLD DIGGERS: A QUICK LESSON IN GOLD

White or yellow 14-karat or 18-karat is the most commonly used gold for wedding bands today; but what do color and karats mean?

First of all, do you remember seeing gold on the periodic table of the elements in your seventh-grade science room—atomic number 79, symbol "Au"? Well, that element in its pure form is way too soft for jewelry; you'd be molding your ring like Silly Putty. So they take pure gold and alloy it with other metals (platinum, nickel, zinc, copper, iron, even aluminum) for strength. And which of these other metals are used determines the color of the gold—white, yellow, rose colored, etc. They can make red gold, black gold, green gold, and—yes, lavender lovers—even purple gold.

Okay, now what about those karat things? When you're dealing with gold, *karat* means 1/24th—so 24-karat gold is pure gold, and 12-karat gold is half gold and half whatever. (You should definitely be suspicious of that guy on the street corner trying to sell you a 28-karat gold ring.)

ALTERNATIVE BANDS

But does your wedding ring have to be a simple gold band? Nah, it can be any material you choose, in any design you choose. When Cindy Crawford married Richard Gere in a quickie $510 Las Vegas ceremony in 1992, the couple exchanged aluminum-foil rings. (Of course, Richard later upgraded Cindy's by giving her not one, not two, but three gold bands.) But our point is this: your wedding ring, symbol of your everlasting love, should be whatever you want it to be.

If you don't like anything you find in the stores, or if you want something unique, you can design your own rings. A good jeweler can help you, either from a verbal description or a rough sketch; he'll then make a wax sample for you to approve.

The wedding rings worn by Tess and Jane were custom-made by San Francisco artist Jeanine Payer, who often uses photographs in her jewelry. Tess's ring has a tiny tiny photo of Jane as a baby, in a little glass box that sits between two gold wings; Jane's ring has a baby Tess. Jane told us: "What better thing to be between two angel wings than a baby picture? It's the purest part of each other, so that whenever we

My partner and I went to a jewelry store in Chinatown in San Francisco to buy rings for our commitment ceremony. We knew we'd get a good deal there, but we were really nervous about getting a reaction to the fact that we're lesbians, so we decided to be really low-key about it. We walked in and told the clerk that we wanted to buy some plain gold bands. He said, "Ah, yes, you want wedding rings!"

—KIT CHERRY

have a fight or one of us wakes up in the morning with foul breath and lines under the eyes, a quick glance at the ring reminds us of what we fell in love with to begin with."

Some other custom designs we have come across:

○ For years, Bob and Jeff had been wearing inexpensive copper rings they bought on a trip to Morocco. When they decided to have a public ceremony, they had the copper rings encased in gold, called the celebration a "Spring Ring Thing," and billed it on the invitations as "exchanging copper for gold."

○ Bob and Rod's rings are platinum, but Rod's has a 1/4 gold-leaf overlay and Bob's has a 3/4 gold-leaf overlay, making each one incomplete without the other.

○ Judy and Talia got exquisite matching rings . . . tattooed on their ring fingers. (If you choose this option, *mean it.*)

You can also find antique rings or use rings that are family heirlooms. (If you go the heirloom route, make certain your beloved is as crazy about the ring as your grandmother was; and if it's truly a family treasure, consider making a prenuptial agreement that it must be returned if—God forbid—you should ever split up.)

PUT IT IN WRITING

The other great thing about rings is that they can be engraved, and in fact have been since the earliest times. Inscribed rings were used for religious, political, and sentimental purposes by the Greeks and Romans, and have been found engraved with such words as ZHCAIC, XAIPE, and KAAH. (You may want to think of something a little more meaningful to the two of you.)

Sixteenth- and seventeenth-century betrothals utilized "posy" (verse) rings, which were inscribed in Old French, Old English, or Latin. Here's a sampling of some of the engravings found on them:

• Till death divide

• Amor vincit omnia (Love conquers all)

• Semper amenus (May we love forever)

• Deux corps un coeur (Two bodies and one heart)

- Love him who gave thee this ring of gold / 'Tis he must kiss thee when thou art old

- This circle, though but small about / The devil, jealousy, will keep out

- My love is fixed; I will not range / I like my choice too well to change

Lots of contemporary couples put the wedding date and each other's names or initials on the inside; others put entire phrases. We've heard of rings saying everything from "The heart is a resilient muscle" (a Woody Allen quote), to Robert Browning's "Grow old along with me! The best is yet to be," to *Ahoovot chaiim* (Hebrew for "beloveds for life"). Use your imaginations and follow your hearts. Remember that the ancients believed rings to have magical powers. Maybe they were right.

WEDDING-RING SUPERSTITIONS: READ 'EM AND WEEP

- Never buy a wedding ring on a Friday.

- It's bad luck to buy a wedding ring if another person has tried it on. (Good luck trying to figure out if someone has.)

- After you've bought it, never try on the ring for fun before the wedding or you will never marry.

- Never drop the ring in the ceremony; the person who drops it will be the first to die.

- If the ring should ever break, there will be a quarrel or separation.

- It's bad luck to lose your wedding band. (We assume this is because your spouse just might ask you why you took it off.)

▼ EAT, DRINK, AND BE MARRIED

FOOD AND BEVERAGES

What you serve your guests and how may well be one of the major things they will remember about your wedding years down the line (even though you yourself will probably not get to taste the food and, if you do, won't remember it). "Oh, yeah, Wendy and Jackie's wedding was really incredible. They had a great seafood station, a vodka bar, and that guy who made ice cream sundaes." This is not to say that your ceremony wasn't unbelievably touching, that you didn't look spectacular, and that you didn't have the hottest band around; it's just that for some reason, most people remember food very distinctly. The food may be just cake and coffee, but you'll want the cake to be made and decorated to your specifications and the coffee to be tantalizing. And if the food tastes bad or you run out, people will remember that too. Since for many people the wedding feast will be the most important and expensive single meal they will ever host, it's no wonder some get tied up in knots over menu and presentation. Don't fall into that trap; this should be a joyous offering, a way to show your love for your guests and to share your happiness. And a simple platter of cheeses accompanied by some lovely breads can be just as heartfelt a gesture as a four-course sit-down feast.

Consider how important food is to you. Yeah, yeah, we *know* you have to eat it to stay alive; what we mean is, how significant a role does it play in your daily life? What does food mean to you socially? There are couples who love to cook together; some who have dinners once a month with the same group of friends where everyone brings a new and exotic dish; and people who are always on the lookout for the newest best restaurant in town. Others are happy having Cheez Whiz on Ritz crackers as their appetizer and Big Macs as their main course. The category you fall into will help determine the direction you want to take when sussing out the eats.

The wedding repast must be delectable whether the menu is simple or elaborate, and it must be attractively served with suitable appointments. All these points should be given careful consideration, as good food served badly and with poor appointments loses much of its appeal; while poor food on beautiful china and silver deftly served is also not equal to the occasion.

—MARGUERITE BENTLEY,
Wedding Etiquette Complete (1956)

If you've decided to have your celebration at a hotel or a restaurant, you probably already know where your food is coming from. If you're planning on using a site such as a bowling alley that allows you to bring in your own caterer or pick one from their recommendations, you may employ the services of a caterer to simply drop off trays of finger food. Or you may be going for a 100% do-it-yourself operation. No matter which of these you end up with, we'll walk you through the steps of what you need to know.

CATERING TO YOUR EVERY WHIM

Caterers may go under a number of aliases (party planner, food-service manager, banquet adviser, director of food services), but they should do what the word *caterer* says: they should cater to you, attend to your needs. Now, exactly what your needs are will vary depending on the size of your guest list, the location of the wedding, how much time you have to spend on the details, how much money you have to spend, and the temperaments of the brides or the grooms and everyone else involved.

For our purposes here, the caterer is the person or company in charge of the food (and drink). However, the caterer's area of responsibility could range from buying the food to cooking the food to delivering the food to setting up the food to cleaning up after the food. You may choose one of those caterers that consider themselves artists and food their medium; or your caterer may be the Chicken Delight down the street that will deliver 45 extra-crispy drumsticks with all the fixings. Either way, what really matters is that *you* understand what is being provided, and that *they* live up to their end of the bargain.

Caterers can offer you tons more than just the consumables. Their gamut of expertise can lend a hand in the following:

✕ *Helping you find your location.* Caterers who have regular corporate clients can give you an entrée to office lobbies, atriums, or top-floor meeting rooms; resourceful caterers might have an "in" with facility managers or owners of private estates.

✕ *A sense of style.* A caterer should know how serving styles work with different age groups in assorted spaces. Creative menu selection tailored to your crowd and presented in a unique way gives the party character. Kegs of imported beer accompanying foods served from pushcarts was one caterer's answer to a reception held on the lawn of a couple's backyard.

✕ *Structuring the day and pacing the party.* When you hire a thorough caterer, you are

FOOD AND BEVERAGES

hiring an expert who will help guide you through many of the details of the reception. The party will be orchestrated in a way that gives guests time to schmooze, munch, and boogie too. A good caterer knows the answers to the following questions: When is it time to serve dinner? Is dinner over yet? Should we cut the cake because some people have to leave? When can *we* leave?

✂ *As an endless source of information.* Because the caterer is at the epicenter of the party-planning business, he or she can steer you to florists, decorators, and rental companies who will all join forces and become your wedding-reception army.

SO HOW DO I FIND A GOOD CATERER?

Choosing the proper caterer can be a cause of great anxiety; in fact, it's part of the syndrome that we call Food and Beverage Apprehension. Catering is the ultimate in ordering in, only the stakes are much higher than you're used to. Food and Beverage Apprehension can also manifest itself when suddenly everything is much more expensive than you had planned and you begin to feel that this highly recommended food-service director is ripping you off royally. (Your internal monologue might go something like: "Yeah, he *seemed* really nice, but I'll bet deep down he's really a homophobe, and he's trying to ruin our wedding!") This is probably paranoia. (Probably.) Do people get ripped off by caterers? Yes, sometimes they do. But if you follow our guiding light, you'll minimize the chances of that happening.

The two best ways to find the caterer of your dreams are personal experience and word of mouth. Personal experience doesn't necessarily mean that you've hired them yourself. Remember last year at your office Christmas party when you went through that buffet line four times? So, who catered that party? Think about restaurants where you love the food; they might do catering. As for word of mouth, check around and ask friends (especially those who have had weddings recently) and any organizations you're affiliated with. If you've chosen your photographer, ask him or her—wedding photographers have probably eaten at more weddings than Zsa Zsa Gabor. Say to everyone you meet, "Hi, who does your catering?" (We personally feel that this is a scintillating conversation opener.)

As a secondary source, let your fingers do the walking and check out your local yellow pages and the gay yellow pages. Depending on where you live, you should find quite a selection under "Caterers" that illustrates the diversity of cuisine and assistance that is available. Don't pick a caterer from the yellow pages just because you think "Flash in the Pan" is a clever name; make sure you run them through the paces that we're about to propose.

EVERYTHING THERE IS TO KNOW ABOUT FOOD SERVICE

Cornell University in Ithaca, New York, offers a masters program in hotel management that includes food service. We're telling you this because you should be aware that there is a lot of information to be had here, and that you shouldn't panic because you're not an expert in the field—yet. We're about to give you a crash course in food service so that you can begin to figure out where you need professional help and where you think you can handle it yourself ("I'll buy that bottled water myself at the Price Club") or throw in your own personal touches ("No one can set a table as beautifully as I can").

For wedding purposes, we can break down the elements of catering into four categories.

The food: Caterers have different strengths or specialties in food preparation. Some are particularly good with regional fare; others are not known for food but offer a fabulous presentation (great if you're looking for custom ice sculptures or fruit carvings); still others can provide something special such as a sushi bar and chef. A good caterer will be game to tailor your wedding to your specifications. Food can be served buffet style, from food stations, sit-down, or passed around on trays by circulating servers. Typically, cost is calculated on a per head basis, and you'll need to find out what that really includes.

The drink: Includes whatever suits your fancy: champagne, hard liquor, wine, kegs of beer, mineral water, Mountain Dew, coffee, tea, or milkshakes. In hotels, halls, and private clubs, liquor can account for as much as 45% of the catering bill, and you probably won't be allowed to supply your own. You'll get more bang for your buck if you're in a space where you can provide your own liquor and hire a bartender who will prep and pour.

The help: These are the folks who actually set up and serve the food. Often the caterer you're interviewing will not be present on the day of the wedding, so you'll want to know who your contact person is. Labor costs include cleaning up after the party so the space looks as good as (or better than) it did before the festivities began. Caterers either include the cost of help in their prices or charge you a separate per-server/per-hour fee. There is often a five-hour minimum, which sounds like a lot but includes setup and prep time as well as breakdown and cleanup. The industry standard figures on roughly one server for every ten guests, but this varies greatly depending on how complex the service is; you'll need more for a sit-down dinner, fewer for a buffet. Also let your caterer know your feelings about the personality types the staff should or should not have. You could end up with a staff of youngish waiters and waitresses who might add to the fun and even end up partying a little with the guests, or a more professional and seasoned group who are almost butlerlike in demeanor and efficiency. But whether you're hiring two servers or a team of fifteen, make sure the caterer understands that the wait staff must be at ease serving at a gay or lesbian wedding.

The rentals: You can rent almost any equipment your heart desires, from twinkle lights to crystal champagne glasses to chandeliers. Caterers rarely come fully equipped with silverware, plates, tables, chairs, and linens, so don't assume these things are part of the food package. Rental charges vary greatly depending on what you need and for how long. Some caterers attach an administrative fee for handling rentals; others will suggest what to rent and whom to call, and let you deal with it. We like the caterer who handles the rental logistics and charges you only the true cost. Rental companies pick up and deliver for an additional fee. (See chapter 13, "Rent Control.")

DOING THE CATERING DANCE

Okay, you're now ready to make some calls. When you first speak with caterers, they'll ask some basic questions about your party. (If they're already completely booked for your wedding date, you may as well save everybody's time and move on.) They may pitch you some ideas over the phone and/or set up an appointment to talk in person. Ask them to send you a sample menu with price breakdowns, which will also give you an idea of their style. They should mail this to you within forty-eight hours. If they don't return your original phone call or mail your information promptly, it's not a good sign; after all, you're hiring someone to be organized for you, and this is their first test.

Once you've looked over the info they send, you'll begin to get some idea of whether they're anything vaguely like what you envisioned and whether you should pursue them. They should give you a minimum price quote per head, along with a description of what they can provide for that amount. If their price is completely out of the question, you might as well bail early; if it's merely more than you planned on spending, don't give up immediately, because you may be able to work something out. Catering costs will vary greatly depending on what part of the country you live in and how well you do your homework. If you bring in a caterer, a punch and cake reception can cost anywhere from $4 to $10 per person; a buffet lunch or supper can tally up at $12 to $20 per person. Full sit-down meals (including passed munchies beforehand) ballpark in the $18-to-$30 range. At hotels, prices begin at $12 to $20 for a tea service and run from $45 to (hold on to your wallets) $150 and beyond per person for dinner on a Saturday night.

If they seem like they might be the caterer for you, and you haven't done so already, now's the time to explain to them that there will be two brides or two grooms, and is that a problem? You should be aware of the chemistry between you and the caterer. (No, no, not sexual chemistry, dummy—you're getting married!) Hiring someone who "gets it" will be much better for you in the long run than dealing with someone whose phone calls will put you on edge. Think about whether they seem comfortable with the fact that you're gay, because their attitude may filter down to their staff, who will be serving you and your friends and family.

You should ask to see pictures of party setups that the caterer has done; get names and telephone numbers of recent events they've worked, and call for reactions. (Any caterer worth his or her salt—as it were—should be able to provide you with at least three recent recommendations.) If you're bringing the caterer to your site, you should ask if they've ever catered there before. You might even ask if you can stop by while they're setting up for their next party, which will give you a good sense of how smoothly their organization runs.

Share your ideas concerning the menu, attire of service personnel, style of rental equipment and decorations with the caterer. Remember, it's more than just the food when you hire a caterer. Steer clear of anyone if you hear the phrase "this is the way it's done—just trust me."

—DON KREINDLER
CATERER, 21 WEST, BEVERLY HILLS, CALIFORNIA

THE PERFECT DIALOGUE
WITH THE PERFECT CATERER

We join the following conversation, which is already in progress. (Important points are emphasized in italics.)

YOU: We're having our reception in the party room of the First Unitarian Church. *Are you familiar with the space?*

CATERER: We work there from time to time. In fact, we did a lovely heterosexual wedding there just last month. They have good facilities—a walk-in refrigerator and lots of prep room. Unfortunately, the stoves aren't great, so I would stay away from anything that needs intense preparation on the premises, like poached salmon.

YOU: That's okay, my friends aren't big fish eaters. But *can you work within my budget?*

CATERER: Within reason. It's important that whatever I serve be of good quality, so if you want lamb and your budget doesn't allow for a choice cut, I suggest you go with a chicken dish instead. You might also think about having the party at a time when your guests won't expect a full meal.

YOU: *What are some of your specialties you'd suggest?*

CATERER: If you want a full meal, people rave over our salmon tartare with chives on whole-wheat toast points, Brie-and-eggplant quiche, medallions of chicken in a light bell-pepper curry sauce, saffron steamed potatoes, and asparagus bundles.

YOU: Frankly, most of my friends aren't the nouvelle cuisine type. In fact, most of the people who are coming are vegetarians.

CATERER: In that case, we make a mean meatless chili. We can serve it with fresh baby greens and homemade jalapeño cornbread.

YOU: Now you're talking. Okay, we're having fifty people, and I want everyone to be free to mingle and dance, so a sit-down dinner is out. *How can we serve* the chili?

CATERER: Well, actually, chili isn't something you'd want to stand and eat; balancing the bowl in one hand and your beer in the other is kind of tricky. Instead of chili, why don't we come up with a variety of finger foods that have some substance to them. We can have them passed on trays, served on a central buffet table, or split up at different tables, which are called food stations. For fifty people, a combination of passed hors d'oeuvres and several stations might be nice.

YOU: *How do we make sure that there's enough food for everybody?* I only *heard* about how good the oysters were at Sally and Mavis's wedding.

CATERER: Rumor has it that Mavis ate most of the oysters herself. But when they selected their hors d'oeuvres, due to cost they probably ordered a lot more minipizzas than oysters on the half shell. We'll choose our selections carefully so that everyone will get a chance to taste everything.

You: Tell me you're not one of those caterers who buy frozen hors d'oeuvres at the Price Club and nuke them at the reception.

Caterer: Food is my life. We make every single morsel ourselves; certain items we have to make in advance and freeze, but those are the exception to the rule. *I can arrange for you to stop by one of our next events and have you taste some of our selections.*

You: *When do I have to decide?*

Caterer: I like to have my menus finalized at least a week before the date, but we'll certainly be in touch, and I can be flexible—within reason, of course.

You: Okay, let's *talk about drinks.*

Caterer: I know that the reception hall has no problem with alcohol being served. What did you have in mind?

You: Well, definitely champagne.

Caterer: Are you thinking a glass of champagne just for the toast, or do you want it available the entire time?

You: The entire time. And beer and wine, too. I think that's enough booze. And soft drinks, juices, and lots of mineral water.

Caterer: Okay, we can work this one of two ways. *I can supply all of the drinks, but it would be less expensive if you bought your own.* I can provide the bartender and set up the bar . . . you know—ice, lemons, whatever. When we get closer to finalizing things, I can give you an idea of how much you'll need. One more thing: I must tell you that I just did a great party where we served outrageous frozen margaritas.

You: Most of my friends don't drink hard liquor, but let me think about that one. But let's backtrack: *Do I pay for the bartender and the other help?*

Caterer: When we know exactly how many guests you'll have and how involved the service will be, I'll make sure there are enough servers and kitchen help. These are people who work for me all the time; they're efficient and friendly. You'll be charged per server, per hour. And if you decide you want to go the margarita route, I can hire the bartender too.

You: You're making this all sound so easy. *Will you be there on the day of the party?*

Caterer: Probably not, but at our next meeting I'll introduce you to Tammy, who will be your coordinator and will run things for you. The church has enough chairs, but we'll need to rent extra tables for the food stations, and Tammy will sit down with you and work out a floor plan.

You: Wait a minute. *We have to rent tables? I thought you supplied all that.*

Caterer: Sorry, but this is pretty standard. You'll choose and pay for linen and dish rental, as well as utensils and glassware. I supply all of the serving pieces such as punch bowls and chafing dishes. And don't worry about renting champagne glasses; I'll take care of them.

You: What if I want to use paper plates and plastic utensils?

Caterer: I think I have to go now.

FOOD, GLORIOUS FOOD

Think of your wedding reception meal as having everyone you know over to eat at the same time. What would you serve?

Unless you've been in a cave the last couple of years, you're aware that American food trends are moving toward lighter fare and smaller portions. Yet during the holiday season and for special occasions, people often throw their Deal-a-Meal cards out the window and indulge. Your wedding will probably be one of these occasions.

Americans are also expanding their food horizons toward more international tastes, so you can offer your guests the very best quality of a food that they know and love, or choose unusual dishes that might be completely new to them. Ethnic food from all over the world is being rediscovered; across the country you'll find Ethiopian restaurants, Thai food, Polynesian cuisine, and Caribbean specialties as well as old-world European-style cooking. You can find a caterer who specializes in a particular ethnic cuisine or go directly to a restaurant and make arrangements for them to cater your party.

What if you want to make this a more sophisticated meal than you would usually serve, but don't feel educated when it comes to food talk? Here's where a good caterer earns his money. If your eyes glaze over at the mention of words like *julienne, terrine,* and *roulade,* don't panic. A proper caterer will explain it to you; all you have to do is ask. If you love crab and the sample menu lists "crab quesadillas with pineapple salsa," but you don't have the foggiest idea what quesadillas are, *ask.* If you don't know an herb-infused oil from Crisco, *ask.* If you don't know crudités from pâté but you think maybe one or the other is something you want to serve, *ask.*

Some food for thought as you chew over your menu choices:

Know your crowd. This shouldn't be too difficult, because these are people you have chosen to share one of the most intimate moments of your life with; you'd better know them. It's highly unlikely that, if you and most of your guests are Orthodox Jews, you'll consider serving ham. Nobody expects you to be an expert on each guest's detailed food preferences ("Now, let's see, does Jared like white meat or dark meat?"), but you should have a sense of what kinds of foods will make the crowd happy. This can even be accomplished by "going against type." One groom told us: "Everyone I know is so diet conscious, we're sick of grilled tuna and salad. So for our wedding Sam and I decided to have deli platters—huge trays of pastrami, corned beef, turkey, ham, cheeses, potato salad, coleslaw. It was a big hit, and I got a real kick out of seeing people eating their third or fourth sandwich of the day."

Know yourselves. You may want to use this occasion as an excuse to serve the foods that are at the top of your own wish list. Melissa and Julie said: "We decided that, hey, it's our party, we want our favorite food. So we sat down and made a list of all of our top take-out, like buffalo wings from Hot Wings Cafe, moo shoo pork from Genghis Cohen, the Chinese chicken salad from Victor's, garlic basil nan from East India Grill, guacamole from Border Grill, focaccia from Il Fornaio, and chicken satay from Tommy Tang's. We called ahead of time and ordered, and the morning of the wedding our best friend took our list and ran around town collecting it all; then the crew we hired did the setup, the serving, and the cleaning up."

You may want to reflect the heritage of one or both of you in the selection of foods that you serve. Ben told us: "Mikel's family immigrated here from Russia; they're very close-knit and very supportive of our relationship. We decided that blinis, smoked fish, caviar, and vodka would make the perfect statement for the afternoon. His parents were so proud to be acknowledged and honored that way."

Consider the nature of the event, and think about eliminating certain foods. If you're all dressing to the nines, skip the barbecued ribs. If you serve shrimp in the shell at a cocktail buffet, your guests will pay more attention to peeling the shrimp than to each other.

At certain times of the day, people expect to be fed certain types and amounts of food. If you're having a cocktail party reception, people will know they'll just be getting finger food and drinks, and won't be surprised if they feel the need to go out to dinner afterward. However, if you've billed your event as a dinner party, your guests will expect to see some meat, poultry, fish, or other entrée land on their plates at some point.

Pay attention to the season. If it's winter in Minneapolis you won't want chilled leek soup on the menu. At 110° in the shade, steer clear of heavy cream sauces. If it's December think about roast goose, glazed sweet potatoes, baked squash, and cranberry ring.

STYLES OF SERVICE

Chances are you'll end up with some combination of the following styles of food service.

BUFFET

At a buffet, guests serve themselves from one central food display. Buffet service pops up in one form or another at almost all parties because you can accommodate more people than at a sit-down dinner, and there are fewer hassles. Guests can munch, mingle, and choose what they wish to eat all at the same time. Your buffet can be casual or dressed up with theatrical displays, or can feature international themes.

While they are often thought to be less expensive than more formal meals, buffets can be more costly than sit-down service because additional food is required for the displays to look fresh. (Also, people can go back again and again, and you know what that means.) Buffets can also be tricky and shouldn't be automatically thought of as the easiest way to go. After people have served themselves a plate of food, they have to eat it somewhere. Do you expect them to stand, holding the plate in one hand and a drink in the other? We think not. With buffet service, make sure you have enough chairs (or room on your living-room sofa or elsewhere) for people to park themselves while they eat. It's also a great bonus if there are a number of small tables or even some pre-set larger tables for the guests to put their plates on so they won't have to use their laps.

If a buffet is sounding good to you, digest the following:

★ Every buffet service is different, but to give you a sense of organization, make sure there are enough designated helpers to serve the food and replenish the buffet, and one or two people working cleanup. We cannot stress how important it is to have responsible help whose sole purpose is to walk around and bus dishes; otherwise, at some point someone will put a foot down into a plateful of tuna salad that your cousin left on the floor.

★ Because guests at a buffet help themselves, "audience participation" foods work well—for example, taco bars, sandwich platters, create-your-own-dessert tables.

★ The perfect buffet food requires no cutting, but if cutting is necessary, it's vital that you not use paper plates. Visualize your beautifully attired aunt with a paper plate on her lap that has bent under the pressure of her trying to cut a bite of turkey. Not a pretty picture.

★ Ideally, buffet food should taste as good cold or lukewarm as it does hot. (Because that's how it's likely to be eaten.) Similarly, it should be able to withstand warm temperatures if you're having an outdoor wedding.

★ Buffets don't have to be full meal deals. They can range from lox and bagels to afternoon tea sandwiches to the ever-popular dessert reception.

LAYING OUT A PROPER BUFFET TABLE

You don't want the buffet to turn into the steam table of your high school cafeteria, with guests waiting in line to get tired Salisbury steak, so ponder the following.

☞ As guests will mostly be serving themselves, it is important that your food be easily handled. Some dishes, like chicken breasts and crepes, can be prepared in individual portions; others, such as quiches, should be presliced. The messier the food, the more you need to think about how to serve it. Finding proper serving utensils like large spoons and spatulas will help your three-cheese lasagna from turning into mushy noodles, tomato sauce, and runny ricotta. Each dish should have a designated serving utensil.

☞ When setting up a buffet table, you want to stress ease of movement and avoid bottlenecks and long waits. To do this, you really have to hand-feed (no pun intended) food options to guests. Guests should move down the line, see the attractively displayed food, get it easily on their plates, and move on.

☞ Arrange the plates, eating utensils, and napkins at one end of the table. It helps if guests can hold all of this in one hand. (Rolling the utensils into the napkin is a big plus on that front.)

☞ As they move down the buffet line, guests should encounter side dishes first—vegetables, pasta, potatoes. These are followed by the main dish—say, fish or chicken. You may want an attendant to help serve the main dish.

☞ Condiments and sauces should be placed next to the food they're intended to accompany. Too often when you get to the end of a buffet table you see this off-white sauce and wonder what you're supposed to do with it.

FOOD STATIONS

Food stations are a variation on buffet service, except that here different types of food are offered on separate tables, each devoted to a specialty, sometimes with a live chef thrown in. Stations are set up around the room, in various rooms, or throughout the garden, which creates a great flow. Stations are also a great way to get people to mix: imagine your Uncle Marvin striking up a conversation with your ex-lover Maria as they're waiting for the chef to complete their chicken crepes.

Food stations can be ethnic in nature (tostada station, dim sum station, curry station), can feature foods of the region (raw seafood bar, Southwest station), or can be based on how the food is prepared (grill station, crepe station). The idea is to offer a selection of foods that will complement each other or stand on their own.

FOOD AND BEVERAGES

THE DESSERT RECEPTION

★ Strawberries Dipped in White and Dark Chocolate

★ Old-Fashioned Double-Crust Apple Pie

★ Chocolate Raspberry Cake

★ Madeleines, Ladyfingers, and Baby Brownies

★ Almond Torte

★ Heart-Shaped Pink Petits Fours

★ Kiwi, Pecan Caramel, and Grape Tarts

★ Cheese Tray and French Bread

★ Champagne, Coffee, and Tea

★ Lemon Wedding Cake

PASSED TRAY

Also called butlered service, passed-tray service involves hors d'oeuvres being passed among guests by wait staff and is often a staple of the catered affair. Don't be fooled into thinking that this is an inexpensive route; in fact, serving passed hors d'oeuvres at a cocktail reception can end up being more expensive than a sit-down meal. For one thing, people never put their drinks down, and that adds up. Also, canapés are not exactly cost effective: at some hotels you can pay $15 or more for six little tidbits, which is what they figure one person will eat.

APPETIZERS THROUGH THE AGES

Herewith, our own historical perspective on the revolving trend of finger foods.

THEN	NOW
Deviled eggs	Vegetable-stuffed sushi
Celery stalks with cream cheese	Spear of endive with goat cheese
Cheddar cheese puffs	Buffalo mozzarella with tomato and basil
Olives rolled in chopped dried beef	Assorted tapenades on baguette
Mini egg rolls	Fried tofu with sweet and sour sauce
Onion soup mix dip and saltines	Guacamole and blue corn tortilla chips
Carrot and celery sticks	Crudités
Mini drumsticks	Hot wings with blue cheese dressing
Chopped liver on a Ritz	Vegetable pâté on whole wheat toast points
Pigs in a Blanket	Melon wrapped in prosciutto

SIT-DOWN

Yes, sit-down is what it says: your guests sit down, and food is served to them. However, there are a number of ways this can happen. Prearranged plates of food are set in front of them ("plated service"), or seated diners are served individually from a tray of food, by one waiter alone who both holds and serves ("Russian service") or by two waiters, one who holds and one who serves ("French service"). Aren't you glad you asked? Sit-down meals tend to be the most formal, and they can also be the most elegant. They do not exactly encourage mingling, except as preordained by your seating chart; however, they are often preceded by a cocktail hour where the guests can schmooze to their hearts' content. Sit-down also means that your guests are at the mercy of someone else's schedule: they'd better be hungry when the food starts in, because if this is the salad, the entrée can't be far behind. Sites such as hotels lend themselves to sit-down, but don't rule it out for intimate home receptions too.

Maybe you're assuming that sit-down dinners are the most expensive. Not necessarily: you can control portions for everyone, which may offset the money you'll probably spend on service.

I GET A KICK FROM CHAMPAGNE: POTENT POTABLES AND OTHER BEVERAGES

It used to be that a wedding wasn't a wedding without what *Jeopardy!* calls "potent potables"—specifically, an open bar with full liquor service and free-flowing champagne. But in this era of raised consciousness, people are keeping a close eye on their health and are also cautious about drinking and driving. This has precipitated the growing trend of what is referred to as the "soft bar."

What's happening is that wedding couples are now serving what they would normally serve at any party, with the possible addition of champagne. This actually makes good sense. You may not want to serve alcohol for religious or personal reasons, and if you are nondrinkers and don't serve

THE QUINTESSENTIAL SOFT BAR

★ Champagne

★ Beer (imported, American regional, and nonalcoholic)

★ Wine (white and red)

★ Sodas (diet and regular; with caffeine and without)

★ Coffee (regular and decaf)

★ Tea (a selection, including herbal)

★ Juices

★ Mineral water (and for purists, bottled spring water such as Evian)

Type of Reception	Start Time	End Time	What Guests Generally Expect
Wedding Breakfast	10 A.M.	noon	Continental breakfast with pizzazz
Wedding Brunch	noonish	3 P.M.	A bigger, better breakfast than they would fix for themselves on a weekday morning
Wedding Luncheon	12–2 P.M.	4 P.M.	A light, elegant meal—not what kids take to school in their lunch boxes (unless you're doing a childhood theme wedding)
Wedding Tea	2–3:30 P.M.	6 P.M.	Not much. (That's why it's the least expensive type of reception.)
Cocktail Party	4–6 P.M.	7:30 P.M.	Drinks, and something to nosh on while drinking them
Wedding Dinner Party	6–9 P.M.	?	The world
Late Supper	8 P.M.	?	Hearty snacks or light fare, and sweets
Dessert	afternoon or after dinner		Sweets (and plenty of 'em)
Midnight Rendezvous	12 A.M.	?	Breakfast fare

What You Can Serve

Fresh juice, coffee, tea, croissants, muffins, sweet rolls, fresh fruit, wedding cake

Buffet: Croissants, muffins, sweet rolls, quiches, fruit, cheeses, cold cuts, dim sum
Sit-down: Fruit, omelettes, eggs Benedict, crepes, huevos rancheros, toast, rolls
Beverages: Fresh juice, coffee, tea, champagne, mimosas, Bloody Marys, screwdrivers
Dessert: Pastries and/or wedding cake

Buffet: Crudités and dips, salad (green, pasta, chicken, potato, fruit), cold poached salmon or
    chicken, cheeses, shrimp, crepes, cold cuts
Sit-down: Passed hors d'ouevres, then: soup or salad; chicken, beef, or fish; rice, vegetables, rolls
Beverages: Sparkling wines, full bar or soft bar
Dessert: Sorbets, fresh fruit, wedding cake

Tea sandwiches (cucumber, cream cheese, etc.), assorted cheeses and fruits
Beverages: coffee, tea, punch with/without champagne, wine
Dessert: Tarts, cookies, wedding cake

Hot & cold hors d'oeuvres (passed or buffet)
Beverages: Full bar or soft bar
Dessert: Wedding cake

Cocktails & hors d'oeuvres first hour. Then:
Buffet: Carving stations, everything listed for "Luncheon," anything else you've ever wanted
Sit-down: 3- to 4-course meal including appetizer, soup, salad, meat/fish/poultry entrée,
    vegetables, rice or potatoes, rolls
Dessert: Sorbets, fresh fruit, wedding cake

Hors d'oeuvres
Light supper: Fish or chicken (no meat), salads, light pasta, omelettes, scrambled eggs
Beverages: Full bar or soft bar
Dessert: Wedding cake

Beverages: Wine, champagne, coffee, tea
Desserts: Tortes, tarts, pies, cookies, cheese and fruits, wedding cake

See "Wedding Breakfast" and "Wedding Brunch." (Go back and start all over again.)

alcohol at home, you're certainly not obliged to serve it at your wedding. Sparkling ciders and nonalcoholic wines can fill the bill.

Oh sure, some couples do still have open bars, especially if they're having a dinner-dance wedding; but it doesn't take a brain surgeon to figure out that a full bar is a lot more expensive than a soft bar. For an open bar at a hotel, you'll either be charged by consumption (on a per-drink basis) or will pay a flat package rate (per person, per hour). Dianne Greenberg-Dilena, manager of food services at the Hotel Bel-Air in Los Angeles, told us, "Drink packages are rip-offs; you'll never drink what's in that package! No one consumes six drinks in a night, but you'll be paying for it anyway." If you do have an open bar, find out exactly what brands they'll be pouring—premium or generic? Decide on how "open" you want your open bar to be; it's one thing to mix a gin and tonic, but it's another setup to deal with those funky drinks like a "Hop, Skip, and Go Naked" and a "Mudslide."

 Taste-Police Alert

No matter what you do, do not have a cash bar! You know how loose we are about rules, but we must hold our ground on this one; it just shows a lack of class. If you think alcohol is important to your guests and you want it to be available, cut back somewhere else so that you can provide it for them. Also, assign someone the task of removing any tip cups that may mysteriously appear on the bar, because you'll have included gratuities in your contract and you don't want your guests to feel pressured into digging into their own pockets. Need we say more?

Research shows (can you believe they actually research this kind of stuff?) that if people are offered wine or champagne, one-third to one-half of them won't switch to hard liquor later on, so to save money, have your guests met with trays of champagne when they first arrive. (We know, the most gracious hosts wouldn't do this, but sometimes ya gotta cut corners somewhere.)

Now, about the infamous corkage fee. First of all, what the hell is it? Yes, it's true, hotels and restaurants charge you for taking the cork out of a bottle of wine you've supplied them with. Well, that's ostensibly what the fee is for, but hey, don't they take the cork out of a bottle you bought from them, for free? Kind of. A corkage fee is about one of two things, or maybe both: (1) hotels must protect themselves concerning liability for liquor consumed on the premises, and charging you the corkage fee will help offset the cost of insurance; (2) a bottle of wine bought by you in bulk may cost one-third or even one-quarter of what the hotel charges for the same bottle of wine. (If you don't believe us, flip through the wine list of any restaurant and notice the markup on the same bottle purchased at a liquor store.) The bottom line is, if they let people bring in their own booze, they stand to lose lots and lots of money. Try to see it from their point of view; what's next, bringing in your own food?

But does a corkage fee ever make sense for the consumer? Sometimes. Check out what the hotel is offering by way of champagne; a bottle may cost you $25, and not be a very good vintage at that. But if the corkage fee is, say, $5 per bottle, you can buy some great champagnes for $8 to $15 a bottle. You'll save money, and your guests will be drinking a better-quality swill. On the other hand, we found some of the upscale hotels charging a corkage fee of $25 per bottle—in which case you probably won't be able to beat them at their game unless you own a vineyard. (And if that's the case, why don't you just have the wedding at the vineyard?)

One other pitfall to watch out for whether you're having the hotel (catering hall, country club) provide the booze or you're bringing in your own and paying a corkage fee: every once in a while you hear a story about a site "pushing" drinks on the guests or opening lots of extra bottles, which then go undrunk. This of course translates into more $$$ for the site. You might think about giving the caterer or reception site a dollar or bottle limit ahead of time, and have them talk to you before crossing that line. While we're explaining cons, make sure to count the number of bottles in their stock before the party begins; if you began with 50 and they charge you for 60, something smells fishy, and it's not the salmon mousse.

If you're working with a caterer but buying your own liquor and beverages, try to get them to refer you to a wholesaler in your area. You can buy by the caseload and save a bundle (you'll get at least a 10% discount), and sometimes you can return unopened bottles.

In your quest to save money, remember that picking up and delivering cases of liquor and soda is back-breaking, time-consuming work. Check out the delivery policies of liquor stores and beverage outlets. You will also need to collect the unused liquor at the wedding site for return and, you hope, refund, so be sure someone will pick it up for you. (Usually your pals are more than happy to perform this task—but if they're anything like our friends, expect a few bottles to get "lost" along the way as they continue to celebrate while you're on your way to Niagara Falls.)

Champagne is the only drink that leaves a woman still beautiful after drinking it.

—MADAME DE POMPADOUR

If I had my life to live again the only thing I would do different is drink more champagne.

—OSCAR WILDE

CONSPICUOUS CONSUMPTION, BY THE NUMBERS

1 to 10: the ratio of servers to guests for a dinner service

1 to 25: the ratio of servers to guests for a cocktail party

3: the number of napkins to buy per guest

6 to 8: the number of glasses per bottle of wine or champagne

1/2: the number of bottles of wine or champagne each guest will drink

4: the number of hors d'oeuvres each person will eat in an **hour**

2: the number of drinks each guest at a cocktail party will consume in an hour

1: the number of pounds of ice you'll need per person, depending on the weather

22: the number of 1.5-ounce shots you'll get from a one-liter bottle of alcohol

CHAMPAGNE SHORTS

🍸 Champagne was first made by the blind monk Dom Pérignon, who was the cellar master of a Benedictine abbey . . . thus the name of (almost) everybody's favorite bubbly. "I am drinking the stars!" he was reported to have shouted after first tasting his creation.

🍸 At some places there is a separate charge itemized as a "champagne toast"—the passing out of glasses to your guests, pouring the bubbly *once,* and collecting the glasses again. Free-flowing champagne is a horse of a different color; don't mix up the two when you're getting price quotes.

🍸 One tried-and-true maneuver is for you to have two or three different champagnes; start with the best for the toast, and as the day wears on and the bottles empty, move on to the lesser-quality stuff. Your guests will never know what hit them.

🍸 You can rent an electric champagne fountain, which circulates five to seven gallons of bubbly through its tiers. It can be used for punch too. One drawback is that most of these fountains don't keep the liquid cold, so you'll want to use one only if you're having a large or fast-drinking crowd.

🍸 By filling champagne glasses three-quarters full, you can also economize on champagne; about 90 glasses can be procured from a case in this way, as opposed to the usual 72.

SOME SOBERING NOTES

Do we even need to say the words? Yes. Don't let your friends drink and drive. For selfish reasons, if nothing else. Do you want an after-wedding tragedy to spoil your memories of the occasion? And if that doesn't put the fear of God into you, how about this? In most states there are laws holding the host liable for allowing guests to drive while intoxicated. If you don't want to be responsible for keeping tabs on your guests yourself, appoint a levelheaded friend to collect car keys from anyone who gets carried away. And we wouldn't be doing our duty if we didn't remind you that you should never serve alcohol to minors. Last but not least, if you're using a caterer, see if they have liquor liability insurance in case a guest drinks too much, drives, and later sues.

Cheers!

QUERIES FOR CATERERS AND SITE COORDINATORS

If you're using a hotel or other site where events are part of their business, you'll get a full-blown contract that will cover the following points. Other suppliers may only give you a letter of agreement; either way, be sure the following areas are taken care of:

❏ Space to be used, including extra rooms, suites, changing rooms

❏ Hours when the event is to begin and end, and options for exceeding those limits. Is there an overtime charge?

❏ Cost breakdowns per guest and for each service

❏ Payment plan—how much do you owe them and when is it due? (There is usually a 20% deposit, and 40% due two weeks in advance, with the balance due the day of the event in the form of a certified check.)

❏ Deadlines for guest counts, postponements, and cancellations

❏ Responsibility for any damage and breakage caused by you or your guests (from a broken glass to a food fight that ruins the drapes)

❏ Display and decorations; (whatever you do to alter the space must not damage the premises)

❏ Setup of tables and chairs

❏ Are coat check facilities and valet parking included?

❏ Number of serving staff

❏ Are gratuities included, and how much are they?

❏ Are taxes included?

❏ Are delivery charges involved?

❏ Breakdown of rental fees, if any

❏ Exactly what food will be served for exactly how many people

❏ How the food will be served and number of serving staff

❏ Who supplies what beverages and how much they'll cost

❏ Who supplies the wedding cake and whether there are extra charges

❏ Your promise to not allow anyone under 21 to consume alcohol

❏ Your promise that games of chance will not be permitted unless legal permission has been obtained by authorities. (We guess they don't want you to lose your new spouse in a craps game.)

❏ Clause protecting all parties from natural disasters, including earthquakes, floods, and nuclear war. (Such catastrophes fall under the category of *force majeure* and are dealt with in every contract in the known world.)

CATERING
WEDDINGS
BANQUETS
DINNERS

Ron Singleton

Photo: Nancy J. Robbins

▼ The Cake Takes the Cake

The Wedding Cake

The wedding cake. Think of the images it conjures up: fluffy and flouncy, with tiers and tears, instant Kodak Moments of the young couple starting out life together as they cut that first piece, finger-feed it to each other, then share it with all the guests (not to mention the incredible sugar shock afterward).

The wedding cake is the grand finale of a full-course meal and a full day, or it is its own centerpiece for a cake-and-champagne reception. It's not only the culmination of the meal but the apex of all the festivities. Look at it this way: you can imagine a wedding without anything—the dress, the preacher . . . hell, even a bride or a groom—but you cannot imagine a wedding without the wedding cake. The cake takes the cake.

Time for some sense-memory. Think back to the wedding cakes you ate as a kid . . . those pretty, white-tiered numbers that looked like a fairy-land castle . . . tasted sweet and gooey . . . symbolized by the wedding whites and sugar blues. These cakes were probably made of a white or yellow cake with a jelly or butter-cream filling and frosted with a sort of lard-like goop.

But times have changed; gays are lucky to be bursting upon the marriage scene just in time to reap the benefits of the Wedding-Cake Revolution. We Americans have become more sophisticated in our eating habits, including our tastes in baked goods. Croissants and scones, once available only in small bistros in the French Quarter, are readily available in the frozen-food section of your local supermarket. Not to mention those New Wave bake shops in even the smallest hamlet that specialize in "decadent creations" and "specialty cakes" and feature cookies in twenty varieties. Forget plain old chocolate chip and say hello to double-white-chocolate-silk praline lemon. And the wedding cake, which is the King (or, okay, the Queen) of desserts, has followed suit.

Photo: Shocking Gray

And so, thanks to this high-end baking trend, your wedding cake is yet another area of your wedding where you can have your cake and eat it too. You may not yet be able to have a legal marriage, but—almost as important—you *can* have a cake of beauty, taste, and personality. The traditional tiered white cake with the Crisco frosting has metamorphosed into magnificent imaginative creations. Today's cakes offer not only fine ingredients, but also intricate decorations and elaborate shapes and presentations.

Sure, the white frosted fairy-land castle cake you are picturing in your mind is still available, but today it can be ordered in half a dozen different flavors and filled with your choice of white-chocolate bavarian cream, vanilla custard, strawberry and raspberry mousse, cream cheese with pineapple, crème anglaise, cannoli cream, amaretto, and so on into the night. Yes, your guests will still end up in sugar shock, but it'll be a much classier state of shock.

In addition to the traditional tiered wedding cakes, large single-layer cakes with sumptuous fillings like rum and walnuts or triple triple chocolate are decorated with spun-sugar ribbons and marzipan bows. Today's cakes can be made in many shapes, such as hearts and triangles, as well as the long, flat sheet cake. There are cakes that have beveled edges or use a solid marzipan icing to give them a Victorian feeling. Artisans specialize in 3-D dioramas, where the sheet cake becomes a stage for frosted and candied figurines molded in the shape of the couple walking through the woods, in a '57 Chevy, or posed with their favorite movie characters—Rhett, Scarlett, Joe & Hank.

HOW MUCH DOES A ONE-WAY TICKET TO PARADISE COST?

Wedding cake, like almost everything else in the wedding, is figured out on a per-head basis. But because you're buying the whole cake, you usually tell the bakery how many people you need to serve and they'll tell you how much a cake that size costs. But for the sake of estimating, the bottom line is that a slice of wedding cake can start at $1.50 and run as high as $10. (Yes, *per slice.*)

Calm down. It all depends on where you buy your cake, what ingredients are used, and how fancy-schmancy not just the cake is, but the shop where you're buying it. Obviously Monsieur Maurice's Puff Pastry Emporium is gonna outcost your local A&P, but there are points in between, too. In addition to shops that specialize in cake design, consider small neighborhood bakeries, gourmet food stores, and upscale supermarkets, which are all out for a share of the wedding-cake market.

If the hall or hotel is supplying the cake, we encourage you to cross-examine your caterer with the same tenacity as you would a private baker. (And don't forget to talk about the cutting fee.)

LET THEM EAT CAKE: SOME SHOPPING HINTS

Order your wedding cake as much ahead of time as possible. Cakes sometimes take two to three days to assemble, and it is not unusual for popular bakers to be booked up several months in advance. The size of the walk-in refrigerator as well as the labor-intensive chore of producing a large cake limit the number of cakes a bakery can turn out and store. So if you have your heart set on purchasing from Kakes by Kathy, call and check on Kathy's availability to avoid disappointment with your kake.

Check around through your wedding network of caterers, site coordinators, photographers, and so on to get recommendations. Often, florists have the inside scoop on bakers because they work with them in coordinating floral decorations on the cake table.

You can browse around in potential bakeries, telling the counter person that you are interested in seeing wedding-cake selections. You'll be quoted a price, and maybe be given a brochure with flavor ideas. You are then handed large photo albums with examples of different styles of cakes they have baked.

The snapshots in bakeries' sample books will most likely be of cakes they have created—though caveat emptor, baby—we have heard of some upscale supermarkets that show stock cake designs that they will try out for the first time on your wedding. Avoid being anyone's wedding-cake guinea pig.

As you home in on possible bakers, ask to taste the cake flavors that most interest you. If they make you buy full slices or tell you that it really isn't possible to taste exactly what you want, look elsewhere. Frankly, this is a case where you should be able to sample the milk before you buy the cow.

You may or may not have a problem ordering a "gay wedding cake." Some shops really won't care if you're marrying a pony as long as you can pay for the cake.

Other bakers may be chatty and inquire about the wedding; if you get one of these, just tell 'em. If you feel they'll throw a pie in your face, go elsewhere.

THE RIGHT ORDER

Now that you have a shop in mind, you need to sit down and "talk cake" with the baker or shop salesperson. It is always best to call in advance and make an appointment. When you go to the shop, have the answers to the following questions well thought out:

? What design are you leaning toward?

? What about the three F's: filling, frosting, and flavor? Which ones are you thinking about? (A cake that you love but that sounds a bit too exotic for the general public—say a zucchini-mango loaf—may turn off all but the most committed roughage lovers.)

? How many people will the cake need to feed? An approximate number is fine for now, as you will have until a week or two before the date to make absolute-positive-no-turning-back decisions.

? When do you need the cake? This includes the time of day, so they can either have the cake delivered or make arrangements for it to be picked up.

? Where will the cake be set up? Indoors or out? (Hint: Unless botulism is going to be a theme for your wedding, you will want to stay away from certain ingredients that don't travel well, or don't do well if they remain outside in the sun for too long.)

? What does the room or surrounding area look like? What is the ceiling height of the room? Some people even take a photo of the reception area to the baker to make sure everything is in sync.

As you contemplate the cakes, remember that in addition to wanting the wedding cake to look and taste fabulous, you also want it to blend nicely with the rest of the menu. Knowing what will or will

BAKERS BEWARE

If your cousin who bakes great Toll House cookies offers to bake you a wedding cake, remember that those tiered numbers aren't just three little cakes piled on a couple of pillars and then frosted. Wedding cakes are an engineering feat, not to be left to the inexperienced or the faint of heart.

not accompany the wedding cake will help you to zero in on flavor choices. A rich whipped-cream cake may put guests over the edge after a heavy meal. If you're planning to serve fresh strawberries in addition to the cake, veer away from a strawberry-based wedding cake. If your friend Bonnie is bringing a hundred chocolate truffles to the reception, a white-chocolate cake is probably overkill.

TAKING THE CAKE

Transporting the finished product may prove to be as difficult as trying to ship glassware from the Orient. You can't simply send your little sister in her Celica hatchback to pick the cake up and hope for the best, because unless it's a single-layer number, it just won't make it. In fact, some places will *require* you to send two people to pick the cake up. ("No, I'm sorry, sir, but my instructions are to release this cake to no fewer than two people. I shudder to think what would happen if I let you take it by yourself.")

So when ordering, talk to the baker about delivering the cake and setting it up. If it has more than two tiers, the baker or owner of the bakery will probably do the setup and assembling at the site, and may or may not include the cost of that in the price they quote you. You'll sign a contract for time of delivery and cake description, and leave a deposit. Some places will want you to return cake stands after the wedding so that they can recycle them. (And if they don't require it, you, an ecologically aware citizen of planet Earth, can suggest it.)

YOU'RE THE TOP!

"Very nice, very unusual, a wedding between two people of the same actual sex," your cousin Bernice will murmur. "But just one question, smarty pants: where in the world are you going to get a wedding-cake top with two men on it???"

Oh, shut up, Bernice.

Same-sex couples have been adorning the tops of their wedding cakes with same-sex couples for literally . . . months now. Look

Even a real health nut will indulge on an occasion as special as your wedding is certain to be—especially if organic flours and natural sweeteners and dairy products are used in making the cake. However, if your crew is diet conscious and you're afraid they'll admire but not eat your wedding cake, consider having fresh fruit on hand as well.

at it this way: you're creating not only a new tradition, but *history,* as you go along. Same-sex wedding-cake tops may just be the Stonewall of modern matrimony.

If you've always wanted those little plastic figures atop your wedding cake, there are two ways to go about it: the political way, and the easy way out. The political way, of course, is to tell the baker that you want two men/women plus whatever on top of the cake (one couple we know had figures for the two of them and their two standard poodles). As in all this educating-the-

straight-world stuff, be firm, confident (even if you're not), and very specific about your needs. Remember, you are enlightening as well as ordering. Chances are that they won't have a same-sex couple in stock, but they can either make one up for you or give you leads on where to find the components.

An easier and possibly more direct approach: those little plastic figures that you are thinking of may be available à la carte at your local bakery supply store, craft store, or hobby shop. What this means is that you will purchase each little figure separately and piece them together with a base to hold a canopy, wishing well, or an arch with wedding bells if that's the look that you and yours are after. You can create exactly the couple, looks-wise, that you want to represent you, choosing from a range of skin tones and hair colors. Also check out little top hats, wedding veils, and other accessories available for the well-dressed little plastic figurine. Malibu Barbie and Dream Date Ken, eat your hearts out!

OTHER WAYS TO GO

• Actually, the plastic toppers are no longer the first or most stylish choice to adorn your finished wedding cake. In fact, some of the more upscale *pâtisseries* just plain don't use them anymore. According to Jane Lockhart, owner of Sweet Lady Jane bakery in Los Angeles, "We don't put brides and grooms on our cakes because traditionally they're plastic, and it just kind of goes against the whole look of an elegant cake. Sometimes people do bring us an heirloom piece—maybe it was the cake top that the bride's parents had on top of their cake." If both sets of your parents have saved their cake tops, you can extract one appropriate-sexed figure from each and put them together. (Won't your parents be pleased?)

• Porcelain couples from the thirties, forties, and fifties are highly collectible and can be found in gift shops—and at antique shows and flea markets at more affordable prices. Of course, antique figurines will cost you less if you go shopping with an opposite-sex same-sex couple who are also planning a wedding ("We'll keep the two grooms; you'll keep the two brides").

• Some bakers can sculpt figurines in your image or put you in touch with an artist who can. So if you always wanted the image of you and your lover captured forever in clay or papier-mâché, this is your chance. If you have an enormously creative friend, see if this couldn't be a potential wedding gift. If you're not that lucky and you have $500 or so to spend, contact Myla at the Beverly Hills Doll Company (listed in the Resource Directory at the end of this book). Working from your photos, Myla makes exact-replica porcelain figures with silk clothes. Order early—it can take her up to a month to get them just right.

• Have you seen those little lifelike statues that are made at photo shops by taking a photograph, mounting it onto foam core backing, and cutting it out? Find a great picture of the two of you, or better yet, get into your wedding duds, grab a snapshot, and use that. People will exclaim, "Why, that looks just like you two!"

• If you tend to be of an understated nature, the usual recommendation is to have the baker or florist top the creation with a spray of fresh flowers that will finish off the look of the cake. They may be lightly sprinkled along the tiers of the cake or individually applied to accent the frosted creation. Just make sure they haven't been sprayed with insecticides.

• Many bakery artists can re-create your bridal bouquets in spun sugar atop the cake. Your florist or whoever is going to make your bouquets can supply a photograph or description of what kinds of flowers will be used.

• We've heard of creative types using twinkling lights (buy the strings with battery packs), dollhouse figures, puppets, framed photographs representing different eras from each person's life, and windup toys.

And if you don't have enough takes on the subject already, we're going to wind up this discussion of cake tops with a quick survey of some of our favorite etiquette gurus:

🍰 "Then there are Temples of Love, and gay little cupids perched on wedding rings, wedding bells in tulle, small baskets of real flowers, and on it goes. It is for you to choose the pinnacle for this cake of cakes!" This, courtesy of Marguerite Bentley.

🍰 A check with Emily Post reveals her personal take on the cake-top dilemma: "Bells or a replica of a wedding ring may top the cake in place of flowers. They are in better taste than the bride and groom dolls sometimes used."

🍰 Martha Stewart, a respected food and entertaining guru, writes in her book *Entertaining:* "For decorations the crowning bride or groom statuette has given way to antique figures, or Kewpie dolls, or other personal whims. One bride I know wanted gnomes; another, who collected frogs, found a chef extraordinaire to create a pair of sugar amphibians dressed in lace and top hat."

THE GROOM'S CAKE

(Which may or may not be served at a lesbian wedding, and of which two may be served at a gay wedding)

The groom's cake began as a custom in the South and at one point was a disappearing item, but it seems to be making a comeback in all parts of the country. Southern belles used to set aside a rich chocolate cake (but much more simple than the bride's cake, with no decoration) to share with their first guests after returning from the honeymoon. At some point the groom's cake evolved into a dark fruitcake; maybe that's why it almost became extinct. This tradition then segued into having a separate cake at the reception that was cut into small squares, packaged in little boxes with the couple's initials, and distributed to the guests to take home. Legend has it that women who slept with the piece of cake under their pillows would dream of the men they would marry.

Mail-Order Brides (and Grooms)

Family Celebrations debuted in 1997 as America's first wedding and special-occasion catalog for gay men and lesbians. The catalog offers couples one-stop shopping for everything from same-sex cake toppers to toasting glasses to rainbow ribbon lace garters. (See the Resource Directory at the end of this book for instructions on how to get a catalog.)

With what you'll be spending on the wedding cake, you may just decide to 86 the groom's cake. Or close friends or relatives might offer to bake and package a groom's cake as a wedding gift. If you want the boxes, you can get them printed at the same time your invitations are; or skip the boxes altogether and invent some sort of whimsical wrapping yourself. (Caution your friends not to put the cake under their pillows without the box, however.)

EATING YOUR CAKE AND HAVING IT TOO

Now about that little tradition of saving some cake to eat on your first anniversary. Folklore says that you must do this to ensure luck and a long life together. The older etiquette gurus talk about taking the entire top *tier* and freezing it; but talk to savvy bakers today and they'll shake their heads in disbelief. Sweet Lady Jane says, "First of all, there's just no way that you can freeze cake for a year and expect it to taste as good as it should. And with what you're paying for a wedding cake, stop and figure out what the top tier is costing you. Then let me know if you still think it's such a great idea." If you want to partake of this tradition, you can do it in a modified way. Take a single slice, wrap it well (several layers of plastic wrap, aluminum foil, and a freezer bag are not overkill), and wait for a year to pass. It's actually a sweet little ritual, and perhaps tasting the same cake you had on your wedding day will turn you into newlyweds all over again.

THE WEDDING CAKE

HOW TO SAVE A LITTLE $$$

Thrifty brides (and their parents) have used this little trick down through the ages, and we pass it along to you:

Buy and display a fancy cake that is smaller than one you would buy to serve all of your guests. Then in the kitchen, have auxiliary sheet cakes that are of the same flavors and frosting. After the cake-cutting ceremony, have the fancy cake taken to the kitchen and—along with the sheet cakes—sliced for serving your guests. For instance, if you're having 150 people, order a wedding cake for 75 and sheet cakes for another 75.

RENT CONTROL

ALL ABOUT RENTING
AND BORROWING

*Y*ou rent your apartment. You rent videotapes. You rent bowling shoes. There is almost nothing you can imagine that can't be rented, as long as you can afford the rental fee. True, money can't buy happiness; but you *can* rent happiness in short spurts.

For almost any wedding, you'll find you need things that you don't own, can't afford to buy, and would probably never use again anyway. Instead of buying (which is forever) you can rent (which is only for the day). Common rental items are the stuff that your reception is made of: tables, chairs, glassware, champagne buckets, and linens. Architectural needs can also be filled by renting *chuppahs,* guest-book stands, arches, kneeling benches, pews, canopies, and rolled red carpet to create the aisle for you to march down. You can even change the entire look of your environment by renting palm trees and large flowering plants.

But by expanding your concept of renting beyond food service and architectural items, you'll open the doors to virtual rental reality, because also available are dance floors, klieg lights, and Jacuzzis; Wurlitzer organs and carousels; stages and large-screen TVs. The world of rentals can be your oyster; you just have to return it by noon the next day.

Along with carpet cleaners, cribs, and lawn mowers, most rental companies handle basic party supplies. Going to Joe's Rent-It-All is like visiting a terrific garage sale. You'll see all sorts of neat stuff that you will want to own—uh, we mean, rent—coffee makers, rolling bars, disco mirror balls, popcorn and snow-cone makers. It's all there to be enjoyed and returned, without the burden of permanent ownership.

Here's the drill:

🏆 With as much advance planning as possible, visit the rental store and choose the items you will need. (Companies can run out of essentials, especially around major holidays.)

🏆 Leave a deposit to keep the merchandise on hold.

🏆 Get an itemized bill, making sure the following are spelled out: cost per item, thorough description of items, date of rental, amount of deposit, and delivery and return information.

🏆 Decide on an approximate time of delivery for all the stuff. (See if you can have everything dropped off the night before at no extra charge.)

🏆 Find out exactly when the goods are due back at the shop. Lots of companies will deliver on Friday and expect the return on Monday, but ask, and make sure it appears in writing on the bill.

🏆 Call several times in advance (two weeks and then one week before is not excessive) to confirm the details.

🏆 Figure out a time when you or one of your posse will be there to meet the truck, since most rental companies will not drop off merchandise without a signature.

All merchandise will arrive neatly packed, and if you're renting something exotic like a fog machine there should be instructions as well. You're expected to return the merchandise in (almost) the same shape in which you received it. (You're supposed to rinse plates to remove caked-on food, but they do the heavy-duty sterilizing back at the store.)

Rental companies carry a basic statement of liability indicating that you will be billed for merchandise damaged or broken. The more exotic the item rented, the more you will want to discuss this clause. For the average renter, a broken glass or a chipped plate is not the end of the world; however, if the disco ball falls from the ceiling and shatters, you might want to know how much it's going to set you back or if it's insured.

I LOVE YOU, BUT YOUR FEE'S TOO BIG

As convenient as renting can be, keep in mind that costs add up quickly. Since the most common rentals in the wedding biz are place settings, let us consider what that might mean to you. For argument's sake, let's say that a 10-inch white china dinner plate costs 40 cents to rent. Multiply that times the number of guests, say 75, and you've got $30. Not bad—but that's so everyone has one plate. So what if you need to put together an entire place setting? Your average charges might look something like this:

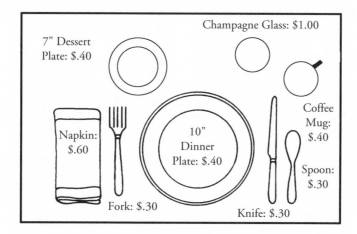

7" Dessert Plate: $.40
Champagne Glass: $1.00
Napkin: $.60
10" Dinner Plate: $.40
Coffee Mug: $.40
Spoon: $.30
Fork: $.30
Knife: $.30

Now we're talking more in the neighborhood of $3.70 per person, or $277.50 all told. The rental bill for a buffet reception can end up being as much as 20% of your total reception costs. We suggest you don't go overboard and run up costs that you will regret later on. Rent *with* your head, not over it.

Now, if you live in an area that has stores with bargains on glassware, for example, it's entirely possible that you can find a great deal on something like champagne flutes. One groom we know of thought he would rent everything, but became a little bit unglued at the thought of having to spend $1 apiece on stemware that he'd have to return. He did a little researching and found that at his local discount warehouse, he could *buy* nicer glasses—for $1.20. Since the glasses were something he figured he might need in the future, he became the proud owner of forty champagne flutes for only $8 more than the rental charge would have been.

Having said that, we return to the premise that renting is a quick and simple way to solve common problems in planning the wedding and reception. No one is expected to have on hand six 8-foot buffet tables or 100 chairs, or have matching cutlery for 60 lying around in their kitchen drawer.

Here are some additional hints for you as you research rentals:

✪ As the medical profession has specialists, so does the rental industry. If you're in an urban area, look around and you'll probably be able to find a company that specializes in party goods. You'll get a larger selection and more personalized service. In some cities, there are even rental houses that specialize in fine merchandise and offer the very best crystal and china available.

✪ Look at the fabric of tablecloths and napkins. White, starched 100% cotton table-cloths and white polyester-blend tablecloths are two entirely different animals.

✪ Be sure to look at a sample of the actual color. ("Dusty rose" napkins can be more like pink; "rose" is a dark red. "Ruby red" is another story entirely.)

✪ If you have a choice between three different kinds of chairs, pretend you're Goldilocks and sit on each one to see for yourself which is the most comfortable.

✪ Recommendations that tell you how many people a table will hold are guidelines, not rules. If you want ten people to sit at a six-foot round table, have the store place ten chairs around it; then sit down and picture nine of your relatives squished around you on all sides.

✪ Take a tape measure along to double-check on sizes and heights, especially for architectural items. "Oh yes, ma'am, I'm sure that gazebo will fit through your gate" is the kind of statement that nightmares are made of.

✪ Notice the weight and the pattern of the silverware; if there's a choice to be made, hold a sample of each utensil.

✪ A caterer gave us this tip for renting chafing dishes for large parties: if you're planning on leaving the dish uncovered for most of the reception, you don't need to rent the ones with silver-plated lids; they're almost double the cost of the basic stainless steel ones, and since the lids will be off, no one will know the difference.

✪ Finally, rentals need not come solely from a party rental house. Some other places you might look for some of your more exotic needs are display houses, tent and tool-supply shops, community theaters, schools, civic organizations, newspaper classified ads, and audiovisual houses.

DON WE NOW OUR GAY APPAREL

WEDDING ATTIRE

"**I** haven't got a thing to wear." You've probably said this at some point in your life, but this time it may be true. Or you might have something waiting in the wings for just this sort of occasion. And this isn't a solo act; you're going to have to coordinate clothing not only with your partner, but with your entire wedding party if you choose to have one. What to wear, what to wear . . . where to start?

   Make a quick trip into your closet. (That's right, this time you are encouraged to go back into the closet.)

   Look around at what's in that closet. What do you like to wear? Do you ever dress up, or are you strictly a 501s kind of guy? Are you a woman of many looks, or would you just as soon wear a comfortable shirt and Birkenstocks?

   Think about how what you wear influences how you feel.

   Walk out of the closet (whew), sit yourself down, and consider the following: How much money is budgeted for clothes for your wedding? Have you been envisioning a white wedding? Do you want to look a special way that will make a certain impression on your future spouse? And do the two of you want to coordinate your outfits?

What you ultimately choose to wear to your wedding may be guided in part by the season, the time of the gathering, and the sense of formality (or lack of same) that has been woven throughout your wedding plans up to this point. (For example, nearly everyone who

Every man should own at least one dress—and so should lesbians.

—LESBIAN ACTIVIST JANE ADAMS SPAHR, 1988

Photo: Marcelina Martin

has their ceremony in a house of worship keeps their clothing conservative out of respect for the location.) In fact, there exist very specific rules of etiquette that purport to spell out the definitive answers to such pressing questions as, Can I wear a morning coat in the evening? Should I wear a long formal train in the afternoon? Is a white dinner jacket acceptable for a January wedding? We, of course, feel you should be able to wear anything you like—sure, even a dress with a train, just so long as you don't trip on it and fall.

Between the fuss that has been made over wedding fashion for the last several centuries and the fact that yours is by nature an unconventional wedding, what you decide to wear will be a major act of personal expression. When same-sex couples talk about choosing wedding attire, their answers are invariably prefaced by some fundamental principle that brought them to their final fashion decisions. Ultimately, the clothes reflect a basic ideology about this whole wedding business.

HOW OTHER SAME-SEX COUPLES HAVE DEALT WITH THE WHAT-TO-WEAR DILEMMA

♦♦ "We wanted our wedding to be like us. We don't share the same sense of style, so we decided before we went to buy our outfits that we could each wear what we wanted. We wanted to feel comfortable as individuals."

♦♦ "I had decided to get a bridesmaid's dress, something understated but classy. So I was looking at the bridesmaid's dresses, but over on the other side of the store were these beautiful white wedding dresses. I started to feel like a second-class citizen. I thought, 'I'm a bride. I want a bridal gown.' So I bought one."

♦♦ "As extravagant women we decided to have a formal event. We each wore long dresses, and our attendants, male and female, were all in black tuxes."

♦♦ "Matthew and I got married on the beach, and decided that Speedos were too casual. So we wore khaki shorts and matching T-shirts."

♦♦ "We did it campy. I wore a fedora, a bustier with sequins, and a long ivory skirt, and Greta wore an electric-blue jacket with nothing underneath, white pants, and shades."

♦♦ "We ultimately decided against it, but John's into themes and at one point we were going to be married in Elizabethan garb. We ended up in tuxes."

WEDDING ATTIRE

GENDER-BENDING FASHION

Same-sex weddings are the perfect occasion to bend traditional gender-related fashions. We all know that it's possible for a woman to look equally as hot in a tuxedo as a man does. Women have dressed in classic men's clothing for years. Consider Katharine Hepburn, whose sense of style in a suit was rivaled only by Cary Grant. From the Annie Hall look to Madonna donning double-breasted suits and a monocle, man-tailored clothes on a woman are smart, stylish, and chic. Two brides all decked out à la Dietrich in *The Devil Is a Woman* are sure to be real crowd pleasers.

On the other hand, if you have your hearts set on a wedding with a groom wearing a satin gown with a hoop skirt, you may have to work a little harder to create an atmosphere where everyone feels comfortable. Your grandmother from Dubuque may have to be warned in advance. Still, for some gay men drag, and in this instance, bridal drag, is the appropriate fashion *and* political statement.

Ultimately, the choice is up you. But put this in your pipe and smoke it: lesbian and gay weddings challenge tradition in a multitude of ways, so if it's what you want to do, why shouldn't you challenge the rules of fashion too?

We're going to split you into two teams now—pants and gowns—and deal with the sexes one at a time. However, please feel free to read outside of the category you technically qualify for.

MEN ABOUT TOWN

There's a famous line from an episode of *The Mary Tyler Moore Show* in which Georgette and Ted, off to a formal affair, arrive in matching tuxedos. "I feel like the top of a gay wedding cake," Georgette tells Mary.
Little did she know.

FORMALWEAR

If a classic look is what you're after, guys have a narrower range of choices in selecting their wedding garb than women do. Formal menswear (and, some would argue, men's fashion in general) hasn't changed much over the last century. This isn't saying that men put less time or planning into wedding attire than women, just that their choices come with less societal baggage. Two men getting married in tuxes just don't make the same statement as two women in full bridal regalia. Go figure.

So what exactly does *black tie* mean? Black tie means serious business. It can also mean waiter or can remind you of a bad lounge act if you're not careful. It's actually an etiquette term indicating that guests (male and female) wear semiformal attire; for men, that starts with a tuxedo.

THE BASIC TUX

"Everyone looks great in a tuxedo" isn't far from the truth. Black (usually) and slenderizing, elegant and spiffy, it was the attire of choice for many of the male couples (as well as many women) we spoke with. There's really nothing quite like a tux. You can rent it and have it tailored for you, and best of all, you can return it the next day, stains and all. Over and done.

The cut can be classic American or tailored European. The lapels are either notched (currently most stylish), peaked (the classic), or shawl collar (a vintage look—like Bogey's white dinner jacket in *Casablanca*.)

Shades of dark gray and black are the only ones the etiquette gurus want to see on grooms in a formal wedding; they suggest saving the powder blue tuxedos and pastel accessories for the prom. (We say, just keep a safe distance from burgundy.) White dinner jackets are kind of a throwback to the fifties but are making a resurgence; they are traditionally worn with black trousers and accessories for a spring or summer wedding.

VARIATIONS ON THE THEME

The cutaway or morning coat. Think of it as tails for daylight hours—a long black or gray coat worn with black or gray striped trousers, pearl gray or black waistcoat or black cummerbund, white wing-collar shirt, and striped ascot or bow tie.

The stroller, walking coat, or sack coat. A looser and longer tuxedo coat without the buttons. The jacket is black or gray, the trousers black-and-gray or black-and-white pinstripes. Worn with a four-in-hand tie (see "Formal Accessories," on the next page) and optional gray gloves. Favored by attendants when the groom wears a cutaway.

White tie. The most formal of formalwear, it is also called white tie and tails or full dress tailcoat. It's what made Fred Astaire Fred Astaire. The suit is black; the tie is—right you are!—white. The front of the coat (which has no buttons) extends below a white piqué waistcoat. The trousers are solid black and are held up by suspenders. The white shirt has what's called a "boiled front" (meaning it has a white piqué bib, never a pleated one) and a wing collar. If you're going all the way and "puttin' on the Ritz," add a pocket watch and chain, a white scarf, white kid gloves, a silk cape, an ivory walking stick, and of course, a black silk top hat.

There are all kinds of threatening-looking charts that tell you when the various incarnations of formalwear are to be worn, and by whom. Use them as guidelines, but don't get too caught up in them unless your greatest goal in life is to avoid offending a debutante. If you want to wear tails in the afternoon, no one's going to have you arrested.

FORMAL ACCESSORIES

The accessories you choose will further embellish the classic quality of the formalwear.

The *bow tie* should be of moderate-width black satin unless you decide to have it match a colored cummerbund. If you go with an *ascot* (a scarflike tie looped under the chin), it's usually either striped or white and requires a stickpin. Then there's the gray-and-black-striped *four-in-hand,* which is what you think of as a generic tie with a slipknot.

A *cummerbund* is a pleated sash worn around the waist and often matches the bow tie in color and material. Since the trousers have no belt loops, they're held up by *suspenders,* sometimes referred to as *braces,* which of course are covered by the jacket but may make an appearance if you take the jacket off as the day wears on.

Waistcoats are nothing more than backless vests (with straps around the back) and are worn instead of cummerbunds. For the purist, they match the tie in fabric and color; but you can go wild and find a brocade, tapestry, or iridescent-colored one. (And what about lavender?)

Shoes are properly black plain-toe *oxfords* or *pumps*—slip-ons of patent leather or calfskin. *Opera pumps* are patent leather, with grosgrain bows on them.

Socks are black; no leg exposed, please.

The *shirt* for your tux should not be an afterthought. Remember the ruffled shirts that the Partridge Family wore for their performances? Run as far away from them as you can. The classic tux shirt is most often a form of white (ivory, pearl, cream) and has a pleated or white piqué bib front. At the neck is either a standard *spread collar* or the more mysterious and elegant *wing collar.*

The formal shirt requires *studs* (never mind the clever definition that we won't lower ourselves to use; they take the place of buttons) and *cuff links* made of anything from mother-of-pearl to black onyx.

Add to this either a *pocket square* (folded handkerchief) or a *boutonniere* (using both is considered gauche) and, abracadabra, you're dressed to kill.

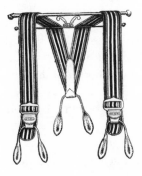

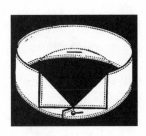

IS THE RENT DUE? TIPS FOR TUX RENTERS

If you plan on having your attendants wear tuxes, ask for package discounts. You should get one free tux rental with the rental of four or five others.

Don't use a rental shop where you select outfits from a catalog. Make sure they have tuxes to try on and be fitted to you in the store.

Take the time to go into the shop for a test-fitting; don't just call your measurements in and hope for the best.

If you want everyone to match, don't let anyone bring his or her own tux from out of town. Out-of-towners should be fitted by professionals from their hometown, then coordinate the measurements with the shop the rest of your attendants are using.

The cost of renting shoes is extra. Skip the rental if you have something appropriate, but make sure they're well-polished.

Find out exactly when everything is due back at the shop, and have your best man or best woman make the return for you.

In some parts of the country you can rent a complete formalwear outfit for $50 to $100, but if you live in a big city where a rental can cost $125 or more, you might think about buying a tuxedo instead. You can actually find some great ones for $200 to $400 (although that Ralph Lauren number will run you upward of $1,000), and if you anticipate needing to wear a tux again in the foreseeable future, purchasing could actually be the prudent way to go. You can also check with your local tuxedo rental shops, which sometimes sell last year's tuxes at bargain rates.

FORMALWEAR ALTERNATIVES

If you feel like black tie is a bit over the top for your taste, a dark suit (navy, black, or dark gray) is elegant and is taken almost as seriously by the etiquette gurus as a tux is for dressy wedding wear. To maximize the look of a suit, we recommend a crisp white dress shirt; one with French cuffs and a spread collar (never a tab or button-down) is a good choice. Add a dark tie (woven silk is the most formal) and your dressiest black shoes.

The obvious upside (and downside) of a great suit is that it can't be rented. If you don't own one, you'll have to buy it, but you'll have it forever.

If you've never been one for rules and want to fight fashion fascism, you can put your individual stamp on your wedding by wearing any of the following:

• Cowboy boots or sneakers with your tux

• A traditional three-piece Nigerian outfit called a *grand buba* that has drawstring pants, a caftanlike shirt with a Nehru collar that hits the midthigh, and a matching robe.

• Worn-in Levis and starched white T-shirts

• Kilts

• Black leather pants, black leather vest, black leather gloves, stud bracelets, black leather hat, and . . . what? white pumps?

• Oriental robes

• Yarmulkes, kufi, or kente hats or other ethnic accoutrements. There are yarmulkes in pearl white and basic black, but we've also spotted them in leopard skin, brocade, and, of course, lavender. (And you can have custom imprinting done, too.)

• Vintage clothing. Shop around in thrift stores or look in your family's attic.

HERE COME THE BRIDES

Straight people say to me, "Oh, a lesbian wedding? What, do they both wear tuxedos?" Big deal. Sometimes they do . . . and sometimes they both wear dresses and sometimes one wears a dress and one wears a tuxedo. A lot of them seem to wear silk pants, blouses, flowing jackets. But they all look stunning, and that's because they're in love.

—THE REVEREND ROSALIND RUSSELL

Historically, the wedding gown was the single most important and expensive dress a woman would wear in her lifetime. As the leading player in the traditional wedding drama, all eyes were upon the bride as she made her entrance and paraded down that aisle into holy matrimony; all necks would crane to see what she was wearing, and a communal gasp would

WEDDING ATTIRE

NO GLOVE, NO LOVE?

Brides and grooms through the ages have learned that gloves and rings are not the finest combination. Does she remove her glove in order to get the ring on? Then what happens? Does she walk back down the aisle wearing a glove on her right hand only? As always, rules of etiquette were developed to take care of this situation. If the bride chose to wear gloves, she was to remove a finger (not hers, silly, the glove's) or slit the glove in order for the ring to be slipped on at the appropriate moment. So we say to you modern brides and grooms alike: either do it with your bare hands or opt for a modified Michael Jackson look.

be heard as people took in her magnificence. This was her day to be queen, to rise head and shoulders above the rest, to feel gorgeous and divine.

Today, regardless of the gender of their intended, women either embrace the notion of "the wedding gown thing" or reject the concept entirely. Some lesbians feel that wearing a wedding dress is taking a political stand, further proclaiming that "there is no difference between 'us' and 'them.'" If you're the kind of gal who went through life daydreaming "Someday, my princess will come," a traditional wedding gown could be for you. Alternately, you may have wanted to *be* Prince Charming, despise the pageantry associated with the wedding dress, and boycott anything that even hints at taffeta.

As two lesbians who are tying the knot, one of you may feel the first way, and the other the second. This is all workable; we've heard of many beautiful weddings where one bride was in a gown and the other in a smashing tux.

QUEEN FOR A DAY

Bridal magazines of the forties and fifties made it all seem so much simpler. You could be "the autumn bride," "the playful bride," or the ever-popular "classic June bride." Contemporary options are, shall we say, more diverse.

THE STORYBOOK BRIDE

"We wanted a big society wedding, the wedding you picture when you're growing up. My dress had a six-foot train."

This is it—the big ball gown with beaded bodice, lace, and petticoats. It screams *Bride!* Echoing the dress and the look are the headpiece, optional veil, and if the cut is suitable, a flowing train that runs behind the gown itself. Wedding dresses come in a variety of styles, with assorted lengths, necklines, bodices, and waistlines, so that nearly everyone can look magical.

This kind of bridal gown is pure fantasy; it is a costume. Unless you go to inaugural balls or perform in a guerrilla theater troupe, chances are you won't find an occasion to wear this dress again. It becomes an instant heirloom and gets packed in a box with special preservatives and sits in a closet for the rest of your life. You take it out every time you move, and try it on to see if it still fits. (Or you'll want your daughter to wear it someday . . . but that's another book.)

If you want to be the classic bride, go for it—but our recommendation is that unless you want the ceremony to feel like a put-on, make sure the style of the rest of the wedding is equally traditional.

THE MODERN BRIDE

"I want to wear something elegant and spectacular, but I want it to be more my style."

Some women want to select a dress or other ensemble that emulates a bridal look, but speaks more to their personal style than to the fantasy. You may splurge here and treat yourself to something that's more formal or glamorous than you would normally consider buying. You can

Photo: Michael Arden

also find gorgeous batiste antique wedding gowns or other vintage dresses that don't scream "bride," but rather whisper it.

Check out stores such as Laura Ashley, where you can get European-style cotton brocade gowns with extremely simple detailing.

There are also a number of possible variations on the modern-bride theme. In Hawaii, there are formal gowns called *holoku,* which are traditional dresses; African wedding designs in boldly printed fabrics or *ashoke* (a handwoven cotton from Nigeria, interspersed with metallic thread) with matching jackets and head wraps are another possibility.

THE PRACTICAL BRIDE

"Our wedding was the perfect excuse to buy something new. We both wore silk dresses."

The practical bride decides to indulge in that Armani suit she has always admired, or puts together a stylish ensemble that's only a touch flashier than what's usually found in her closet. Her M.O. is to find a look that complements her lifestyle so that she really *can* wear it again and again. She might wear a simple white pantsuit but dress it up with an elaborate veil, or wear a black sheath and a wreath of wildflowers in her hair.

In our ecologically minded world, it seems foolish to some to spend a lot of money on a piece of clothing that will be worn only once. You can go with a more contemporary styling; then by dropping the accessories you use to make the outfit special for your wedding day (such as a wide-brimmed hat and elbow-length gloves), or raising the hemline six inches, you have an outfit that will work in other circumstances. (And each time it's worn, it carries a special memory of one of the best days of your life.)

Oh, and one more thing about the practical bride: she wears sensible shoes.

THE REBEL BRIDE

"My mother asked me, 'Why did you wear pants?' I said, 'Mom, when have you ever known me to love wearing a dress? I've got news for you, I'm not going to be buried in a dress either.' This was my occasion, and I was going to be comfortable."

The Rebel Bride, the Leather and Lace Bride, or the Bride of the Future—cousin to the Storybook Bride but with extraordinary flair. She will make a broad statement, but not specifically of a classic bridal nature. Wild headdresses, period costumes, and theme outfits all fall into this category.

WEDDING ATTIRE

You don't have to create this look yourself if you've got the bucks to go designer. Check out Betsey Johnson's thermo-cotton wedding dress with crib-cover veil, or Claude Montana's baroque bride in silk-satin quilted coat, velvet chenille dress, and feather earmuffs. Or you can go environmental with a ball gown made of newspaper, plastic garbage-can liners, or recycled aluminum. You can wear jeans and hand-appliquéd tux jackets; satin nightshirts from Frederick's of Hollywood; or long ranch-style calico skirts and cowboy boots. If you have a taste for the outrageous, here's your chance to be the belle of the ball—on your own terms.

YOU'D BETTER SHOP AROUND

Bridal fashion is an industry unto itself, so if you're thinking of buying a wedding gown and want to see what's popular these days, pick up one of the many specialty magazines and flip through the pages. Or, if you really get into it, you can attend a bridal show. These are held in major cities at hotels and convention centers. Check your local newspapers in the fashion or entertainment sections for listings.

If you're traveling down Wedding Gown Lane, be aware that in theory, bridal attire is one of the last bastions of the apparel industry in which garments are customized to each client. For certain lines, there is no such thing as "off the rack," and it's not unusual to order a wedding gown five to eight months in advance of the wedding date. Other manufacturers will offer ready-to-wear, but you'll still need alterations for the correct fit.

Also keep in mind that the average wedding gown costs $780. (You think that's a lot? Well, a Pat Kerr designer gown can run you twenty grand, so start saving those pennies.) And the pity of it all is that you usually don't get a great-quality dress for your $780. If you were going to spend that much on any other dress, you'd get something pretty incredible for your money, wouldn't you? No such luck with the bridal-gown industry; it might be of synthetic material and unlined, with unfinished seams and loose threads. Add a veil or a headpiece for $150 or so, plus the shoes, the undergarments, and other accessories, and you're probably pushing $1,000. Double that if you've both decided to go for it.

DOING YOUR COLORS

No matter what anybody says, regardless of age, size, or marital history, you can wear white. "But I *hate* the way I look in white," you're thinking. So don't wear white. Wear a color. Ecru, off-white, eggshell, ivory, cream, or champagne can be wedding colors that are white—but aren't. And it's not just the color that makes it a wedding gown, but the choice of fabric and style as well.

Historically, the only unacceptable color to wear for bridal garb is green because it's the color reserved for fairies and it's the color of jealousy—so unless you're a bitchy fairy, don't wear green. Chinese brides wear red (the color of celebration); Spanish and Icelandic ones wear black.

Red was also big during the American Revolution, signifying rebellion. (Might be a good choice for you, no?)

WHERE TO LOOK

THE BRIDAL SALON

The bridal salon carries everything you could ever imagine wearing to a wedding—not only for the bride but also for the attendants, the mother, the grandmother, and the flower girl. Here you can buy a tiara. Here you can get sixteen dresses in varying hues of lavender.

Salons today focus on personalized pampering. A consultant will put you through the bridal paces and oversee style selection, alterations, and the total accessorized bridal package. Bridal salons sometimes have true bargains—as much as half off at sample sales (you may be purchasing a gown that's been tried on countless times, so you'll want to look it over for lipstick stains) and closeout sales. Sale gowns are usually nonrefundable, so give the dress a thorough inspection for defects and make sure it's the one for you. (If you change your mind, your only hope is to talk your lover into wearing it instead.)

You can locate bridal salons by looking in the bride magazines' listings, or in your yellow pages.

Ask the shop owner if you can get a two-for-one deal on wedding gowns.

 Consumer Alert

Don't buy accessories like gloves, undergarments, garters, and so forth from bridal salons; the markup on these items is outrageous.

DEPARTMENT STORES

Department stores are worth a look, especially after Christmas and in August, when clearance sales are held. Though many major department stores do not have departments devoted exclusively to bridal fashion, their formalwear section may have exactly what you're looking for. One of the best things about department stores is that if you get the dress home and freak ("What could I have possibly been thinking?!? I could never wear this thing!"), you can return it. Most department stores will also take care of alterations.

BRIDAL DISCOUNTERS

Bridal discounters sell off the rack from suppliers that range from designers (who give you last season's stock), to salons that have gone out of business, to someone who has samples he or she couldn't get rid of. Sometimes they're nomadic companies that set up business for a weekend at a time in hotels, or even sell out of the homes of "representatives." The labels and identifying tags are usually gone, so you don't really know what you're getting, and the service will be slim to none. But the savings can make it all worthwhile (from 20% to 40%, and sometimes even higher), plus the entire process here is so swift that you can buy a gown and be married in it the same day! If you don't have a lot of time and are an easy fit, check them out.

RENTALS

Rentals are a modern-day answer to some brides' dress dilemmas. Men have been renting formalwear since time began, so why not women? This trend is cropping up in major cities and offers you the chance to have the look you're after without . . . well, without being married to it forever. Rental prices start at about $75.

There are rental stores such as Just Once Ltd. in New York City that specialize exclusively in couture wedding dresses. Gowns by major designers like Carolina Herrera and Scassi that sell for upward of $3,000 can be rented here for $350 to $750. Arguably, if you shopped till you dropped you might find an inexpensive dress for about the same price as you'd pay to rent the designer gown, but if you've set your sights on top of the line, this could be the way to go.

P.S.: If you're into this sort of thing, you *will* have to worry about the karma that comes with the dress and can't be removed at the dry-cleaners: Who else has worn it, and what emotions coursed through them while they were wearing it?

MAKING YOUR OWN

Pattern companies like McCall's and Vogue sell patterns that mirror the styles found in the bridal magazines and salons. If you or a loved one wants to tackle the project, remember that formalwear is extremely complicated to fit, and unless you really know what you're doing, the results could be disastrous. You can also farm out the production to a good dressmaker or seamstress and still come in under what you'd pay for a ready-made dress.

YET MORE IDEAS

Thrift shops and consignment shops can carry "pre-owned" designer clothes; and vintage clothing stores are a popular alternative for a different spin on bridal attire.

Check the classifieds or local shops for gowns that were bought and never used because the wedding was canceled. (Boy, talk about questionable karma.)

WEDDING ATTIRE

You may be fortunate enough to have your mother's or grandmother's dress in a trunk; at one time you probably thought it would never be worn again, but here you are, about to be a bride. The heirloom dress becomes a sentimental part of the ritual. Do you have a close friend or sister who has a wedding dress that you love? They might not want to lend it, but if your budget is tight, it's worth asking. And hey, you're taking care of "something old" and "something borrowed" at the same time.

THE ACCESSORIES

VEILS

Yes, yes, veils did historically mean veiling the woman so no other eyes could gaze upon her until her future partner got his hands on her. But consider: Salome's Dance of the Seven Veils was sexy, with each veil revealing just a little bit more. (There's a fashion tip in here too: instead of one veil, wear a whole bunch of them—seven?)

Veils can be made for $2 by taking a headband and pasting some tulle or lace on it to cover your face. Or you can pay hundreds of dollars and have a veil that will rival the one Julie Andrews wore in *The Sound of Music*. There are plenty of options in between. A general rule of thumb: the shorter the dress, the shorter the veil.

SHOES

If the shoe fits, buy it, but don't wait until the last minute. If you're wearing a gown, you'll want to wear the proper shoes for fittings, so plan ahead of time.

Finding the right shoes seems simple enough, but this is not always the case. You need to find shoes that will be comfortable yet work with what you're wearing. Before you buy those spike heels, consider how long you're going to be on your feet and, maybe, dancing. Break them in ahead of time.

One simple and elegant solution is to wear ballet slippers. But if the slipper doesn't fit, you can wear heels for the ceremony, then

Over the course of two to three weeks we took ourselves to the Goodwill stores located all around the city. Jessica McClintock off-loads their unsold stock (for a considerable tax advantage I'll bet) to these stores. We bought similar (but different!) brand-new dresses by the same designer for a grand total of eighty dollars!

—BETH AND PATTI

change into tennies to dance, dance, dance at the reception. Rachel gave us this tip: "Buy a size bigger and put in inner soles. When your feet start to swell, take the inner soles out and it's like putting on a new pair of shoes."

For the ultimate fashion statement, wear Dr. Martens.

THE GARTER

In olden days, the garter was a sash worn just below the bride's knee to keep away the wandering hands of the groom and his men. Today you might wear a garter belt to hold up your stockings, but a garter? It's just a prop. You can buy garters at bridal shops, novelty stores, or by mail order; or make your own. Buy two if you're thinking of throwing one to the crowd. If you hate the lacy stuff, tie a piece of suede or purple grosgrain ribbon around your leg.

JEWELRY

Keep it simple for a classic bridal look, or shoot the moon for a more theatrical take. Pearls are classy wedding attire, and can be in the form of earrings, a bracelet, or a single-strand necklace. Diamonds are always nice, as are heirlooms of any kind. Best of all is a pendant, locket, or anything similar given to you by your lover (preferably the one you're marrying).

The higher the hair, the closer to God.

—K. D. LANG

HAIR DO'S AND DON'TS

Do practice on your hair a few days ahead of time, with whatever headgear you've chosen. You don't want to have a bad hair day on your wedding day, so prepare in advance.

Don't end up like Lucille Ball in that *I Love Lucy* episode where she fell down the staircase in her Ziegfeld headpiece. If you're wearing a veil, crown, tiara, comb, headband (in tribute to Hillary Clinton), flower piece, or Carmen Miranda basket of fruit, try it on ahead of time and walk around with it.

Do have someone style your hair (and makeup too, if you go in for that sort of thing) on the day of the wedding if you can. You'll be nervous enough without worrying about poking yourself in the eye with the mascara wand or having a pesky burn mark on your forehead from the curling iron that got away.

WEDDING ATTIRE

IT'S MY (WEDDING) PARTY . . .
AND I'LL MAKE YOU DRESS ALIKE IF I WANT TO

Legend has it that originally the wedding couple was surrounded by many friends, family members, and neighbors all dressed similarly so that evil spirits could not distinguish them from the nuptial pair; this is one of the reasons members of the wedding party all dress alike today. Pop folklore has it that the bride chooses dowdy matching outfits for her wedding party to make sure she stands out from the crowd and no one steals her thunder (or, perhaps, her groom).

If you want to do the pretty-bridesmaids- (or groomsmen-) all-in-a-row thing, check out the following:

• Some tux rental shops or bridal salons also rent bridesmaid dresses. If you're determined to have everyone match, this might be the most inexpensive way to pull it off.

• If it's a batallion of tuxes you're after, coordinate the kind of tux each person is going to wear. Otherwise you'll be unpleasantly surprised when they all show up in black—except your Cousin Selma, who's wearing a Wayne Newton look-alike red satin ruffled number.

• The wedding party is traditionally responsible for paying tux rental fees or purchasing the gowns you want them to wear. By the time the shoes are dyed and the bag is bought, you could be talking about a lot of money. If someone can't afford it and you really want her or him in the wedding, you should figure out a way to pay for it.

• Since everyone is not the same, not everyone likes the same clothes. Tread lightly as you zero in on a fashion ensemble appropriate for your nearest and dearest pals.

• As you choose the ensemble, remember the sizes, shapes, and weights of those who will be doing the wearing. Will the color be subtle or frightening when mixed with the varying hair colors of the attendants? Will the style make your Cousin Maxine look like Barbarella? Will the cut make your Cousin Vinnie look like Tennessee Tuxedo on acid?

• Each tux or dress will need to be fitted, so make initial arrangements for your attendants to have their alterations done. If renting, get everyone to reserve their garb enough in advance that you won't be disappointed by coming up one outfit short.

• If you don't care if everybody matches, just have your wedding party wear their best clothes—but be sure to consult with each of them to eliminate any major fashion gaps.

• There are actually good designers of bridesmaid gowns who make the outfits look (and feel) like they are fit for a wedding and (yes, it's true) that can be worn again and again. (What a concept.) Look for gowns by Watters and Watters or Jessica McClintock.

VARIETY, THE SPICE OF LIFE

There are many other options for same-sex brides and grooms (wasn't it so much easier back in the days when the only gay fashion tip was which color handkerchief should be worn in which pocket?). For both the boys and the girls, there are other ways to have a unified look without making everyone wear a uniform. Here are four of them:

Pick one basic color that will integrate the wedding party. Shades of black or white are popular and easy (and nobody minds having one more black outfit). Pastels tend to work as well; but when you start going into shades of, say, blue or pink, you could be asking for trouble, unless you're in a position to see everyone's outfit well before the wedding. You don't want your wedding party mistaken for a Halloween party.

Pick an accessory, any accessory (a scarf, a necklace, a boutonniere or corsage, a hanky), to coordinate everyone. Whatever you choose, it just has to have the "feel" of matching; you don't necessarily have to have a total look-alike chorus line of people behind you.

Pick a period—for example, lacy Victorian romance, the Gatsby look, fifties funk, punk, etc. The decision is yours, but remember, you're making quite a statement (especially if, for example, your entire wedding party has their noses pierced for the occasion). Watch the line between clothing coordination and costume design.

Find your own distinctive look and use it to set you off. You can choose to wear a different color or cut of coat. If the grooms or brides are both resplendent in full tuxes or other formalwear, have the attendants decked out in tuxedo shirts and jackets—over jeans and sneakers.

Photo: Michael Arden

The Flower Hour

FLOWERS

*Y*ou might think, "I know nothing about flowers." But if you've ever been sent a congratulatory bouquet, or bought a single long-stemmed rose from a street vendor, you already know more about flowers than you might think.

Unless you're Ebenezer Scrooge or someone with a wicked case of hay fever, you won't want to get married without flowers to complete the ritual. Flowers are nonessential essentials; they don't do anything but look magical. We think of them as a necessary luxury.

You'll find that as you meet with florists and are shown more and more elaborate arrangements, you can quickly blow your budget big time as you notice how dramatic the effect becomes "simply by doubling the amount of flowers in an arrangement." And the "once in a lifetime" inner monologue begins anew. Your flower budget may range from $10 for a couple of boutonnieres to thousands of dollars for elaborate creations, so you'll need to know what you're doing.

So how do you avoid floral fallout?

🌷 Decide exactly where and how you want to use flowers. Flowers can be worn, carried, and used to create a mood in a room, pull things together, and cover imperfections.

🌷 Brides traditionally carry bouquets and grooms wear boutonnieres. You do whatever suits you. Bouquets, corsages, and boutonnieres are a great way to give the wedding party a coordinated look; and for the nervous attendant, a bouquet provides something to do with fidgety hands.

🌷 For the ceremony, fresh floral garlands can decorate the entrance and large arrangements can be placed on either side of the vow site. Reception flowers create a distinctive ambiance with centerpieces and exotic greens scattered about serving stations.

Every flower is a soul blossoming out to nature.

—GÉRARD DE NERVAL

❦ Flowers set the stage as backdrops for numerous photo ops. And they do wonders covering up the wood paneling if you get married in your den.

BEAUCOUP DE BOUQUETS

Carried down the aisle by brides and attendants, then preserved forever in Lucite or tossed to singles anxious to be the next to wed, the bouquet sets off the chosen attire whether it is a gown or jeans. The most traditional of the traditional is a bouquet of white roses for the bride, but by all means don't rule out flowers that "speak to you" or exotics you simply find fabulous.

If you choose bouquets for attendants, consider who will be doing the carrying. A petite attendant cuddling a massive cascading bouquet of hothouse tiger lilies can look funny, so pick a style that's in proportion to the size and weight of each person. Men can certainly carry full bouquets, but this is a look that tends to be more bridal. (However, if you're looking to make a statement, go for it.) Carrying a single flower is also a stylish option whatever your gender. If you're trying to coordinate an array of attendants' outfits, come up with a floral color scheme that is neutral or one that will work in concert with the styles and colors of the chosen attire.

The following are some of the more popular bouquet styles.

The cascade: A large, tear-shaped arrangement with blossoms trailing downward. This is the most popular bridal bouquet and complements a full ball-gown look. "The larger the dress the larger the bouquet the taller the bride the further the flowers will cascade downward" is a good rule of thumb.

The arm arrangement or presentation bouquet: Think beauty pageant or the kind of flowers given to opera divas and you've got it. A dozen white roses or a more elaborate variety works well here. The arrangement should lay cradled comfortably in your forearm (usually the left so you can wave with the right) and coordinates nicely with attendants carrying presentation bouquets composed of different flowers.

Loosely tied or country garden bouquet: Increasingly popular in floral design, this bouquet has an "I just picked these out of my English garden that happens to be in the backyard" feel. The bouquet has an unstructured look and can be made up of many different flowers or wildflowers. The stems aren't pruned as in other bouquets and are tied together with ribbon, lace, or fabric.

A single stem or solo bouquet: You can create an effect that's either sexy or Zen-like minimalist by carrying a single calla lily, one perfect rose, or a solo orchid.

The nosegay: A round bouquet in various sizes, the nosegay could have a ruffle of fabric (like grandma's hankie) or lace around the edge. One type of nosegay that's especially popular today (and dates back to Victorian times) is the "tussy mussy," which is a smaller, tighter cluster of flowers, perhaps baby roses or peonies. Or use fragrant herbs such as lavender, rosemary, and scented geranium.

IF YOU DON'T WANT TO CARRY THEM . . .

The boutonniere: The male version of the corsage—that carnation or single rose you're picturing, the one you wore to your prom or frat formal, pinned to your lapel, with fake leaves taped to the stem. Boutonnieres have come a long way, and can be created from most hardy flowers or several different buds put together. Etiquette tells us that all the male attendants should have matching boutonnieres—except for the groom, who can get something special, perhaps from the bridal bouquet. You certainly offend no one if you follow tradition, but if you want to mix and match boutonnieres the results will be more interesting. A single flower such as a rose or a small gardenia is classy and always appropriate.

The corsage: The corsage either pins onto the dress by the shoulder or can be worn on the wrist (though it tends to get knocked into things and get mussed up). Favorite corsage flowers include gardenias and jasmine. Traditionally corsages are presented to the mothers of the brides and grooms, and can tend to give off a promlike or matronly vibe. So if you're considering giving a corsage to an attendant, you might want to consider other floral alternatives.

The lei: Leis are becoming increasingly popular for weddings, and can be worn by brides, grooms, attendants, and family. They smell incredible, require no carrying, and can be easily removed for close dancing.

If you can't stand the thought of carrying an ordinary bouquet, you can always carry:

• a Bible or an old book that means something to you, whether it's *The Prophet* or *Franny and Zooey*

• a fan or lorgnette

IF YOU'RE GOING TO SAN FRANCISCO . . . BE SURE TO WEAR SOME FLOWERS IN YOUR HAIR

❀ A full wreath of flowers is a good solution to headgear if you don't want to wear a veil.

❀ A comb with fresh flowers, baby's breath, or a white orchid worn on the side of the head can look exotic or sweet.

❀ Loose baby's breath scattered throughout your hair (especially if you have longer hair) gives you that neo-romantic look.

- a miniature poodle or other small pet

- a piece of fabric from a shirt or some other memento of a special friend who passed away, whom you want to honor as being at the ceremony in spirit

- soft-sculpture flowers, painted wooden flowers, bouquets sprayed black, and, yes, beaded flowers have all been carried down aisles. (As Vincent Price once told us, "Bad taste knows no bounds.")

CEREMONIAL FLORA

If you're getting married at a religious site, talk with your contact person there before you purchase a truckful of delphiniums and lilacs and find out if there are specific requirements or restrictions on decorations. Fire laws may prohibit flowers arranged around burning candles, for example. Or your setup and breakdown schedule could conflict with other events in the same space. You could be expected to buy one or two large arrangements for the altar and then to leave them there as a donation. Or you could be expected to make do with existing flora; some synagogues and churches have fresh flowers and plants already in place, depending on the season.

Once you know your limitations (we mean with the flowers, not in life), sit in the space and consider the architecture or lack thereof. Does the look need to be enhanced? Often an intrinsically interesting building with stained glass or windows that allow for sunlight to stream in needs only a minimum of sprucing up, and doing more will produce diminishing returns. Ask around and see what other couples have done in the way of decorations in the same space.

Look at the ceremony site from the viewpoint one would have when walking into the room. Picture any of the following:

🍃 a canopy or gazebo decorated with flowers and twinkle lights

🍃 long-stemmed irises arranged in tall urns at either side of the aisle

🍃 a sprig of fresh herbs, such as basil and sage, and flowers on all the doors in the ceremony site

🍃 scented geraniums mixed with rosemary and mint in large oversize pots accentuating separate areas

🍃 large wreaths of bright red chili peppers hung on the walls

Remember that the ceremony site will be lovely by virtue of the fact that you will be married there. If you're on a limited budget, you might save most of your money for reception flowers and keep the look of the ceremony simple. (Your guests will probably be at the ceremony site for only about half an hour anyway.) Or think in terms of transportable flowers that can travel from the ceremony to the reception site.

A Flowery Reception

Blooming buds need not be busting out of every crack in the plaster to give the aura of beauty. Used cleverly, flowers and plants can actually fool the eye architecturally or transport the wedding from your community hall to a tropical rain forest. (Well, almost.)

By renting large plants, trees, and even potted hedges you can redesign any space. In a large industrial space, trellises can delineate the dance floor and create intimate nooks and crannies. Renting flowering plants and turning the hall into a greenhouse will warm up even the coldest of high-tech spaces.

To adorn the hall or your home for the reception, consider the following possibilities.

- eclectic vases filled with lots of different flowers to give an English-garden feel
- terra-cotta-potted plants and low baskets filled with fresh cuttings as centerpieces, suggesting a casual country look
- fruits and vegetables such as ornamental cabbages, oranges, garlic braids, and figs are popular and give a back-to-the-earth kind of aura
- buckets filled with miniature sunflowers for a happy, optimistic feel
- for a whimsical reception, small topiary trees in shapes such as hearts, animals, and free-form sculptures, used as centerpieces and around the reception area
- fragrant fresh petals sprinkled around the guest book and on tables, as you would dust sprinkles on an ice cream sundae

FLOWERS

At our reception we had two-step dancing and a chuck wagon buffet, so for centerpieces we collected pairs of cowboy boots, and put cut flowers in paper cups and set them inside. Of course, we cleaned them up a bit. We had a small problem when guests tried to take the centerpieces home!

—GEORGE AND DAVID

FIND ME A FLORIST

"Gosh, can't I go to the corner store, buy a few carnations, stick them in water, and call it a day?" Well, of course you can, but if you shop around a bit, you might find a florist who will work with you within a reasonable price range. As you set out in search of your florist, take the following into consideration.

Individualized service and personal commitment. When you meet with a florist, ask yourself if it seems that this shop has a sense for weddings and large events or if the bulk of their business is delivering orange-and-black FTD arrangements on Halloween. Is the florist familiar with the spaces you're using, and if not, is he or she willing to check out the locations ahead of time?

A specific style or specialty of the house. Victorian English gardens, an architectural approach to floral design, or a slant toward the exotic are all styles that different florists might work best in. A tip-off is often the flower shop itself. Some florists have magnificent spaces that feel more like a whole environment than a retail store. Shops can be lush with fresh and dried flowers next to bundles of hay and branches, or the essence of simplicity, with a few gardenias floating in oversize bowls. Always scope out the selection in the cooler to get an idea of specific flowers that are most often used in their designs.

What the florist has done for other events. Since about half of your total floral cost will be eaten up in labor, you're paying for the florist's taste, experience, and skill—so ask to see pictures of past creations. Some shops might give you standard design books or floral magazines and ask you to pick what you want. Avoid this type of catalog flower shopping because you will rarely end up getting an arrangement that looks anything like the one in the photograph.

Florists tend to fall into one of three categories:

THE SHOP DOWN THE BLOCK

On the few occasions you bought someone flowers, you went to this little shop in your neighborhood with the nicest people running it, and gee, you'd love to give them your business. Should you? Well, smaller shops are able to keep only a limited variety of flowers on hand—and a lot of burnt orange chrysanthemums. Maybe they're capable of special events, in which case you'll get very personalized service. On the other hand, they might not be able to handle large orders and will send you elsewhere.

THE BASIC FULL-SERVICE FLORIST

Births, weddings, funerals, proms, horse races—the basic florist repertoire includes all of life's monumental moments. Most florist shops fall into this category and could be perfect for handling bouquets, boutonnieres, and table arrangements. If they do special events, there is probably a large staff on call that will step in to decorate for weddings, so check out references and see what kind of rapport you establish with the shop owner.

Some shops welcome new ideas; others have been cranking out these dove and mum arrangements for years and have a wedding package all set up: in the wedding package you'll get white-carnation centerpieces that for no extra charge can be spray-painted to match the colors of your bridesmaid dresses exactly.

THE FLORAL DESIGNER

On the other end of the spectrum you have the floral designer as Artist, the one who will give you the Garden of Earthly Delights. This flower connoisseur really fuels his or her work with imagination. Some florists will set up a shop that is also a crafts store or an antique store and use the eclectic articles along with your flowers to create a total look.

Your most reliable source for finding a floral artist or designer is through word of mouth. Some designers will be more than willing to work within your budget and will welcome the challenge of putting their thinking caps on to reach new heights of floral fantasy. Other florists are beyond snooty and will not touch a project unless they have total design control.

Once you have a sense of your needs, interview several florists to find the one who strikes your fancy and will be able to work within your budget. And, since flower fees can potentially break you (the flowers for society weddings typically run in the tens of thousands of dollars), if you don't gel with the florist, bail early and begin again. Here are some thoughts to help you prepare for the task.

✿ If you're not a flower maven, visit nurseries and flower shops and learn the names of the flowers you've always loved the sight or scent of.

✿ Find out which flowers are in season during the month of your wedding; making choices around seasonal flowers can save you money. Clip pictures or arrangements that catch your eye and keep a file of flower ideas so you can show rather than explain what you would like.

✿ If you're coordinating colors between clothing and tablecloths, bring in fabric swatches. But don't become obsessive about matching flowers to fabric; you're dealing with Mother Nature here. Flowers are just plain miraculous, and the last thing you should be worrying about is if they "match."

THE SECRET GARDEN

Once you've found a friend in your florist, take the following steps to make sure that what is in your dreams is what shows up the morning of the wedding.

TRULY REAL

When deciding exactly what you want, ask again to see actual photos of their work or visit a site and examine their arrangements in the context of a wedding. Some florists will do a mock bouquet or arrangement using flowers in the shop as a sample for your approval. Take photos so whoever has to duplicate the flowers the day of the wedding has something to work from. (The person who is making decisions with you isn't always the one to ultimately do all of the hands-on arranging.)

JUST THE FACTS, MA'AM

Get a written contract that spells out the date, time, place, and specific flower arrangements to be created. Each separate bouquet or arrangement should be listed individually so you can keep track of the number of centerpieces and boutonnieres you ordered and what everything costs.

DETAILS, DETAILS

Spell out specific details, such as whether roses are to be closed or open, whether vases are to be returned afterward, and what substitutions are allowable if specific choices are not available a few days before the wedding. (If there's suddenly a huge frost that wipes out the country's larkspur crop, you've got to have a second choice in mind.)

EXTRAS

You really should get free delivery for a large order, but most florists will tack on a setup fee because part of what you're paying for is their artistic eye. If this fee strikes you as unusually high, question it, and consider simplifying labor-intensive decorations.

TIMES AND DATES

What time do they come to the reception and ceremony sites, and what will they need when they get there? If they're setting up a few hours in advance, you'll need to coordinate the services with your key person at each site. If they plan on a large time gap between the setup and the ceremony, ask the florist if the building will be too hot or too cold—because after all, you want the daisies to be fresh as . . . (You got it.) Also ask how many weddings they'll be doing that day, and what their staffing is like. If they're doing too much on the same day, the florist could arrive late *and* with the wrong flowers.

WHERE DO FLOWERS COME FROM? . . . THE GROUND, SILLY.

Florists buy from wholesalers, usually at a flower market or in the flower district of large cities. Wholesalers get their flowers flown in from overseas and from around the country. The market changes based on availability, and availability changes according to your location, the time of year, and the weather. If you trust the florist, ask her or him to choose the bulk of the flowers by *market value,* meaning the best prices on in-season flowers on whatever day the florist goes to buy his or her stock. Make sure you discuss specific colors and the list of flowers you absolutely hate.

SIX PLANTS AND FLOWERS HISTORICALLY ASSOCIATED WITH HOMOSEXUALITY

❀ **Violet.** In a poem by Sappho, she talks of herself and a lover as wearing garlands of violets. Violets were also worn in sixteenth-century England by men and women to indicate that they did not intend to marry.

❀ **Pansy.** When Puck gathers pansies in *A Midsummer Night's Dream,* they are said to have the power to "make man or woman madly dote / Upon the next live creature that it sees"—man or woman.

❀ **Calamus.** The title that Walt Whitman chose for the most homoerotic part of *Leaves of Grass,* this flower's name comes from Greek mythology: Calamus was the lover of Carpus, and was changed into a reed after Carpus drowned.

❀ **Ladslove.** Need we say more than the name itself?

❀ **Hyacinth.** Another origin in mythology: Although Apollo loved Hyacinthus passionately, that didn't stop him from accidentally killing him with a discus; so Apollo turned the body into a purple flower.

❀ **Orchid.** Our local gay printer tells us: "Lesbians love orchids—they're all over their wedding invitations." Hmmm . . . we wonder if they know that the name comes from a Greek word meaning "testicles." (No, the flower doesn't look like them—the bulbs do.) The term *orchid-eater* was used in nineteenth-century erotica as a euphemism for "gay man."

(as listed in Lavender Lists, *Alyson Publications, Boston, 1990)*

ROSE IS A ROSE IS A ROSE IS A ROSE

Gertrude Stein once wrote: "Rose is a rose is a rose is a rose," which means something to the effect that a rose by any other name is still a rose. (At least we think that's what it means—or maybe she had just eaten some of Alice's brownies and was only rambling.) Oh, if it were only true when it comes to quality control and prices. Roses fall into three categories:

- ❦ Select: the crème de la crème
- ❦ Extra fancy: middle grade
- ❦ Fancy: sounds great, but indicates the lowest quality of graded roses

When you see advertisements for one hundred roses for $22.50, they're probably fancy, and a few days old to boot. If you want to be assured of quality, be sure to ask the florist about the grade of roses available; and think about how your choice will affect your checkbook.

THE ART OF FLOWER ARRANGING

If you can't find someone you trust, or if you yourself are a friend of flora (as well as a friend of Dorothy), you can coordinate the flowers yourself. Even if you're totally confident, be sure to coordinate all of your activities so you don't end up spending the morning of an afternoon wedding up to your elbows in potting soil. Here are some ideas that came from do-it-yourselfers:

❧ Take a trip to your local crafts store, or better yet to a wholesale house in the flower district. Some wholesalers are entirely closed to the public, but within the district you'll find a few shops that deal in both retail and wholesale. You might have to buy in bulk, like getting a case of 5-inch bud vases, but the savings will be unbelievable.

❧ Locate a farmers market and get bunches and bunches of cut flowers. (A large quantity of one or two varieties is more effective than a few each of lots of different kinds.)

❧ Don't worry about all of the vases matching: use any kind of container you can dig up that you like. Eclectic is very "in" now, you know.

❧ To save money, think in terms of living plants rather than cut flowers. A dozen cut roses in season could cost you around $25; a flowering 5-foot rosebush can be yours for about the same price.

❧ Take a trip to the greenhouse and buy all sizes of perennials (flowering plants that will bloom again and again). Have your guests take them home, or keep them yourself and plant them after the wedding. (They'll become your Wedding Garden.)

❧ Use fewer fresh flowers, and augment them with "bouquets" of brightly colored balloons.

JANE'S BRIDAL BOUQUETS

I wanted to include flowers from my own garden in our bouquets, so I went down to my friendly florist and explained the situation, and he gave me—gratis—two specially made bases that are used to construct wedding bouquets. I also purchased from him extra flowers that I wasn't able to grow—fragrant tuberoses and freesias, bright blue bachelor buttons, and of course the ubiquitous and very bridal baby's breath. I decided to make the bouquets and headpieces the day before the wedding, because the last thing I needed the morning of my wedding was to be nicking my fingers on floral wire. The florist recommended that, in order to keep them fresh until the next day, I put them in a plastic bag, exhale into it, and seal it up: the carbon dioxide from your breath is an excellent preservative.

Things you need: flowers, a base (a plastic holder with special material to keep the flowers fresh), something to wrap around the holder (a hankie, a ribbon, antique lace, a cowboy scarf).

Suggested flowers: most important is to honor the season, unless a flower has particular significance to you. You can use anything; these are my favorites:

> *For color: baby roses, bachelor buttons, sweet Williams, coreopsis, iris, daisies, cosmos, yarrow, larkspur, baby's breath.*

> *For fragrance: tuberoses, jasmine, lavender, freesias, sage, scented geraniums, rosemary, mint, roses, bay leaves, gardenias, narcissus.*

—JANE

P.S. A dear friend of ours who had been looking for love for years caught my bouquet; six months later, he fell deeply in love. That was two years ago, and they're still together.

Photo: Lynn Houston

▼ # YOUR PRESENCE AND YOUR PRESENTS

PARTIES AND GIFTS

We know that material gain is not the reason you're getting married; but one of the nice things that happens when you have a wedding ceremony is that people want to give you wonderful things and celebrate with you often. It's the kind of pick-me-up that you really need when you're in the dumps, but here it is, one of the happiest times of your life, and everyone keeps trying to make it even better. Go figure.

Anyway, that's what this chapter is about—the celebrations and the gifts. And what you might do for the givers in return.

WEDDING GIFTS

Wedding-gift giving and receiving has caused more hurt feelings than anything else about a wedding (except maybe not being invited to the wedding itself). How many times have you heard a gift giver wail, "She returned my gravy boat!" or "I never got a thank-you from them, can you believe it?" Or, from the other end, "Oh, sure, they got me something *Robert* would like, but they know I *hate* Lucite!" Or how about this one: "Can you believe it—with all his money, he gets me a dumb cow milk pitcher! And he knows I'm lactose intolerant."

TEN WEDDING-GIFT RULES THAT REALLY MAKE SENSE

 Gifts are a great by-product of having a wedding. However, if you are getting married just to receive gifts, you shouldn't be getting married (and *we* certainly aren't going to be buying you a gift).

I told Brian, "You do this for love. I am not going through all this for a pickle dish."

—DAVID

🎁 Gifts are intended to be bestowed and received with good intentions. "It's the thought that counts" may be a cliché, but it also happens to be true. Keep this in mind at all times.

🎁 Gifts are not supposed to compensate for the price of the meal and champagne a guest consumes at the reception. This is not a fund-raiser.

🎁 If a chum hosts a shower or an engagement party, or lends his or her home for the wedding itself, don't hold your breath for another wedding gift. Your friend's generosity already reads loud and clear.

🎁 Understand that everyone's time is valuable and folks might consider the hours spent helping you address envelopes or creating a dish for the reception to be wedding gift enough.

🎁 If you receive a large engagement gift or shower gift, consider it The Wedding Present.

🎁 Never *ever* announce in the wedding invitation where you're registered; it's really rude. Tell a good friend and allow him/her to spread the word; or if you're asked directly, by all means tell.

🎁 If some of the people you send an invitation to can't attend the wedding, traditional etiquette says they're still supposed to send a present. We say, a loving note from them is just as good.

🎁 Gifts are supposed to be sent to the couple, not brought to the wedding, thus relieving the couple of the responsibility of finding a safe place to put the gifts during the festivities. Everyone breaks this rule, so assign someone the task of keeping track for you and making sure all the cards are taped to the correct packages.

🎁 If you don't get a present from some people within a few weeks of the wedding, don't be insulted and don't despair that they don't love you anymore. The etiquette gurus say that they have a full year after the wedding to find and send you just the right gift. (And allow your closest friends to apply for an extension if need be.)

And finally, here's a single rule for givers and receivers alike: Wedding gifts are supposed to be unexpected, delightful, and given with love to start the couple out on a new chapter in life.

Enough said.

Well, not quite enough.

Let's face it: aside from your wedding, when else do so few get so much from so many? Couples can get carried away and obsess about not blowing this golden opportunity to haul in the loot. Their minds turn to the countless wedding and shower gifts they bought for their nongay friends, and they begin to see each guest as another person who can chip in for that CD player they want.

And on the other side of the cash register you have the would-be gift giver who is going through his or her own traumas. ("Should I give them something practical or something they'd never buy for themselves?") Some want to give something that will remind you of them every time you look at it. One bridesmaid hated the idea of buying her friends two wineglasses through a gift registry because she thought, "When there are a dozen glasses on the table, how will Karen and Emily know which two are from me?" Then there's your pal from college who shows you how much he loves you by giving you a healing crystal to hold when you need faith and inspiration, not knowing that the crystal you were hoping for was more along the lines of Baccarat.

Everybody, just relax.

To help organize the good intentions of gift givers in such a way that they can help you to achieve your nuptial-gift goals (sounds like a contract, doesn't it?), the convention of the gift registry has been adopted. Here's the lowdown:

IS IT REGISTERING?

To Cousin Bernice, "picking a china pattern together" is just a euphemism for getting married; she would never consider one without the other. You on the other hand may have let out a scream when we mentioned this convention. We know, registering seems like something right out of the 1950 version of *Father of the Bride*. And yes, we are aware that the original point of registering was to assist the young bride in assembling a set of heirloom-quality bone china, silver, or stemware. This insured that the bride got exactly what she desired, and guests felt that they were contributing something important to civilization: a butter knife.

But look at registering this way: who knows better what gift to give than the couple receiving the gifts—i.e., you? All of your guests wants you to be happy with your gift, so telling them what would make you happy in advance should make everyone happy all around, no? Plus, the fact that you register doesn't mean that your guests have to choose that gift option. They're always free to do what they feel most comfortable with.

For gay couples, registering is much more than making a wish list of wedding gifts. When you register, you are telling the world and your guests, "This is the real thing going on here, folks." People who get married register for wedding gifts. When you walk over to that department store counter, look the blue-haired lady in the eye, and explain that you want to register for a nontraditional wedding, you become an ambassador for same-sex marriages. And in a way, the guests who choose to use your registry are also making a political statement by publicly supporting your union.

HOW TO AVOID GETTING A BLENDER

If you don't choose to register, you're certain to be asked, "What can I get you for your wedding?" If your answer is, "Oh, I'm sure we'll treasure whatever you get us," you'll end up with several blenders. How is your Uncle Barry supposed to know that you wanted His and His terry-cloth bathrobes or Hers and Hers hand towels? So prepare some real answers: "We really love to travel" might prompt a passport wallet or luggage (or two tickets to Tahiti); "We're both avid readers" could produce the latest best-sellers. Or tell them outright, "We certainly have everything we need for the kitchen," which should help you avoid that blender. If you do register, you can let them know: "Oh, we're registered at Williams-Sonoma." And don't register for a blender.

    Warning

We should mention here that most stores call the place where you register the "bridal registry," which may not settle so well with two grooms. Some stores have services that are equivalent to bridal registries but are called simply gift registry or self-registry. These services are available for anyone for any occasion, such as graduations, birthday parties, or housewarmings.

THIS IS HOW IT ALL WORKS

❶ Before you begin, take stock and think about what you really want to own together as a married couple. In America today, people are getting married at an older age and often already have the essentials that would normally be associated with a bridal registry. So in thinking about gifts, before you go to register, consider what items you want to "upgrade" and what needs to be added to in terms of what you already have.

❷ Go to prospective stores and look around. If you choose a large department store, take advantage of the home-electronics department as well as furniture, clothing, and sporting goods.

❸ Always call in advance to see if it's necessary to make an appointment. (Plus, if you have any uneasiness about coming out to Macy's as a same-sex couple, it might be easier for you to approach the subject over the phone.) Then it's down to business: walk into the registry section and tell them that you need to register for a wedding. They'll ask you the names of the bride and groom. If you haven't told them your tale over the phone, this is the time to hit them with "Well, you see, it's like this . . . "

❹ You'll be asked to fill out a general data sheet on which there is a space for the bride's name and another for the groom's name. You can cross out the inappropriate title on the form, but your correction will not appear on the computer printout. This is how things are set up . . . for now. (We're working on it, we're working on it.)

❻ Your selections go into a directory (often computerized) under your name and wedding date. This info is fed into the computers of any other branches the store may have. As your friends and family select from the list at the registry and gifts are bought, a notation is made so that there is no chance of duplication.

A TALE OF TWO REGISTRIES

Registry One

Randy, who works at the bridal registry at Bloomingdale's in New York, explained that for same-sex couples, "we make a note on the account so that correspondence from the store isn't automatically written 'Dear Ms.' or 'Dear Mr.' just because one name is in the bride's column and one is in the groom's. We also register for any occasion you want at the self-registry. But I feel that for a gay couple to do that—to 'make something up'—well, that's a cop-out. Bridal registry implies commitment, so if you're having a ceremony, whether it's same-sex or heterosexual, come to the bridal registry and register as a couple. If you register in another way, you're tiptoeing around the issue."

Registry Two

Michael, who registered at a large Atlanta department store, had a somewhat different experience: "I have to say, registering is the only place that we got a little attitude. We went in and I said, 'I'd like to register my china pattern,' and the lady said, 'Is the bride with you today?' Meanwhile I have this six-foot man standing next to me. So we told her what was going on, and everything seemed to be fine. But when friends started calling up the registry, the way the store filled things out, they had me listed as the bride. So I went back to the lady and complained and she said, 'Well, there's no way for us to switch it around.' I said, 'Look, I realize that this is a gay wedding, but I am a groom and I should be listed under 'groom' and that's that!' By the time I left, we were cross-referenced on both lists. In other words, we were both down as 'bride' and 'groom.' No way could anyone not find us."

OTHER TIPS ON REGISTERING

$ Register in stores where you and your guests feel comfortable shopping. It's actually best if it's a store where you shop on a somewhat regular basis. Tiffany and Cartier will certainly register same-sex couples, but before you decide to go with them, really think about the items they offer and how those things would fit in with your lifestyle.

$ You can register at a couple of places (three, tops)—say, a department store and a specialty store—but don't duplicate merchandise.

$ Choose a store that's in a central location for both you and your guests. Many large department stores have branches around the country and a toll-free number for shopping by phone.

$ China and silver are traditionally popular for registry because they can be extraordinarily expensive. If you're registering a pattern, figure in how many guests might decide to buy this against the number of pieces in the set. If you pick a set with many pieces and you have a small number of guests, you'll end up with one set of salt and pepper shakers, and maybe a cup (with no saucer).

$ Register in several different price categories. Two or more people might want to go in together on a higher-ticket item, but be sensitive to your guests' budgets.

$ Do not attempt to do this all in one day. Take your time; after all, you'll be living with these choices for a long while.

REGISTERING FOR LUMBER

Gay couples have entered the wedding-gift market at a time when the rules are broadening. Rather than working on Limoges place settings for twelve, traditional and nontraditional couples alike are registering at Home Depot and with environmentally correct mail-order companies. Garden centers, CD stores, even travel agencies will work with you to set up a gift registry. If the roof needs fixing, "register" with your local roofer. Or how about registering your special "asphalt pattern" at the hardware store so you can finally redo your bumpy drive-

One gal came in and said, "I don't know what I want. I'm not even sure what I like." It's very hard when people don't have any taste or any ideas, so you try and show them things, and some of them they like. Then it's "How will I know I'm going to like this in ten years?" "Well," I say, "how will you know if you're going to like your partner in ten years?" If you can't make up your mind, leave it off your list.

—BARBARA HELD,
BARNEY'S NEW YORK

way. Recently we heard about a home-mortgage company on Long Island that established a registry to help couples pay for the down payment on a house. This current trend is a reaction both to changing personal values and to cold hard economic realities.

Getting a registry going at a garden center or local antique store is a lot simpler than you might think. First, see if they already have a gift registry system set up. If this is new to the store (not the same-sex stuff, the registering stuff), work with them on putting in place a system to keep track of your gifts. (A simple list of selections and prices can be kept behind the counter if the shop is small.) Few stores will pass up the business; most likely they'll stand on their heads to make it happen.

MARRYING FOR DOLLARS

In some cultures money is the appropriate gift, and the presentation of the gift envelope is part of the wedding reception. (You remember the wedding scene in *The Godfather* where Connie Corleone was walking around with a big bag filled with cash.) If this is your background, you'll probably get some checks from relatives who either don't know what to get you or know that money never goes out of style.

We have heard of several cases where same-sex couples let it be known to friends that cash would be the most appreciated gift they could get; perhaps this is because same-sex couples are more likely to be paying for the entire wedding themselves. While the etiquette gurus would have a field day with this one, it should be said that none of the guests we spoke with were offended by the request and in fact were thrilled to be able to help their friends out in the way they needed it the most.

BRAVE NEW WORLD PLACES TO REGISTER

- Tower Records
- The Metropolitan Museum of Art
- Sprint, AT&T, and other long-distance carriers
- universities and schools
- wine sellers
- The Price Club
- Amtrak
- Quality Paperback Book Club

WEDDING-GIFT SUPERSTITION

One must never give a sharp or pointed object as a wedding gift, because it will sever the romance.

SWEET CHARITY

There are couples who would rather have guests make donations to a charity than spend the money on wedding gifts they don't need. They may have all the worldly possessions they want, or they may just feel that donations are more in keeping with the spirit of their particular union celebration. In this case it is acceptable to include a separate card along with the invitation that informs the guest of the specific charity or foundation. For example:

In lieu of gifts
please make contributions
in honor of our ceremony of commitment to:
The NAMES Project
310 Townsend Street, Suite 310
San Francisco, CA 94107

Make arrangements with a representative at the charity to handle the collection of checks; if possible, list the contact person by name on the enclosure card you send and set up a record-keeping procedure by which you are kept up-to-date with who has sent donations. This way you can acknowledge the gesture with a personal thank-you note. (The NAMES Project sends out a card to the gift giver; but even if the charity acknowledges the donation, you really should too.)

TEN GREAT FANTASY WEDDING GIFTS TO ASK FOR IF ANYONE IS STUCK ON WHAT TO GET YOU

★ A signed David Hockney (either a print or a painting is acceptable)

★ A personal trainer to come to your house for the rest of your life

★ A year's worth of fresh flowers, delivered daily

★ Two seats on the space shuttle

★ Five years' worth of groceries—shopped for, delivered, and put away

★ Bette Midler to sing at your next birthday party

★ Coupons that say things like "Cut Me Some Slack" that you can give to your friends and that actually work (that's the fantasy part)

★ An industrial ice cream maker, and a dairy farm for the source material

★ Really great personal stationery—and an assistant to answer all of your correspondence

★ Tickets to the ballet, opera, or theater—in Paris

PRE-WEDDING PARTYING

SHOWER POWER

Wedding legend has it that a young Dutch woman fell in love with a miller who had given away most of his flour to the poor instead of selling it to the bread factories in town. When the girl's money-hungry father forbade the marriage and denied the couple a dowry, the townsfolk took pity on the poor young couple and showered them with gifts to help them set up their home, where of course they lived happily ever after. And thus was born the wedding shower.

How accurate this story is, and what happened to the girl's dysfunctional father, we don't know. But we do know that it's a nice story in that the friends and other assorted happy towns-folk became the young couple's family and supported them in their decision to marry.

The shower has evolved into a pre-wedding party, usually with a theme centered around gift giving. Some showers can be truly practical, like a linen shower where everyone pitches in to take care of all the household sheets and towels. Other showers are silly, like the lingerie showers that single-handedly keep Victoria's Secret in business.

The shower was typically a bride's "date with the girls" until the groom was included and the "couples shower" became popular. Yes, it reeks of straight tradition, but a shower is a great opportunity for small groups to celebrate, so why not once again skew tradition to your own situation?

A lesbian or gay shower can be given for the couple together, or individual parties can be thrown for, say, Groom One and Groom Two, which can be a healthy break from the constant pre-wedding togetherness. A Last Hurrah where you're the center of attention and get gifts—how bad could it be? Most of the gay couples we spoke with had some sort of a pre-wedding party that combined a shower with another tradition such as the bachelor or bachelorette party or the pre-wedding luncheon. Rod and Bob's friends threw them a surprise "BASH," so named "because it was a combination BAchelor party/SHower."

SHOWER THE PEOPLE . . .

As we said, showers are usually based on a gift theme. It's fun to be showered with gag gifts, but if a well-stocked refrigerator will make a stronger contribution to your ultimate well-being, tell your friends to toss the erotic lollipops out the window and bring in the groceries.

Several shower ideas follow—some tried and true, others brand-new.

THE SPRING CLEANING SHOWER

Each guest brings a beautifully wrapped cleaning utensil such as a new mop head or a can of Drano. (Pretty sexy, huh?) If the couple have just moved into a new house or apartment, everyone could pitch in and help clean up the place or even do some painting. Or maybe not.

THE CHEAP THRILLS SHOWER

For the couple who have everything. The gifts must cost five bucks or under; free is best of all. Some possibilities:

🎁 Everyone brings a story about the couple during their earlier days.

🎁 You must *make* a decorative gift using found materials from around your home.

🎁 Have a talent show: guests present performances (three minutes, tops); they can sing, dance, do a skit—whatever. The more unusual the better.

THE LITERARY SHOWER

Everyone brings books under one unifying theme such as "I should have read this years ago" or "No home should be without a copy" or just plain "love."

THE MEN 'N' WOMEN DAY O' BEAUTY SHOWER

Everyone contributes grooming products like cologne, aroma-therapy bath salts, and rub-on tattoos. Get out the moisturizing cream and hair treatments, do your nails, and give each other facials. Read trashy magazines and dish the couple.

THE I DON'T WANT THIS ANYMORE SHOWER

You bring an item that you don't want in your home one minute longer but feel that the couple really needs. Lava lamps, Abba posters, and porcelain statuettes all become gift fodder for this category.

Along with gift giving (everyone watches as the gifts are opened to choruses of oohs and aahs), there are other customary occurrences at wedding showers:

🎁 The ribbons that were beautifully wrapped around your packages are made into a ribbon bouquet to be carried during the wedding rehearsal and then treasured for years.

🎁 A friend is appointed to record who gave you what gift so you can later write thank-you notes. Another friend writes down your reactions, and at the end of the gift-giving session the remarks are read back and modified with the phrase "under the covers" or something equally as clever. For example, "Oh my God, I've always wanted a waffle iron . . . under the covers."

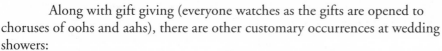

🎁 You play your own version of *The Newlywed Game* or couples trivia.

🎁 Give a *This Is Your Life*–type presentation or a slide show of childhood memories.

🎁 Have everyone bring in ideas about "ways to keep love alive" or "tips for a successful relationship" and put them in a book for you to keep.

🎁 Of course you take lots of photos, run a tape recorder, or get out those camcorders.

🎁 And if you must, there are a plethora of marital aids (okay: dirty gifts) at your local novelty store that were created for just this kind of occasion. Edible undies, anyone?

Bachelor/ette Parties

Caution

If you have your heart set on going out on the town for a night of burlesque or "wanton merrymaking," remember this: If you do something stupid, the person you are about to wed will find out. They always, always do. It's in the rule book.

Bachelor/ette parties are probably more popular on old television shows like *Love, American Style* than they are in real life. Maybe because many gays and lesbians had years and years of "boys' and girls' nights out," they just don't feel the need to kick out the jams at this point. But just F.Y.I., here's the scoop on the conventional bachelor party (with apologies to *Love, American Style*).

Historically, the straight bachelor party was a men-only affair to mourn the groom's disappearing freedom and to tempt him with a last chance at forbidden delights (that is, nekked girls jumping out of a cake)—an entirely odious tradition no matter how you slice it. And then the women got into the action by having their own hot time to mourn the passing of *their* singlehood. They accomplished this by stuffing dollar bills into the G-strings of the Chippendale's dancers, telling raunchy honeymoon stories, and other assorted racy merrymaking.

Just so you know this for your marriage education (and not, we repeat *not*, because we're recommending it), some of the popular hen/stag party activities are rumored to be:

- ♥ renting "blue" movies
- ♥ reading aloud love letters from old paramours
- ♥ looking at pictures of old boyfriends/girlfriends
- ♥ hiring a stripper
- ♥ having the stripper jump out of a cake
- ♥ having cake
- ♥ going to singles bars and announcing, "This is Frank's last night as a free man"
- ♥ playing a rude practical joke on the groom or bride (like having someone pretend to be an old lover who has returned to reclaim forgotten love. If you really want to do the whole joke, have the lover be of the opposite sex and carrying a baby).

'TIS BETTER TO GIVE: GIFTS YOU GIVE TO OTHERS

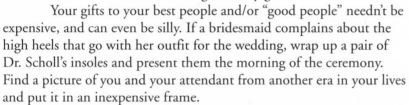

In addition to honoring the people closest to you by asking them to be a part of your wedding party, it's customary to show your gratitude in the form of a little gift. The attendants' gifts are traditionally keepsakes, something sentimental in nature: a locket with a thoughtful inscription, cuff links, or an accessory that can be worn or used the day of the wedding. More important than the gift itself is the card that goes along with it. The card can hold the sentiments that will be remembered long after any gift.

Your gifts to your best people and/or "good people" needn't be expensive, and can even be silly. If a bridesmaid complains about the high heels that go with her outfit for the wedding, wrap up a pair of Dr. Scholl's insoles and present them the morning of the ceremony. Find a picture of you and your attendant from another era in your lives and put it in an inexpensive frame.

There are actual prefab attendants' gifts that are available through wedding catalogs and bridal salons. Examples? Cute little key chains that say "Best Man." Champagne glasses with the word "Bridesmaid" and beer steins with "Groomsman." Pink coffee mugs with the titles "Matron of Honor" and "Bridesmaid" silk-screened across the front. (Just think how many times a young bridesmaid gazes at the mug of the older and wiser matron of honor and dreams about the day in her life when she too will receive the matron of honor mug!)

If any of these sound amusing or campy or just plain fun, they could be the perfect keepsakes. Don't forget the ring bearer, the flower child, and anyone else who helps make the wedding happen, as well as people who address envelopes, sing at the wedding, or prepare food. Remember that giving a gift is not a requirement, but acknowledging kindness with a thank-you note is.

And while you're out shopping, don't forget the guy or gal that this is all about—you know, your future spouse. It's a romantic touch to bestow a little trinket on your beloved that she or he will always identify with the wedding day. The gift could be a new piece of jewelry that is worn during the ceremony, or a surprise back at the house like a piece of furniture or artwork. Whatever you choose to give on this day will have special memories, even a goofy stuffed animal or a distinctive

Yesterday: Elizabethan brides gave guests knots of lace and ribbon as favors; they were decorative and served as a memento of the couple "tying the knot." Gloves were also given as wedding favors, with an accompanying verse that read, "Take away the 'g' and make us a pair of loves."

Today: The Italian term *confetti* describes the little pastel-colored Jordan almonds tied in tulle that are a standard favor given to guests as they leave the reception. The almonds symbolize the bitter and sweet aspects of life.

bottle of cologne to wear for the wedding. And if you really want to be a hero(ine), write a love letter and have it delivered by a friend to your beloved on the morning of the wedding.

DO ME A FAVOR

Giving favors to all the guests is a way for brides and grooms to express their thanks for helping them celebrate their union. The favor is sort of the final punctuation mark on the day and can be anything from a little thank-you sweet such as a Godiva chocolate heart to a bottle of champagne with a customized wedding-day label. For many gay couples having their names out in the world, proud and linked together, is part of becoming a married couple.

THINGS YOU CAN HAVE PRINTED WITH YOUR NAMES AND THE DATE

▼ One-size-fits-all T-shirts that say, "I went to Joel and Greg's wedding and all I got was this lousy T-shirt."

▼ Buttons or badges—great for those who love their jackets covered with P.C. buttons. They can have pictures of the couple or sayings like, "Ask me—I went to a lesbian wedding."

▼ Pride gifts such as pink triangle pins, a little rainbow flag, multicolored "freedom" rings, or a key chain to which you've added a dog tag with your wedding info.

A good engraver or silk-screener can personalize almost anything. Look under "Monogramming" or "Party Supplies" in the yellow pages, or look for a marketing and promotions supply company. See your names and wedding date emblazoned on: coffee mugs, baseball caps, handkerchiefs, playing cards, Post-its, calendars, pens, and candy dishes. The range of these choices extends as far as your vanity will allow.

A less elaborate way to personalize a favor is to have yards of ribbon printed up with your names and wedding date. Anything wrapped with the little personalized ribbon will do the trick, from individual chocolate bars to bouquets of flowers.

Customizing isn't always necessary; a couple we know spent several months collecting old cup-and-saucer sets; guests kept the cup and saucer that was next to their place card. A potter made sixty small bowls and set them out on a table for guests to take home.

There is a Native American tradition called a *giveaway,* which calls for the couple to honor all of their wedding guests with a gift chosen especially for them. The two women we spoke with who followed this tradition made many of the gifts themselves, and presented their friends with baskets and jewelry.

These little parting gifts don't have to be terribly costly, but if you do decide to give them, take care that no one who attends the wedding goes home empty-handed.

TRACKING AND ACKNOWLEDGING GIFTS

THANK YOU, AND GOOD NIGHT

With all this generosity going around, it's easy for a gift here or there to fall through the cracks and not be properly acknowledged. Yes, we're talking about written thank-you notes.

Ideally the note should be mailed as soon as you receive the gift. A general rule of etiquette says a thank-you note should be sent no later than four to six weeks after receiving a wedding gift, and within two weeks of receiving shower or engagement gifts.

Send notes to all gift givers, hosts of parties and showers, telegram and mailgram senders, people who send flowers, and anyone who helped out a great deal.

KEEPING TRACK

If you talk to recently married couples, they'll tell you they feel like they'll be spending the rest of their days writing thank-you notes. It doesn't really have to be that bad. Rule #1 is that the better records you keep of who sends what and who does what, the easier your life will be as you sit down to write and tell everyone how much you loved the . . . whatever.

If you have a general wedding notebook, set up a section on gifts and thank-you notes. Or use the index-card method or, if you're lucky, your computer wedding program that has a special file in it for

INSTA-FAVOR

❶ Print up little labels with your names and the date of the wedding.

❷ Appoint a chosen few to take Polaroids throughout the event.

❸ Stick a label onto each picture and leave the labeled pictures in baskets, where guests can rummage through them and help themselves.

just this very thing. You can also purchase a bridal-gift book at stationery stores and from wedding catalogs. Make note of:

- ☑ the gift
- ☑ who sent it
- ☑ where it was purchased
- ☑ how it arrived—mail/UPS/FedEx?
- ☑ when acknowledgment was sent (that is, when you wrote the thank-you note)

Keep all the gift cards, and write a brief description of the gift directly on the card. This all seems elementary, but even masters of organization can mess this part up. If you don't keep the gifts straight, you'll cause the givers undue stress. They'll be wondering, "Did Sean and Emilio receive the carved beech-wood wind chimes?" Not to mention causing you anxiety as well: "Emilio, who would send us carved wind chimes?"

Your thank-you notes don't have to be lengthy, thank goodness. You should, however, make sure to acknowledge the specific gift so that the giver knows you paired her or him up with the right box ("We just love the espresso maker . . . "), and maybe say something about the plans you have for it (". . . and we can't wait to make cappuccinos to drink while we read the Sunday paper"). It's nice if you both sign the notes, and it's even nicer if you split the pile in two and each write half.

If writing notes sets off an anxiety attack ("They'll compare notes and realize I wrote the same thing to everyone!"), get your hands on a "how to write thank-you notes" guide that gives you samples. (Yes, they exist; use them without shame.)

OOPS!

If a gift arrives without a card or the information was misplaced, use the following procedure to sniff out the gift giver, **Cagney and Lacey** *style.*

1) If the gift arrives from a store, call immediately and explain what happened; if it was charged, they may be able to tell you who purchased it.

2) Check for a number on the label or tag that indicates the date of purchase. With this information in hand you can cross-examine the appropriate salesperson.

3) Was the gift purchased near where any suspect lives or from a suspect's favorite store?

4) Wait until all the gifts are received, and then by process of elimination discern the gift giver.

5) Have a friend go undercover and drop hints about the mystery gift.

RETURN TO SENDER

It happens. After all that, you still end up with four blenders. You want to return some of them (probably three), but you're not quite sure what the protocol is in this area. Here's the drill on typical gift problems:

DUPLICATE GIFTS

If you end up with duplicate gifts, don't go out of your way to tell the giver. (In fact, don't tell the giver—period.) By all means return any duplicate gifts and pick out things you can use. Or keep the extra blenders and give them away as wedding gifts. (Just make sure you don't give a couple the same gift they gave you.)

YOU HATE IT!

Is it rude to return that cheese tray in the shape of a cow or the twig wall hanging that reads "Share the Joy"? Well, sorry, but there really are no "right" answers on this one. If you're really *really* close to the people who gave it, you might want to discuss why a certain present doesn't work for you—because if you pretend to love it but don't put the wall hanging up or use the cheese tray for every function they attend at your house, they'll know you were lying. On the other hand, if you're really *really* close to them, how did they err so badly in choosing a gift for you? We don't know. You'll just have to treat each case on an individual basis. But remember, at all costs, be gracious and acknowledge everything with bountiful delight.

Thank you.

Q. When is a gift immediately returned to the sender?

A. The moment the wedding is called off.

Ron Singleton

D. J. Davis

T H A T ' S E N T E R T A I N M E N T !

M U S I C , D A N C I N G , A N D O T H E R R E C E P T I O N F E S T I V I T I E S

*I*f you're planning on a postceremony celebration that says "Party," in addition to food and drink you're probably thinking about entertainment of some sort. This entertainment most often takes the form of music (for listening and/or dancing) but can also include games, performances, and variety artists.

MUSIC TO YOUR EARS

In chapter 9 we talked about the role music might play in your ceremony; similarly, music is the thread that weaves the reception together. It can mark the dramatic entrance of the newlyweds with a fanfare, keep a buffet line moving with a brisk salsa beat, and create a serious party hardy atmosphere.

First off, see if either of you has a strong preference or predetermined music concept by asking yourselves the following questions.

♫ Is there a certain feeling or look that you are going for?

♫ Should the music help carry through a theme?

♫ Are you planning on having dancing, or will the mood be more intimate and subdued?

♫ Are there monetary restrictions that limit your options? (If you answer no to this, we'd like you to contact us immediately.)

There are so many choices these days in providing music. No longer are there just four guys in powder blue tuxes whose songs all sound like "Proud Mary." There are various ethnic bands, entertainers who put on a complete show, and disc jockeys to spin records or CDs. As you look over the possibilities of music that will fit your reception, consider the following.

LOCATION

Loud music in a small space can blow the lid off the building, annoy your guests because they can't hear themselves think, and/or cause guests to leave early. It used to be that the larger the room, the more pieces you needed to play in the band. But nowadays thanks to newfangled synthesizers, high-tech instruments, and sound equipment, three pieces can sound like fifteen. So look at the space and search for music that will not over- or underwhelm your reception site. If you're having your reception in a ballroom, a solo acoustic guitarist will likely go unnoticed; if it's in a small backyard, a twelve-piece swing band is probably overkill.

LENGTH OF FESTIVITIES

If you're planning a long celebration, six hours of flamenco guitar is probably excessive.

GUEST LIST

Hip Hop or Hokey Pokey? With a varied guest list, the music should have something in it for everyone, so look to compromise. Yes, it's your wedding and you can have your favorite kind of music, but this attitude must be tempered by the fact that you're throwing the party of your life, which means that everyone should get off on the music. A string quartet might thrill your Aunt Ethel but will inflict pain on your friends who are too hip for the room; likewise, a great heavy-metal band will undoubtedly please your headbanging pals but unhinge your older relatives.

BUDGET

We'll state the obvious here: live musicians will invariably cost more than recorded music, unless you plan to hire Casey Kasem to spin some platters for all the groovy guys 'n' gals. And generally speaking, the bigger the band, the bigger the bucks.

IT'S LIVE, NOT MEMOREX

You've no doubt at some point in your life heard someone say, "The band made the party." If this is what you have in mind for your wedding, you'll need to find just the right group. Yes, you can dance to a solo accordion; you can also hire a twenty-six-piece orchestra with six vocalists for background music.

Traditional wedding bands are a special breed unto themselves; they play at functions where the ages can run from eight to eighty and everyone wants to get in on the action. Also

known as society bands, they do not only weddings, but bar mitzvahs, silver anniversaries, sweet sixteens—you name it. They can usually play a mean cover of "I Saw Her Standing There" but can also pull off "That's Amore" and know at least one polka. Their repertoire invariably includes a few show tunes, Top 40, some swing, and classic rock and roll.

There are also society bands with a specific style that might work well for your wedding. In just about every town or its environs, you can locate a sixties band, a fifties band, a big-band band, a good danceable jazz band, and a variety of ethnic bands. So if you're into a theme or have a real passion for a certain era, see if you can hire a group that specializes in it. If you're lucky, they might also be able to perform most standards and have experience pacing a reception, but with a little extra flavor. (There's nothing quite like hearing the hora played by a reggae band, mon.)

You'll also be able to locate local bands that play regularly in clubs and at parties. Generally speaking, don't expect such a band to be able to smoothly segue from their own music to "You Light Up My Life" without missing a beat. On the other hand, they'll probably be enthusiastic and spontaneous. And who knows? Maybe they'll turn out to be the next Van Halen and you can say that they played for your wedding.

FINDING THE RIGHT BAND

If you have your heart set on a particular band, check their availability before you set your wedding date. Popular bands book up months in advance, and having your first choice can be a deal breaker as you finalize dates. ("I'm sorry, honey, the E Street Band isn't available until 2007. We'll just have to wait until then.")

If you're having your wedding on New Year's Eve or some other major holiday, be forewarned that you may have trouble finding a band that's available. Even the worst band imaginable gets booked for New Year's Eve; everyone from an apprentice accordion player to Doc Severinsen is playing at someone's party somewhere. Peak party season actually goes from the second week in November through January 1. After that, bookings slow down again, and you'll get a larger selection of groups for a smaller fee.

When finding and hiring a band for your wedding party, it's best to ask around and get personal recommendations. Begin with your wedding army of caterers and photographers; talk to the musician who is performing your ceremony music. Other leads might be:

♩ Call up a radio station you love and ask the disc jockey for suggestions. Unless you live in a large urban area, he or she will probably be more than happy to take the time to help you out.

♩ Check with your local college music department, which can put you in touch with student musicians who love to play at parties and are considerably less expensive than professionals.

♩ Call a booking agent. In Woody Allen's *Broadway Danny Rose,* agents are portrayed as cigar-smoking guys always trying to make a fast deal for an easy buck. In some cases, this depiction of agents is dead-on accurate, but most of the time an agent can be very helpful in hiring for social events. Booking agents handle the marketing, billing, and paperwork. For this service they receive a commission, customarily 10% to 15% of the total fee you are paying. You do not pay the agent's fee—well, not exactly. It's built into the price quote you're given up front. Agents can be useful if you have less time than money, and often you can negotiate with them.

For your garden-variety wedding band of average talent, you'll probably pay prices starting at $100 to $200 per person, for about four hours of tunes. A Saturday night may be more expensive, and depending on the band's popularity and what city you live in, the going rate may be as high as $5,000. A traditional wedding band should have their own wardrobes (if you want them in tuxes you shouldn't have to pay extra) and provide their own PA system, sound person, and tapes for their breaks. Be sure that these details are spelled out in the contract, even if you have to write them in yourself. Tipping isn't required, but if you're really moved by their performances, we're fairly certain some extra cash wouldn't be refused.

SOUND SHOPPING TIPS

♫ You should get a video or audio demo tape of the band in performance, which will give you an idea as to their sound and should let you know if you have the slightest interest in them. Don't be as concerned about the sound quality of the tape as you are about the style, the vocals, and the musicianship. But if there is poor sound, be sure that it's due to the recording.

♫ Ask the agent or band if you can crash a party they'll be working, and watch the band do their thing.

♫ Note how the band interacts with guests, how chatty the bandleader is, if the guests are responding to the music, if the volume is site appropriate, and what the group's physical presentation is.

♫ See if during breaks the bandleader takes care of providing taped music to spell the musicians.

WHAT TO LOOK FOR IN A BAND

Wedding bands (the performing ones, not the ones on your ring fingers) are usually made up of professional musicians who play these kinds of gigs regularly. You want musicians who enjoy playing at receptions and pride themselves on making the best out of any situation. They should also *look* like they're having a good time; musicians with bad attitudes can kill a party.

If you've hired a versatile band, they should take requests cheerfully (even from the guy who's had a little too much champagne and keeps shouting "Stairway to Heaven"!). Within reason, they should be open to participation by the guests, so if your friend Tom wants to get up and belt out "Stand by Your Man," and dedicate it to the two of you, the band should not only handle it but try to make Tom look good.

THE LEADER OF THE PACK

Most musical groups come with the musical group leader. The leader of the band is the musical director; he or she will work with you to choreograph the order of certain musical selections. The bandleader is also the one you'll want to talk to about the unique circumstances of the wedding; the last thing you want is for the drummer to yell out as he's setting up, "Oh, man, it's two chicks!"

Go over set lists with the leader, especially if there are particular requests. Tess always knew her wedding-day dancing had to include "I Knew the Bride (When She Used to Rock and Roll)," so the band she hired learned it just for the occasion. And even though the bandleader understands that it's not a traditional wedding, if you don't want to hear "Daddy's Little Girl," let it be known ahead of time.

The band leader can also be the emcee for your reception if you work this out in advance. Bandleaders can call guests up to the microphone to make toasts, and can announce the events of the party. The amount of bantering the emcee does with the crowd should be up to you.

DEALING WITH THE BOYS (AND GIRLS) IN THE BAND

Band members are human beings who get hungry and thirsty, and who require rest periods. Break times are usually ten to fifteen minutes per one-hour set (union rules may even require it), but this can vary greatly. Bands typically book in three-to-four-hour blocks of time; many will throw in an hour of "lite sounds" to dine by before they really get down and rock the house.

Your contract may require that you provide food for the band. Booze is an entirely different matter. Technically speaking, it's not considered professional to drink on the job. Some hosts and hostesses feel that offering the band a drink or two is being cordial, and may even increase the musicians' creativity. The choice is up to you.

IT'S MEMOREX

In the heyday of disco, the mobile DJ became popular, traveling to parties with a stack of albums in one hand and a strobe light in the other. DJs have since expanded their musical collections, offering selections that go beyond dance music. With the right DJ, you can go from Garland to the Grateful Dead in ten seconds. If you want rock and roll, New Wave, or other contemporary music, dancing to the real thing instead of to a live band just might sound better. After all, locals can only do so well covering Bruce Springsteen, Sting, or Melissa Etheridge.

DJs are less expensive than bands (say, about $200 to $700 for four hours of entertainment) and come complete with all the equipment they need to run the party—sound systems, smoke machines, etc.—and yes, some still come with that strobe light. Ask all the questions you would of any entertainment when you book a DJ. How extensive is their library, and is it appropriate for your crowd's tastes? Make sure that he or she carries backup equipment in case the turntable should happen to short-circuit. The DJ should also check out your site ahead of time to see if it presents any particular problems.

You'll need to have a little chat with the DJ ahead of time concerning their shtick; it may be perfect for a bat mitzvah but over the top for a romantic wedding. How much do you want the DJ to talk, if at all? Do you want songs identified? Is the DJ to be an emcee for announcing the first dance and the toasts?

Consumer Alert

The boys and girls in the band often play or sing with different musical groups. When a band member wants a night off, someone will take his or her place and you get a band with the same number of players; unfortunately, it's not the exact same band that you fell in love with. Sometimes there's no detectable difference, but in the case of a featured player it could spell disaster. Get the musicians and instrumentation specified in your contract. You're not being paranoid; you're simply covering your bases.

IN THE MOOD

If you don't have a dancing crowd, and want background music and only background music to set a mood, CDs and tapes played over a good stereo system can do the trick. Select music in advance so it's ready to go at the appropriate times. Two brides we know used "The Theme from Twin Peaks" to announce their arrival at the party. Period music from the forties and fifties usually sounds better from a recording than from live musicians; c'mon, who can do justice to vintage Ella Fitzgerald or Tony Bennett? Assign a friend the job of DJ, and make sure he or she is familiar with all the nuances of your requests.

Of course, you can also find live musicians who will help create the mood you're after. Think about what a flutist (or is that flautist?) and classical guitarist will add to your meal or cocktail buffet. Soloists and small ensemble groups are available for very reasonable fees. Sometimes, even if you have a full-on DJ thing later in the evening, it's nice to greet people by having a classical musician playing as they enter the party. It's like being welcomed by a glass of bubbling champagne for the ears.

DO YOU DO YOU DO YOU DO YOU WANNA DANCE?

The classic wedding band is etched in our memories as we remember doing the Bunny Hop as kids, or seeing our parents slow dance to "Feelings." As we grew up we got a kick out of dancing the Hustle with Cousin Shirley or teaching Uncle Mitch to do the Mashed Potato. No doubt about it—dancing can add a whole new dimension to your celebration.

Though entirely nongay in tradition, there are some wedding dance things that are worth doing. (What the heck, you've gone this far. Why not complete the picture?) The Jewish custom of lifting the nuptial couple up on two chairs is almost "required dancing" at weddings. There's the classic conga line with everyone snaking through the

If your fondest dream is to have Madonna perform at your wedding, you have the following options.

✪ Hire her. Unless she is a close friend, she'll probably run between $75,000 and $150,000. (Better go back and double-check the budget.)

✪ Have your band play her tunes. Your party will take on a surrealistic aura if Guy Smiley and His Four Guys sing "Vogue" and it sounds like "The Locomotion."

✪ Hire an impersonator, female or male, to perform as Madonna.

✪ Have a DJ play her latest album.

room while holding each other's waists. And there's not an Italian alive who doesn't have a soft spot for the tarantella.

There are also specific dance styles that are capable of forming a core for the reception theme. If you go all out with one of these, make sure there is enough interest among a significant number of guests. Some current trends include square dancing, the tango (remember that it takes two to do this), ballroom dancing, and folk dancing.

TEXAS TWO-STEPPING

If you think your crowd would be into it, and you have the resources, look into the following possibilities:

- Doo Wop Groups
- Marching Bands
- Choral Ensembles
- Female Impersonators
- Dixieland Jazz Bands
- Dance Troupes
- Exotic Dancers
- Elvis Impersonators
- Motown Acts
- Rappers
- Bagpipers

Two-stepping and country-and-western line dances such as the Electric Slide, the Shadow, and the Tush Push are big in clubs (gay and otherwise) across the nation. Country-and-western dancing is kind of like square dancing but it involves more people, and (forgive us, square-dance lovers) is a lot more fun. Not to mention that when done well, it's an incredibly sexy kind of dance, which brings us to your wedding. We're hearing about two-step weddings (not to be confused with Twelve-Step weddings) where people come in cowboy and cowgirl duds, the food is barbecue, there's a teacher for those who don't know the steps, and everyone dances until they can't take any more. If this strikes your fancy, get yourself a country band or use canned music, polish your boots, and cowboy up!

PERFORMANCE ART

You can hire a group to perform an act, either in addition to or instead of a regular dance band or mood music. Rather than boogie, your guests can watch as though they were audience members in a nightclub. (Make sure there's seating.) Other musical acts can actually move around the reception and perform for small gatherings of guests, so you won't necessarily have to stop everything else while the show goes on.

THAT'S ENTERTAINMENT, TOO

Randy and Joe told us that they knew from the start that after the ceremony and after the food, "we wanted to create a magical environment. We wanted something to 'change.' Putting on a wedding is too much work to have everyone disappear after the cake was cut." So they hired a service that sets up a casino. Everyone got $1,000 worth of chips (not really worth anything, of course), and at the end of the night, the guest with the most chips got a gift certificate to a local restaurant. One of the guests there reported to us that "the best thing about it was that it was a great mixer. You'd find yourself next to a complete stranger at the roulette table; the next thing you knew the two of you were screaming, 'C'mon, red even!' and hugging in celebration over your winnings."

If your friends love a little friendly competition, have board games set up in one room. When they get tired of eating and dancing, they can sit in on the marathon game of Trivial Pursuit or join in a backgammon tournament. Buy silly prizes for the winners, the big losers, and the most enthusiastic players, or let them take home the centerpieces.

Finally, consider an idea that's becoming big especially in urban areas where there's a supply of unemployed filmmakers and video production houses. They form businesses on the side that will make a video of your personal history by editing together stills and footage you might have around, writing a script, and producing a *This Is Your Life* kind of movie. For an added fee, they'll even come in to your reception with a big-screen TV and take care of the setup and playback all day. (Note: This should be considered only if you have a separate viewing area so that your guests do not become a captive audience, forced to watch a loop of your life stories in perpetuity.)

Photo: Lynn Houston

Photo: Barry Michlin

▼ MEMORIES

PHOTOGRAPHY AND VIDEOGRAPHY

Probably all of us want to have some good documentation of our wedding day. If you're a little bit spaced during your ceremony, it's comforting to know you can see a super slo-mo replay later on. (The tape can also be used for verification somewhere down the line: "See, Phil, you *did* say in our vows that you would love me when I was productive and when I was at rest.") And if you're having a large reception, you can't possibly be everywhere at once; a good photographer or videographer will enable you to experience things you missed after the fact.

Since everyone knows someone who has a camera or a camcorder, you'll probably get offers from friends who will want to shoot your wedding for you. But don't let your cousin who "just finished a course" take the only snapshots and hope for the best. Understanding exactly what you get when you hire a professional will help you to make the right choice for your wedding day.

A professional photographer doesn't just have a good eye for pictures and lots of gadgets that attach to a Nikon. Photographers and videographers have the ultimate responsibility of documenting for posterity everything that happens the day of the wedding. If they blow it, you'll have to content yourself with mental images (which get fuzzy with age, you know).

Life is all memory, except for the one present moment that goes by you so quickly you hardly catch it going.

—TENNESSEE WILLIAMS

PAPARAZZI, PLEASE!: PHOTOGRAPHY

Once you pick yourself up off the floor after finding out what a professional photographer costs, you'll probably want to try to cut corners. However, good wedding photographers are worth their weight in gold. (Which coincidentally is just about what they'll charge you.)

How much can you expect to pay for a professional wedding photographer? The average cost in most U.S. cities is $1,000 to $1,500; in smaller cities, around $500. We've heard of couples paying name photographers up to $5,000 (although you probably wouldn't be able to get Herb Ritts for that). No, this is definitely not going to be like those "50 Photos for $19.95!" specials that you always see advertised in the department stores.

There are a number of things that you are potentially buying when you hire a photographer. Let's break them down:

Proofs: Most often take the form of a sheet that contains positive prints of several negative strips ganged together. From a proof sheet you choose which shots you want to have enlarged.

Prints: The finished product, suitable for framing or to put in an album. The size can be anywhere from 3" x 5" snapshots to that 30" x 40" wall portrait that will run you around $500.

Albums: Everyone's seen those photo albums of the bride and groom caught in various poses throughout the wedding day—at the altar, in the receiving line, throwing the bouquet, etc. The quintessential album tells a story from beginning to end. Many wedding photographers include an assembled album in the cost of a package.

Equipment: The photographer will supply all necessary equipment, and you need to make sure it's compatible with your wishes. For example, if he or she relies heavily on the use of a full flash (which eliminates the shadows of natural light) and you're the kind of person who isn't comfortable knowing there's a camera pointed at you, better think twice.

Materials: The price should include all film and processing charges. A good wedding photographer wouldn't think of taking fewer than 150 shots from which to cull the prints you'll want to keep.

Philosophy and attitude: When all is said and done, this is probably the most important part. There's a sort of catch-22 here in that you want someone with a good deal of experience at shooting weddings, because it's very tricky; a good photographer needs to wrangle people, be everywhere at once, and yet not be too obnoxious. He or she must have a feel for you as a couple: after all, this isn't an advertisement for detergent the photographer is shooting, it's two breathing human beings (plus entourage). On the other hand, the more experience someone has at this, the more likely it is you'll find "burnout" that manifests itself in a kind of jaded "Okay, you two lovebirds, smile like you mean it" approach to everything. But in your case you have a trump card to play—you're a same-sex couple! This of course means that you'll have to find someone who's comfortable with that; but chances are, she or he probably won't have shot many same-sex weddings before (if any), which makes you a brand-new challenge. You might even get a great deal because the photographer will want to expand the boundaries of his or her portfolio.

MAMA, TAKE MY KODACHROME AWAY

black-and-white photography echoes a bygone era while also being timeless. A side note to classic black-and-white photography is color tinting, a process whereby black-and-white photographs are hand tinted. This can result in a funky paint-by-numbers look, a cool sepia-toned antique feel, or bright, vivid pastels. Adding attitude to black-and-white photography with hand tinting can turn a photo into art.

◗ When you're examining the photographer's work, notice how many portraits versus candids make up the albums. What style does he or she favor?

◗ How many rolls of film will be shot? Make sure the photographer doesn't skimp on this. For what you're paying, the film should be the least of your worries.

◗ How many hours of coverage are included? (A package will generally guarantee at least four hours.) Will she cover you before the ceremony, getting ready; will he remain at the reception until you leave? Are there overtime costs?

◗ Are there any additional charges for visiting the location ahead of time, traveling fees, or assistants?

◗ How many proofs will there be?

◗ What is the payment schedule?

◗ How long does the photographer keep the negatives? A good studio will keep them in a fireproof vault for 3 to 5 years. Some photographers will let you keep the negatives as part of the fee if they feel this will make or break the deal (unless you're two celebrities getting married, in which case they'll sell the negatives to *People* magazine).

◗ How long after the wedding will the proofs be delivered? What about the album?

Say you've found the photographer of your dreams and you're ready to sign a contract. Go over the following checklist to ensure that what you see is what you'll really get.

❑ Is he or she familiar with the locations? This is most important in terms of the ceremony site, since lighting is likely to be tricky there. Ask if the photographer can visit the ceremony site for the rehearsal. This will give her or him a chance to scope out the room and meet some of your key players.

❑ Does your ceremony site have any restrictions concerning where photographers can stand or what kind of equipment they can use?

❑ If you're hiring through a photography studio, make sure the contract has the name of the photographer on it; some

THE GREAT DEBATE: POSED VS. CANDID

Classic wedding photographers can be compared with the great portrait artists of the past centuries: they record an idealized version of the couple. Think of the classic wedding photographer as George Hurrell, the man who shot movie stars in the thirties and forties with soft, studied lighting and a dreamy look in their eyes. A classic wedding photographer has a whole list of "stock shots" culminating with a photograph of you waving good-bye at the exit for the final shot in the wedding album. Even the candid shots can look posed. The photographer might have you mime throwing the bouquet so the lighting will be just right, resulting in a somewhat studied moment of "excitement."

The photojournalist approach couldn't be more different. As opposed to the fantasy of the moment, they want to record the reality. They'll be as inconspicuous as possible, following the flow of the action but not being a part of it. To get into a photojournalist frame of mind, think of your wedding as being shot by Annie Liebowitz for *Vanity Fair* magazine.

Most couples these days want something in between these two approaches, with an album that incorporates a few of those corny portraits of the two of you superimposed inside of a cameo, as well as a number of candids that show you and your guests in real life moments. Decide how this percentage will break down for you, and let the photographer know this in no uncertain terms.

So how do you go about choosing a photographer? You should interview several, and discuss portraits and candids, lenses and lifestyles. Try and get a sense of the photographer's dedication to wedding photography. Is this a sideline hobby, or is she or he really into building a reputation? Is she blasé about her job? Does he appear to be excited about photographing a same-sex union? Make sure to cover the following:

◑ Look at samples or portfolios. Is there emotion in the photographs? Is the technical quality good? Are colors crisp, and is there a sharp contrast in black-and-white photographs?

My brother-in-law did the video, and it, uh, well, it didn't turn out exactly right. He had borrowed someone else's camcorder, and when it was on he thought it was off, and when it was off he thought it was on. So what we have is a tape that has the audio of the ceremony, only the video is of the carpeting. Then the battery went dead and he didn't know it, so the rest of the thing is just plain blank. It was the only disappointing thing about the whole day.

—BOB

unscrupulous studios pitch their best players to you and then send in the second string at the last minute.

❑ Give the photographer a written list of any special people you want shots of. (You might want to assign a friend who knows everyone to be a liaison here.) Also supply a written list of the general schedule of events.

❑ Decide whether you want to have posed shots taken at the ceremony site ahead of time or afterward. Most people these days opt for the preshoot, when their makeup and clothing are fresh. This also allows you to get right to the reception after the ceremony, without keeping your guests waiting.

❑ Nail down the exact amount of time the photographer is to show up and the length of the full period contracted for.

If you can't afford the full cost of a professional photographer, there are some other ways to go:

$ Hire a professional for the ceremony only, then ask friends to bring their own cameras to cover the reception.

$ Buy disposable cameras for the guests and put one on each table or in a basket by the front door. You'll get some, shall we say, unusual shots that a professional could never dream of.

$ Keep a small camera with *you* at all possible times; shots from the point of view of the brides or the grooms are unique. (While we suggest you not carry a camera during the ceremony itself, as with all wedding-day decisions it's ultimately up to you.)

MEMORIES, LIGHT THE CORNERS OF MY MIND . . .

Once you're ready to preserve those memories, there are a few things to keep in mind.

If you've signed up for a package and they're going to give you an album, make sure the quality of the album itself is good. The photos need to be stored in such a way that they won't fade or discolor—not in your lifetime, anyway. If you're assembling your own album, use one with acid-free paper, or some other album of quality. (Art Leather of

ADVICE FROM A PRO

We asked photographer Lynn Houston what the single most important issue between couple and photographer was. Her reply: "You absolutely *have to* discuss what kinds of shots you want ahead of time. I can't tell you how many couples have said to me, 'Oh, we don't want traditional pictures.' But if you don't get a great two-shot of them, believe me they're going to be really disappointed. Basic communication is the key."

Elmhurst, New York, is the world's largest album/folio manufacturer and is used by most reputable photography studios.)

When you have copies made, think of other people who might want each shot. Some people (the incredibly organized ones) include prints with their thank-you notes. Remember that it's usually cheaper to order multiple copies at one time than it is to go back and have reprints made.

LIGHTS, CAMERA, ACTION!: VIDEOGRAPHY

Fade In: A Wedding.

Eighty percent of nongay couples these days have their wedding video-taped. The bride's brother, with his new camcorder, may be shooting everything he sees; or a professional may be making a series of slick edited tapes of the festivities—for up to $5,000.

Looking for the right videographer is similar to finding the right photographer; in fact, some photography studios have branched off and now offer this service as well. However, in addition to the same questions that you posed to the potential photographer, there are some special things you'll need to ask the videographer.

Is the person a professional or just someone who bought a new piece of equipment and is trying to cash in on a fad? Your best bet is to ask to see a demo reel. (And if there is no demo reel, your best bet would be to fast-forward out of there.)

What kind of equipment does the person have? Today there are excellent low-light cameras that can shoot even by candlelight; there's no need for glaring lights every time the camera is turned on. To ensure a good picture, lighting is often augmented by low-wattage lamps mounted on top of the camera and portable floodlights pointed upward.

How is the audio recorded? We've seen videos that looked great but needed to have play-by-play coverage of what was said because the sound was so muffled. See if the videographer can use a wireless mike for the ceremony to make sure every word is captured. Hand-held mikes work fine for on-camera interviews and commentary, and the bulk of the reception can be captured by using the microphone attached to the camera.

What if the equipment fails? Is there backup equipment? Most videographers carry an extra camera or have 24-hour access to equipment close at hand. But ask.

What is the format? These days, most professional videographers will shoot in Super VHS or Hi-8 format, then transfer the finished tape to home-compatible VHS.

What will the finished product look like? Some packages include some special effects, and some even offer a "deluxe" (maybe even personalized) cassette storage case. (We feel this probably serves the same purpose as the average cassette case.) But basically your concern is how that tape is put together.

- *Raw footage:* Everything that is shot, good or bad, will be on the tape. This means you may end up with three or four cassettes that yes, have the wedding ceremony on it, but which also have 17 minutes with your Aunt Minnie crying over how happy she is for you. (You'll probably watch that once, and then go into scanning mode on subsequent viewings.) If you can afford only the raw footage right now, don't panic; later on you can always have that footage edited down.

- *Edited in camera:* The cameraperson makes on-the-spot choices during the shooting, and will actually go back and erase unnecessary things that have just been taped in order to make a more cohesive final presentation.

- *Postedited:* This is state-of-the-art video: the cameraperson or another editor goes through everything and edits together different sequences. He or she can add all sorts of special effects such as dissolves and fades, making your wedding day look like an MTV video: you can be posterized and freeze-framed; you can have subtitles or super-imposed descriptions such as "Old Girlfriend of One of the Brides"; the editor can use computer-animated titles, throw in credits at the end, and even create split-screen effects so, later, you can watch your own reactions while your best friend sang, "What I Did for Love" with the band.

A typical edited tape will run about 60 to 90 minutes. In addition to the longer edited version of the wedding, some places will also provide a "wedding highlights" tape that's about 15 minutes in length; needless to say, you are approaching expensive options when you want to produce both a full-length theatrical version and a documentary short subject of your wedding.

A really fun wedding video doesn't limit itself to the same kinds of things a photographer would shoot; it often has interviews with family and friends as well as a pan of the buffet table. You might talk with the videographer ahead of time and come up with a few standard questions that can be posed to your guests, such as "Do you remember the first time you met Stanley and Joey?" or "What are your predictions for the future of Marla and Sandy?" (Aspire to having this footage look like the interviews with the witnesses in *Reds,* but be content if you just see your friends talking coherently.)

Photo: Michael Arden

▼

PART III

THE BIG EVENT

THE FINAL APPROACH

THE WEEK BEFORE THE WEDDING

*I*t's getting close. It's getting *really* close. Chances are that you're either nervous or excited, spending your days worrying about details, picking up your college roommate at the airport, making sure there's food in fridge. (Don't tell us—you've been so busy that you forgot to go to the grocery store, right?) You may be having to entertain in-laws and parents in between writing checks and making last-minute changes with the caterer. Whew. You're certain you'll never get everything done and the wedding will be a total disaster. Why did you ever agree to this dog-and-pony show anyway?

It's not really so bad. Let us narrow everything down to two basic categories: you must tend to your personal needs, and you must put the final touches on the wedding. You can do that, right?

You know what your personal needs are better than we do; but since you've been distracted lately and your window of vulnerability is wide open, we're going to remind you of some things that may require your attention and that only you can do: teeth (have them cleaned?), hair, nails, sleep (are you getting enough?), diet (are you existing on Ding Dongs and Butterfingers?), and schedule (have you left yourself just a bit of private time?).

The other list has to do with making sure everything is in place for the wedding. It's about reconfirming every commitment you've gotten and made over the last months. You'll want to go back to your contracts and lists, and make phone calls to double-check times, places, dates, balances due, and specifics of what is being provided. Don't be surprised if somewhere along the line a supplier has spaced out and forgotten that the wedding is *this* Saturday, not *next* Saturday.

Once these things are off your back, you'll feel more capable of focusing on and savoring the joys of the days to come.

How idiotic people are when they are in love. What an age-old, devastating disease!

—NOEL COWARD

PRACTICE MAKES PERFECT: THE WEDDING REHEARSAL

The wedding rehearsal is a dry run of the ceremony that allows you to put your mind at ease on such pressing questions as "After the ceremony is over where do I go?"; "What do I do with this candle after I blow it out?"; and "How will I know not to be in the bathroom when they start the processional music?" Things like that.

Not only does the rehearsal put to rest nasty details for the brides or grooms, but it also helps the members of the wedding know exactly what's expected of *them*. It's best to let everyone get their footwork down before they go in front of an audience.

We aren't saying that your wedding is supposed to look like a finished professional production, all squeaky clean with no room for spontaneity or surprises. Not at all. In fact, once you've got the basics down pat, you'll be prepared to field any necessary ad-libbing. We know an

actress whose picture-perfect ceremony was moving along as planned . . . until the vows. The bride discovered she had misplaced the paper on which the vows were written; she handled the situation by announcing to those gathered, "Please stand by. We are experiencing technical difficulties." Everyone had a good giggle and waited while an attendant located the missing paper.

The rehearsal is most often held the night before the ceremony with a dinner following, but it can take place earlier than that or even the morning of the wedding. When you do it is not nearly as important as *that* you do it. And it's best to have everybody on hand, including attendants and musicians and of course the officiant, as well as all hand props (the ring, the veils, etc.).

REHEARSAL RECOMMENDATIONS

✔ Assign a helper bee—that anal-compulsive friend of yours who is not in the ceremony and who is organized enough to stage-manage. (This can also be someone you hire, but come on, we *know* you know someone like this who lives to tell everyone what to do.) Ask your helper bee to take notes and keep a to-do list of things needed for the big event, such as tape for putting "Reserved" signs on chairs or, if it's an outside wedding, a broom to give the area a quick sweep before guests arrive. Someone who'll cover all the details details details so you won't have to.

✔ If you're having an officiant, she or he can suggest ideas for processional order and will talk through the broad strokes of the ceremony.

✔ Write or have the helper bee write an outline of events (including the order in which the wedding party enters), notes on who does what when and who carries what. Post this outline in an area offstage where it can be seen by all the participants (but not the guests; you don't want to give away your secrets).

✔ Walk through the mechanical details of the ceremony to figure out things like who has the rings, who has the matches (if you're lighting candles—or planning on smoking), where your wedding-party people will stand and sit, where the musicians or entertainers will perform and then sit, where your ushers will sit, etc.

✔ Your helper bee should keep track of all the props (candles, flowers, and of course the rings) used in the ceremony, and later check to make sure everything is in place before you begin. This person should also collect any personal belongings that might have been left behind at the wedding site.

✔ Music (live or taped) should be incorporated in the rehearsal so that the musicians and/or whoever is in charge of turning the canned music on and off knows what and when to play, and how loud everything should be. Working with the actual music will help you and your attendants to time out the walk down the aisle so the song doesn't end in the middle of your entrance.

✔ If you're using a sound system for your voices, practice with it, set volumes, and do whatever is necessary to avoid that annoying feedback effect. (Unless you're looking to create a Woodstock atmosphere.)

✔ If you're wearing a long dress with a train that someone will carry, pin a large piece of fabric to the back of your jeans so you can practice walking and they can practice holding.

✔ Practice all entrances and exits.

> ✔✔ Check out the space and see where you will be making your entrance. If you're not walking down a central aisle, but are instead entering from either side of the ceremony site, make sure that the doors are unlocked. We hear it's an awful feeling to be locked out of your own wedding. (Imagine your embarrassment.)

> ✔✔ If you're using a carpet runner for the aisle, figure out when and how the carpet gets rolled out. And who does it.

> ✔✔ If you're entering while someone is singing, you should wait for one verse or part of the first verse, to let the song establish the mood, before making your entrance.

> ✔✔ As you rehearse, pay attention to your pacing. There's no need to rush as you walk down the aisle. Take your time and enjoy it . . . let's see those pearly whites!

✔✔ At the end of the ceremony, there is usually a recessional or a march off of the "stage" and out. This too should be rehearsed with exit music, if any, so the end of the ceremony doesn't look sloppy. ("Quick! Let's blow this burg!")

ON YOUR MARK, GET SET, GO!

At the Indy 500, they say, "Gentlemen, start your engines." Who's going to make the call at your wedding?

Decide exactly how the actual ceremony will begin. Will it begin at a predetermined time, or will you wait until certain people are there? Remember to take into consideration weather and the late arrival of out-of-towners.

Put your helper bee in charge of keeping you informed. He or she should check with the officiant and other star players to see that everything is ready for blast-off and that your key guests are present and accounted for. Then they should check with you—say, five minutes before the processional is to begin. (Just like in *Funny Girl,* they'll knock on your dressing room door: "Five minutes, Miss Brice.")

This gives you a few minutes to put the final touches on your makeup, bite a fingernail, pace—whatever it is you want to do before your single life is over forever.

After five minutes, the helper bee could check with you one more time before telling the attendants to move into their places; then he or she gives the cue to begin. From here on, the ceremony takes on a life of its own and keeps rolling along. (Just try and stop it!)

If you're not beginning the ceremony with music, dimming the lights is an excellent way to change the atmosphere in the room and give those assembled notice to quiet down. If the lights are to be dimmed, practice this also so you don't trip and humiliate yourself.

"If there is one issue that has captured our hearts over the past year, it is the issue of gay marriage. Gay and lesbian Americans deserve the same benefits and responsibilities of marriage as other Americans. Our relationships are miracles. Let's give them every chance by working together to win the legal support they deserve."

—ELLEN DEGENERES AND
ANNE HECHE

THE WEDDING of JENNIFER & TINA
Any Questions? Ask Scott, your favorite helper bee!

11:00
- Guests arrive
- Don turns on taped "mood" music
- all in bridal party should have boutonnieres or tussy mussys, little Harry gets basket of flowers

11:15
- Scott tells Barbara and Elliot (Best People) to remind the brides that they have 15 minutes!

11:20
- Everyone in the Processional starts getting into position to walk slowly down stairs
- Rachel tells Soloists, musicians and minister to take their places
- Scott asks Barbara and Elliot to double check that key guests have arrived, then gives brides "5 minutes"

11:30 ish
- Elliot gives Scott the OK Sign, Don turns off "mood" music.
- (hopefully) guests take their seats and are quiet
- Rachel checks that Harry has basket of flowers
- Scott signals musicians to begin Processional

Helen sings "Amazing Grace", enter AFTER first chorus.
1. Rachel and David
2. Elizabeth and Tyrone
(stand at either side of minister)
3. Suzette and Rick
4. Harry (with the flower basket)
5. Barbara walks with Jennifer
6. Elliot walks with Tina

Elliot waits until Tina joins Jennifer, takes little Harry's hand and moves Left of the minister

NOTE: Wait a moment at the top of stairs so everyone can see you, take a beat, then walk slowly to the tempo of the music

★ REMEMBER EVERYONE TO BREATHE AND SMILE!

SIZZLER, ANYONE? THE REHEARSAL DINNER

The wedding rehearsal often segues into the rehearsal dinner. Financing this event has traditionally fallen on the shoulders of the parents of the groom because by this point the bride's parents have taken a second mortgage on their home. Whoever foots the bill, this is a wonderful way to share your final meal on the final day before the wedding with family and friends close at hand. Held at someone's home or in a restaurant, the rehearsal meal is a means of gathering all the families together (hers and hers, his and his, biological, chosen, and so on), the out-of-towners with the in-towners, and is a gracious way of saying thanks to the people in your wedding party.

At the rehearsal dinner, those special gifts to honor attendants can be distributed (remember the beer steins?) and any last-minute

glitches can be ironed out. If your rehearsal dinner is held the night before the wedding, try to keep it short and simple. Don't stay up late or eat or drink too much and get sick . . . and spoil your wedding day. You'll never forgive yourself.

SHOULD WE OR SHOULDN'T WE? THE NIGHT BEFORE

Seeing your spouse before the wedding ceremony is supposed to be bad luck for superstitious and embarrassing reasons that hold little meaning for any modern couple. But we do know some couples who, though they had been living together for years, abstained from seeing one another the night before the wedding as well as the morning of, "because it's just romantic as hell to wait until the last possible moment when you see each other walking down that aisle." Abstinence makes the heart grow fonder, and all that.

One big disadvantage of total premarriage seclusion is that these days, photographers often take wedding photos before the ceremony begins. But if your heart is set on isolation from your intended on the wedding day, for whatever reason, you have to have your act together so that everything is taken care of well ahead of time. If you go to stay with your best friend for the night, you want to make sure you didn't leave your cummerbund and bow tie back at the house where your lover (and soon to be spouse) is.

ALL DRESSED UP AND SOMEPLACE TO GO

Think of every possible little item you're going to need when getting dressed and to get you through the day. Create a "just in case" kit to take with you to the ceremony site and reception, and pack it the night before. Here are our nominations for what should be included. (We've tried to be as gender-neutral as possible, but where we've failed, try to figure it out for yourself.)

- aspirin
- baby powder
- Band-Aids
- bobby pins
- bottled water
- breath mints or gum
- comb or brush
- contact-lens solution and extra pair of contacts
- copy of Serenity Prayer
- extra undershirt/teddy
- eyeglasses and/or sunglasses
- hair spray

- makeup
- nail file/clippers
- needle and thread
- Q-Tips
- razor and shaving cream
- safety pins
- scissors
- spare panty hose
- tissues
- toothbrush and toothpaste

I'M GETTING MARRIED IN THE MORNING: FINAL CHECKLIST FOR THE NIGHT BEFORE

❑ Remember to set alarm clock or arrange for a wake-up call.

❑ Locate all essentials that you might forget in a panic—wallets, keys, airline tickets, rings—and put them in one safe place.

❑ Read over your vows and put that piece of paper in a prearranged spot, whether it's in your tux pocket or with your best person.

❑ Double-check that your wedding attire is neat and you have all the accessories: the right color socks, belt, cuff links, shined shoes, headpiece, handkerchief, undergarments, jewelry.

❑ Pack your getaway clothes separately from the luggage you'll be taking on your honeymoon.

❑ Take all pertinent contract information and any other organizational tools you've collected.

❑ See that you have all required balances, gifts, and tips for people such as the caterer, officiant, musicians, and helpers.

❑ Make sure, if you're going out of town, that all arrangements have been made for mail collection, newspapers, and so forth.

❑ Try to sleep.

ON THE DAY THAT YOU WED

WEDDING-DAY DETAILS

*E*ach wedding day is as different as the people who partake in it. However, in the Western world there are a number of popular wedding-day occurrences (think of them as part of Weddings 101) that everyone is familiar with and that you may want to include in your festivities. The trick is to take these heterosexual and sometimes chauvinistic rituals and put your own spin on them for the perfect gay affair. In addition to these dilemmas, there are details that must be worked out that simply have to do with good common sense . . . such as, how do you get to the wedding?

DON'T HITCHHIKE TO YOUR WEDDING

Getting a ride to your wedding shouldn't be difficult. Chances are, you know someone who's going in that direction anyway. (Sure, tell that to Rhoda Morgenstern. Remember the episode when Rhoda married Joe? When her friend Phyllis forgot to pick her up and she schlepped to her own ceremony on connecting subways, wearing her full wedding drag yet? "Some weirdo tried to write graffiti on me," Rhoda lamented.)

Enlist a friend (maybe your best person) to drive you from your house to the wedding, and for goodness' sake, give this job to someone who is reliable. You really don't need the extra pressure of waiting around for anyone whose '72 Lincoln is constantly in the shop for repairs.

Some couples choose to go all out and rent a car and driver to chauffeur them for the day. In some circles, a veritable fleet of cars is hired to transport the entire wedding party. You can't really call renting a limo a necessity; however, it's something that newlyweds often choose to indulge in.

Chains do not hold a marriage together. It is threads, hundreds of tiny threads, which sew people together through the years.

—SIMONE SIGNORET

MATRIMONIAL BOND

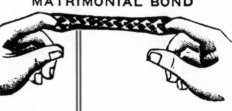

You don't have to hire one of those flashy ultrastretch numbers; most transportation companies have a range of models to choose from. There's the luxury sedan or town car, which is really just a large car with a roomy backseat that will be perfect for the two of you. Next comes your basic limousine, which is big enough to allow you to say to the driver, "James, please put up the divider window . . . We want some privacy." Then there are stretch limos—the ones that can accommodate a party of eight, and we do mean party. The more elaborate stretch limos might come with moon roofs, bars, sound systems, televisions and VCRs, and yes, we've even read of one with a hot tub.

So how much is a ticket to ride? A basic sedan begins around $50 an hour; the super stretches might run into the hundreds. An hour. With a two- or three-hour minimum. And a mandatory 15% to 20% tip added on. (See why we consider it an indulgence?) You might be able to get a package deal or arrange to have the car drop you off and pick you up at prearranged times. Ask around or hit the yellow pages to get leads on reliable and reasonable car services.

Getting from point A (the ceremony) to point B (the celebration) can be as straightforward or complex as you desire. Couples have been known to be whisked away in vintage cars, horse-drawn coaches, hot-air balloons, even helicopters. If you don't have far to travel and you love a parade, you can walk en masse to the party. We heard of two newlyweds who were shielded from the sun by large oriental umbrellas and of others being serenaded by strolling musicians as they led the promenade.

If you go by car, this is a chance to toot your own horn, as it were. The car you're in can lead a long line of other cars, all honking and announcing to the world that you two are indeed "Just Married."

BETTER TO RECEIVE

The receiving line ties the ceremony to the reception and is a formal way for the wedding hosts to welcome guests—and for the guests to meet you for the first time as a married couple. The custom guarantees that the couple get to be kissed, hugged, and congratulated by everyone and alleviates you of the responsibility of "making the

ME? SUPERSTITIOUS?

The following are some wedding-day superstitions that have evolved through the years. Read and heed.

• The couple will be assured of good luck if the bride is kissed by a chimney sweep on the wedding day.

• If a bride cries on her wedding day, her marriage will never cause tears again.

• Bad luck befalls those who stumble on the wedding day. (So don't forget to tie your shoes!)

rounds." This is also an organized way of meeting any guests you might not know yet. Plus—who're we kidding?—the receiving line is glamorous as hell, with everyone kissing you and shaking your hand and treating you as if you were the Queen Mum.

At nongay weddings, the receiving line is usually set up in this order: first the mother of the bride; then the groom's father; groom's mother; bride's father; and then the couple. If you'd like, you can also include grandparents, aunts, uncles, your cousin from Seattle, your florist, ad nauseam. Anyone you feel should be there, should be there.

The downside of a receiving line is that it can slow down the reception. Make sure people are offered something to drink and nibble on while they are waiting (and waiting) in line. Some music to listen to couldn't hurt here, either. (Just make sure it doesn't drown out the comments about how stunning you look.) An honor attendant might also mingle among those in line and tell some jokes or do a softshoe to keep everyone amused.

If you don't want to go the whole nine yards with the receiving line, that's okay too. An abbreviated version with just the two of you greeting the guests makes for an equally warm welcome, maybe even warmer.

MAY I HAVE YOUR AUTOGRAPH, PLEASE?

In a conspicuous place somewhere near the entrance to the reception you may have a blank book for guests to sign. This not only will help you keep track of everyone who attended, it also becomes an instant souvenir of the day. You can buy a book that says "Guests" or "Wedding Guests" on the genuine imitation leatherette cover and has numbered lines inside for signatures. But limiting your guests to signing their names only may choke their creative

CHALK IT UP

Falling somewhere between performance art and a political act is a new gay tradition in which couples write their names in chalk inside a heart, usually after the ceremony, and usually outside on a sidewalk. However temporary this may seem (the names will soon wear down or wash away), same-sex couples' names in chalk symbolize that "we were here and it happened" . . . kind of like leaving a rainbow pride flag on the moon.

Photo: Michael Arden

Marianne and Tammy's wedding was based around the theme of a fifties sweetheart dance. Instead of having a receiving line, their friends crowned them Queen and Queen of the Sweetheart Dance: they were presented with crowns and scepters and were made to sit on two matching thrones. The DJ invited the "court" to greet the royalty. For the first forty-five minutes of the reception Marianne and Tammy relaxed while guests visited them. Said Marianne, "It was great. No one waited on line, we got to meet everyone, and it was really funny sitting on the thrones and having our picture taken with everyone. Just a couple of queens. . . ."

expression. Why not get a large blank book, or even an artist's sketchbook. Have a member of your inner circle start by writing a few lines or drawing an appropriate doodle; not to be outdone, everyone else will follow suit. Don't forget to furnish a writing implement, be it a felt-tip pen, a box of crayons, or the wedding industry's favorite—the fancy feathered pen.

MR. MARRIAGE SEZ

The good wedding hosts/hostesses:

introduce themselves to each guest they don't know but "have heard so much about."

review the guest list so names they might forget will be more familiar to them.

make an effort to spend a few minutes of Quality Time with each of their guests.

don't chew gum, smoke in their guests' faces, or look bored or unfocused.

don't ask their guests, "What did you bring me?"

THE TOASTS OF THE TOWN

After the receiving line is finally over and all guests have full glasses, the best man/woman/person usually makes the first toast to the new couple. Fortunately, that toast is the responsibility of that person—and it's the one thing you don't have to worry your pretty little heads over. Just stand there, listen, and smile/cry at the appropriate times. (Don't worry, you'll know which is which.) Make sure the toast is coordinated with the caterer, so that your guests aren't standing there with empty glasses—or no glasses at all.

Now it's your turn. One of you makes a toast to your spouse, and maybe to all your guests who have schlepped here to be part of this historic occasion. Then it's the other partner's turn to toast. After that, anyone can have a go at a toast; the only real requirement is to get everyone's attention. If there are telegrams, they should be read out loud.

TIPS FOR TOASTERS

Y Tell everyone who you are and how you know the brides or grooms.

Y Relate a story or an experience you shared together.

Y Avoid going overboard and becoming sappy and maudlin.

Y Try to include something about the couple and their life together.

Y Don't be stiff; be natural, and speak from the heart.

SAVE THE FIRST DANCE FOR ME

The first dance traditionally starts with the wedding couple all alone on the dance floor. This dates back to ancient Prussia, where the noble bride would have the first dance with the king, followed by the prince and on down, ending with maybe a page. The groom followed suit starting with the queen, and by the end of the evening, everyone had gotten a chance to dance with the newlyweds.

The music for the first dance is customarily a waltz, or anything slow. You should try to choose music that has significance for your relationship—"your song." It could be the tune that was playing on the jukebox the night you met; it could be "My Guy" or "My Girl" (choose one). Tradition says that during this one song, the wedding couple dance together, then the groom switches to the bride's mother and the bride to her father; then the father and mother of the groom join in, and then guests begin to join the new family on the dance floor. It's pretty confusing, but it's nothing compared with what we know you'll be able to pull off with your permutations of gender and family. And we want to see those mothers dancing together!

WEDDING-DAY DETAILS

When asked the question, "What was the highlight of your wedding day?" many people told us that it was the toast. We think this is because the toast presents family and friends with the opportunity to express emotions that otherwise might remain hidden.

BOB'S FATHER'S TOAST

I had three wonderful children, and hoped that they would all marry in the Jewish faith. When my daughter got married to a Jewish man, I was happy. When one of my sons married a lovely Southern Baptist, I was happy again. Then Bob met Jeff, who isn't Jewish and isn't a woman. But I've always said I'd stand behind him no matter what, and I'm very proud of him and happy for him. So here's to Bob and Jeff.

IT'S A PIECE OF CAKE

Another photo op and a big wedding custom is the couple cutting the first slice of the cake and feeding each other little morsels. This whole cake bit symbolizes breaking bread, many shared meals together, and a home filled with prosperity. It's such a universal wedding ritual that it may be hard for you to avoid the temptation of buying a personalized knife for just this purpose.

Decide in advance who feeds whom first. Then each of you puts a hand on the knife (*Smile! Flash! Flash! Smile!*), and together you cut a slice of the cake and put it on a plate. (The caterer will help here, or you should have a serving plate handy.) With your fingers, feed each other a bite of the cake. Listen to the crowd cheer. Please, please, try to resist that tradition of smashing the cake all over the face of the person you allegedly love most in this world.

THE PARTY'S OVER

If your guests know their Emily Post, they won't dare leave the reception until you've cut the cake. Once the cake is cut and any other dessert is being served, it's a tip-off that the party's winding down. The band might play its last song, kids are getting cranky, guests take off their shoes and put their feet up on chairs, ties are loosened, and it's time for you to move on.

Before you take off from your reception, there are a few matters that must be attended to. (If you want to, that is. Hey, maybe you just want to sneak out the back door while *your* father is dancing the mambo with *her* father.) The following are the final steps to the getaway.

THE TOSSING OF THE BOUQUET AND GARTER

History: The pagan bride used to take a bouquet of herbs and garlic with her to the new home; she'd set it on fire and smoke out any evil spirits that might be lingering; then she'd toss the charred bouquet outside.

The old way: The bride tosses her flowers over her shoulder to the throng of unattached females who have been waiting for this moment ever since the engagement was announced—because the one to catch it is destined to be the next to marry. Then the groom takes the bride's garter and does the same routine for the single men.

The new way: Depending on what you've decided to wear and carry, you may or may not have two bouquets and/or two garters. We say, use what ya got and have it be a unisex throng you're tossing to. And don't limit yourselves to flowers and garters. Jane felt so bad that certain people hadn't caught either of the bouquets that she threw the sash off her dress and an antique lace handkerchief before she could be restrained. Guys can have garters too, you know; or how about your boutonnieres? Or have a special bouquet made just for throwing.

THE FINAL APPEARANCE

You sneak away from the party and change into your going-away clothes, which are anything that's more comfortable. You then appear on a balcony above the crowd, like Evita, and say your good-byes. ("And would the last one to leave please turn out the lights?" is a good exit line.) This gives everyone a warning that it's time for another tradition:

THE THROWING OF THE . . . RICE

History: In days of yore, wedding guests threw seed-bearing plants (wheat, nuts, dates), an act that some scholars claim was to assure fertility; others feel the plants were bribes for any hovering evil spirits. (Feed 'em and they won't notice you zooming away.)

The old way: Everyone makes a lot of noise and throws rice.

The new way: Since it really isn't environmentally correct to throw rice anymore, you have your choice of rose petals, birdseed (the ultimate self-cleaning product—but only if you're outdoors), or biodegradable confetti (which you can find in those wedding catalogs). Or throw oregano or other herbs, which are supposed to guarantee the couple a "spicy" life together.

THE GETAWAY

History: This is the part where the caveman groom was running with the bride over his shoulder and the bride's father was chasing them, throwing rocks, and screaming at the top of his lungs. In a later era, when man had invented shoes, the father took his shoes off and threw them.

The old way: Dick and Jane speed off in a car that has been garishly decorated, with some of those symbolic shoes and noisy tin cans dragging behind.

The new way: Dick and Tom speed off in a car that has been garishly decorated, with some of those symbolic shoes and noisy tin cans dragging behind.

I JUST LOVE YOUR DECOR

There are a number of things that can be used to decorate your car; in fact, there are even kits that contain "everything you need for great results without damage to the car": crepe-paper streamers, balloons, tissue bells, and a Just Married sign. Or use shaving cream, Silly String, white shoe polish, flowers, and photos. Buy a sign that says, "Newlyweds on Board." But do not, under any circumstances, let anyone use paint (even water-base paint); it will never, ever, come off, and you'll have to drive around for the rest of your car's life with "Sue and Maria, Off To Do the Wild Thing!" on the side of it.

We were driving down the freeway at one in the morning with a Just Married sign on the car, and everyone kept honking. Then they'd drive by and look at us with faces that said, "I don't understand."

—MARK

HAVE WE FORGOTTEN ANYTHING???

As you prepare to take your leave, think about the following:

❏ Double-check that your helper bee has cash on hand to pay the help (don't forget the tips).

❏ Make sure someone will be transporting your gifts and other personal belongings back to your home.

❏ Don't forget those leftovers. Decide in advance who gets to keep them (maybe you can set it up so that a local food bank or homeless shelter gets them—and don't forget the cake).

❏ Make arrangements regarding who gets to steal the centerpieces.

❏ Appoint somebody who, after you leave, will make sure everyone is in okay shape to drive home safely.

Oh, and one other thing:
Congratulations.

▼ THE HONEYMOONERS

*T*o honeymoon, or not to honeymoon—that is the question. Your decision usually comes down to time and money (which we'll get to in a minute), but some gay and lesbian couples we spoke with said that honeymoons seemed like another of those useless heterosexual conventions. Wrong. This is one of the wedding traditions they really got right.

Here's the setup: You've been working your butts off pulling everything together. No matter how many of the tasks you farmed out, you've still been worrying about deliveries, learning your lines, picking up friends at the airport, schmoozing with family . . . well it's downright exhausting. The two of you probably haven't had a conversation in weeks that didn't start with "The caterer called today . . . " or "We got the response card from your ex-lover. I thought you said she'd never accept in a million years."

And then there's the wedding day itself. Physical exhaustion is a pretty sure bet, and emotional exhaustion is almost guaranteed. Now . . . doesn't a nice little vacation sound like just the thing?

It may be that you can't get any significant time off of work. See if you can at least get a few days off after the ceremony, and then plan an extended trip for sometime later on that you can call your second honeymoon. If you can't even swing a couple of days, see about checking into a romantic spot close to home just for the first night. (We especially recommend this to any couple having a home wedding; there is just no tactful way to get lingering guests out of your living room when you feel like you're going to drop.)

Now, it may be that you've shot your bankroll on the celebration, and you're just going to have to stay home. In this case we prescribe the following:

Niagara Falls is only the second biggest disappointment of the standard honeymoon.

—OSCAR WILDE

Photo: RSVP Travel Productions, Inc.

ACT LIKE YOU'RE GOING AWAY

🏠 Gather leftovers from the caterer, stock up with goods from your favorite deli, or keep restaurant delivery numbers by the phone.

🏠 Keep that phone unplugged except when you're ordering something to be brought to you.

🏠 Rent some romantic videos. (How far you want to go with these is a matter of personal preference.)

🏠 Sit around and be in love, and when you need a little break from that, open some wedding presents.

Even if you've been living together, a honeymoon is a wonderful occasion. You need time alone and a chance to put everything on hold. If you're changing your names, you'll undoubtedly practice calling each other by your new ones. ("Why, good morning, Mr. Johnson-Meyers.") Or you'll have long discussions about how you're going to introduce each other from now on: "'I'd like you to meet my spouse.' No, 'I'd like you to meet my wife.' No, how about, 'This is my old lady'?"

DESTINATIONS: NO MATTER WHERE YOU GO, THERE YOU ARE

Let's say you're blessed enough to have the dough to take you on a trip somewhere. You have a series of decisions to make. Some are about the same things any newlywed couple need to consider:

❓ Do you want to go one place and stay there, or do you want to travel through various areas?

❓ Do you want lots of activities, or do you want to lie on a beach and read?

❓ Do you have any weather requirements?

HONEYMOON HISTORY

After the caveman stole his bride, his main goal was to avoid the vengeance of the bride's family. So he "went to the mattresses," so to speak, and hid out with his new wife for thirty days—the cycle of the moon. While they were hiding, they consumed the current drink of choice, mead, which contained . . . honey. Thus, "moon of honey."

? Have you ever traveled together before?

? Do you want to be alone (alone together, that is), or do you want to be with a group?

And some are specific to you as a same-sex couple:

? If you travel with a group, do you want it to be exclusively gay and/or lesbian?

? How out are you when you travel?

? Do you want to tell everyone you meet that you're newlyweds?

If you do any traveling at all, you know that it presents all kinds of challenges to the gay couple. Let's say you go on a cruise. If you go on a "regular" cruise, you'll find yourself in one of two positions: either you'll be in the closet or you'll have to be prepared to spend time and energy explaining yourselves.

You might want to consider a gay or lesbian cruise, cattle drive, Amazon adventure, tour to China, sail up the Nile, or any number of incredible trips arranged by exclusively gay travel companies. There are gay Club Med weeks and lesbian cruises to Lesbos; Mardi Gras packages and African photo safaris. The advantage of an all-gay tour is, of course, that you can do things that straight people take for granted in a romantic setting—like hold hands and dance with your new spouse.

Or pick a city such as Provincetown or Key West where you know there's a large gay contingent. There are numerous gay-owned and gay-operated resorts, hotels, and bed and breakfasts to choose from.

WHERE IN THE WORLD?

The favorite honeymoon spots for nongay couples are, according to *Bride's* magazine: Hawaii, Mexico, the Virgin Islands, Jamaica, the Bahamas, Canada, Bermuda, and Europe. (What happened to Niagara Falls and the Poconos?!) There are no stats available yet for same-sex honeymooners, but we *can* tell you . . .

THE HONEYMOON

There's a brochure you can send away for called *Answers to Most-Asked Questions About Cruising* (see the Suggested References in the back of this book). It may or may not have answers to the questions you had in mind, but it's sure to make an impact sitting on your coffee table.

THE FAVORITE DESTINATIONS FOR GAY AND LESBIAN TRAVELERS

The following were named in a survey by the International Gay Travel Association.

DOMESTIC

1. Key West
2. San Francisco area
3. Provincetown
4. New York City area
5. Southern California
6. Miami/Fort Lauderdale area
7. Hawaii
8. Washington, D.C.
9. New Orleans
10. Phoenix

INTERNATIONAL

1. London
2. Paris
3. Mexico
4. Amsterdam
5. Caribbean Islands
6. Toronto
7. South Pacific Islands
8. Australia
9. Rio de Janeiro
10. Berlin

Come Fly With Me

According to the *Out and About* 1998 ratings, the following U.S.-based airlines allow same-gender spouses to use each others' frequent-flier miles and VIP lounge access rights:

American West
American
Northwest
TWA
United
U.S. Airways

SPECIFICALLY GAY HONEYMOON IDEAS

PALM SPRINGS

Palm Springs has a gay guide; it also marks gay-friendly accommodations (with a lambda symbol) in its general visitors guide. According to the Palm Springs Gay Tourism Council, "In Palm Springs, gay people—both visitors and the large local contingent—lead a relaxed life knowing they are accepted and welcomed, not merely tolerated. The gay lifestyle is seen as just another element that contributes to the cosmopolitan, sophisticated atmosphere of this world-class resort." You can stay in one of the numerous hotels listed as catering to gays: some are exclusively gay; others are mainstream hotels that are reaching out to the huge gay travel market.

COPENHAGEN

Because Denmark is the most progressive progay nation in the world, to some gay couples Copenhagen is better than a Hans Christian Andersen fairy tale. There is an almost seamless acceptance of gay life and a public kiss from your new spouse that would stop traffic in America goes unnoticed in Denmark. Plus there's that old-world splendor, and almost everyone speaks English fluently. It can be expensive, but it can be worth it.

HAWAII

Since Hawaii is one of the most popular honeymoon destinations, you might want to do the whole thing on the islands. There's a company on Maui called Royal Hawaiian Weddings that offers a number of complete packages for same-sex couples (actually, they offer the same ones for nongay couples as well—totally egalitarian). They provide welcoming leis (no wisecracks please), beachfront accommodations, an officiant to perform the ceremony, photos, a wedding certificate or copy of your vows done in calligraphy, and much more.

INTERNATIONAL HOME EXCHANGE

There is an organization called Mi Casa Su Casa that will set up a home exchange between you and other gay couples throughout the world.

ON THE ROAD AGAIN

As we all know, the true pleasure of travel is not in the arriving but in the journey. So why not take your act on the road? Set out in a rented or borrowed RV, camper, or pickup truck; take your sleeping bags or just drive from motel to motel. Or plan your honeymoon around an activity that you both love—cross-country skiing, golfing, fishing.

TRAVEL TIPS

Wherever you travel, especially if it's outside the United States, be sure to do the following:

Know what your rights are. European laws are generally more progay than American ones are, but don't assume anything. And there are some resorts in Jamaica that limit occupancy to heterosexual couples; no singles, children, or same-sex couples—and it's legal.

Know what to expect at customs. Yeah, yeah, *we* know you're married, but *they* don't know that. You and your new spouse are not considered a "family" and must abide by customs restrictions for individuals.

Take a copy of a notarized power of attorney. It doesn't have the weight of a marriage license, but it can specifically authorize you to visit each other in hospital intensive-care wards and make legal and medical decisions for each other.

BOOKING THE ROOM

Now that you've decided where you're going, how can you guarantee you won't have to push single beds together in hotels? Well, you can never be entirely sure; sometimes it even happens to nongay couples. But there is a system developed by Lindsy Van Gelder and Pamela Robin Brandt, authors of *Are You Two . . . Together? A Gay and Lesbian Travel Guide to Europe.* (This is an indispensable book if you're lucky enough to be going to Europe.) Pamela and Lindsy tell us that "the ease of getting a double bed varies from country to country and according to the fanciness of the hotel.

"Method A, the simplest: Make your reservations for double-bedded accommodations before you leave home. Method B, a variation on the same ploy: One of you books the room while the other waits at the railroad station or in the car with the luggage. Arrange all the details and get the key. When you return with a husband instead of a wife, or vice versa, just head directly for the room and hope for the best."

There are additional approaches to getting what you want—the honeymoon suite, the basket of fruit, the chilled champagne, the whole ball of honeymoon wax—wherever you go. In a gay-owned or gay-friendly environment, chances are they'll be supportive and really go to town welcoming you, so be sure to tell them you'll be newlyweds.

If you decide to go to a mainstream hotel or resort, you can certainly make the reservation yourself, but to confirm that you'll be going somewhere you'll feel welcome, you might want a travel agent to book the room. In addition to having a contact with whom they have a good working relationship, the travel agent might have knowledge of the hotel's or resort's politics.

But once you're at the hotel—then what? One way for the out-and-about gay honeymooner to find things to do/places to go/people to meet is to have a chat with the hotel's concierge. Simply put, the concierge deals with the needs of the hotel's guests. A good concierge will have the Rolodex from Heaven, with contacts to help you get tickets to a sold-out sporting event or dinner reservations to "hot" eateries. If a guest wants it, the concierge will work to get it, or find someone who can—within legal restrictions, of course. At the request of a woman guest, one concierge had the bed turned down and scattered with rose petals to surprise her female spouse when she checked in.

Personal service and confidentiality are key here, and you should feel free to ask a concierge about gay night life. "Concierges are philosophers, psychologists, and jacks-of-all-trades," says Robert Duncan, concierge of the Westwood Marquis Hotel and Gardens in Los Angeles. They've heard and seen it all, and what they haven't will probably intrigue rather than shock them.

Not every hotel has a concierge who will turn somersaults for you—or even has a concierge at all. Sometimes there's just an employee who answers the phone and transfers you to another department, or a front-desk manager who gives basic directions and recommends places to eat. But should you require their services, they should try to help you. Unless you've checked into the Strom Thurmond Motor Lodge, a same-sex couple shouldn't send them into hysteria.

And think of it this way: it's a good bet that at least 10% of the hotel's staff is gay.

THE HONEYMOON

HONEYMOON HIDEAWAY

If you have your heart set on soaking in a heart-shaped tub, spend the night at a honeymoon haven that specializes in honeymoon kitsch. Such a place can delight you with gel beds and mirrored ceilings; you can get a rococo velvet settee, an all-pink guest suite called the Love Nest, or an all-blue one called Just Heaven. You can find seven-foot bathtubs, pink cocktails called Cupid's Arrow, rock quarries complete with little waterfalls or Roman-villa themes. Hang out the Do Not Disturb sign and enjoy.

Photo: Marcelina Martin

Photo: Lynn Houston

The Aftermath

*I*t's been said by far wiser folks than ourselves that the first year of marriage is the hardest. We're not about to walk you through the entire year with its trials and tribulations, because that's not what this book is about. But we thought it would be unkind to leave you hanging at the honeymoon, and not prepare you at least a little bit for what lies ahead.

I HAVE AN ANNOUNCEMENT TO MAKE

Do you want to formally announce your marriage in the local newspaper? Well, you just may be in luck. Some mainstream newspapers around the country now list same-sex unions just the same as they list heterosexual marriages, and more are climbing on the bandwagon all the time. The first to break the barriers are:

- Austin *American Statesman* (Texas)
- Brattleboro *Reformer* (Vermont)
- Everett *Herald* (Washington)
- Marin *Independent Journal* (California)
- Minneapolis *Star Tribune* (Minnesota)
- Philadelphia *Inquirer* (Pennsylvania)
- San Jose *Mercury News* (California)
- Santa Cruz *Sentinel* (California)
- Atlanta *Journal Constitution* (Georgia)

> *A happy marriage is a long conversation that always seems too short.*
>
> —ANDRÉ MAUROIS

This is a great start, but we think the list needs to be expanded, don't you? You may initially meet resistance from a publication that hasn't caught on; maybe they'll say, "But how can we list you under 'Marriages' when you're not legally married?" For an answer, look to George Pyle, editor of Kansas's Salina *Journal,* who dealt with backlash from the *Journal*'s decision to print same-sex marriage announcements and wrote in an op-ed piece in the *New York Times* on August 11, 1993: "We quickly decided that we could not argue on the editorial page, as we had, for equal treatment for homosexuals and then deny equality on our own weddings page. . . . There is no reason why newspapers that print other marriages should reject gay announcements when they're offered. We can't claim it's not news. And we can't hide behind the excuse that it is not legally recognized. Since when did newspapers let the government decide what they should print?"

Or tell your local newspaper that the Minneapolis *Star Tribune,* for example, changed the name of the heading from "Wedding Announcements" to "Celebrations," so that now a variety of different events can be listed. We think this is a smashing way to make the straight world more aware of same-sex commitments.

If you want to pioneer same-sex wedding announcements in your area, do the following:

❶ Call up the editor of whatever section prints wedding announcements—style page, society page, "In and Around Town," etc.

❷ Ask them what the newspaper's policy is on listing same-sex unions.

❸ Ask them to send you a form that you can fill out so that you and your new spouse can be listed.

❹ Ask what their policies are regarding photographs—what size they need to be, whether they will be returned, and so forth.

❺ Do it!

THE NAME GAME

One of the big decisions faced by a gay or lesbian couple who have gotten married is whether to change their names. The responses to this question range from "We felt it was an important statement to make to the world" to "I wouldn't do that even if you paid me huge sums of money."

For some, changing last names brings up unsavory images of old systems of men "taking possession" of women, and so on; for others, changing to the same last name is symbolic of creating a new family. Donny told us: "It was important for us to change our last names because we are our own family now. There used to be two families; now there's one. We changed our names to reflect that."

Let's say you're considering changing your names. What are the options, and what is involved? We have found four different variations on the New Last Name Game:

Hyphenating. This seems to be the most popular choice: you combine both of your last names, separated only by a tiny hyphen. The two catches here are that: (1) you must decide what order they go in (usually one way just sounds better than the other) and (2) if you're planning on having kids, and they someday marry someone whose last name is also hyphenated, their kids will then have *four* last names, etc. The best thing about hyphenating is that you get to keep the name you've lived with your entire life; you just add to it. When Rod and Bob got married, they decided to become Mr. and Mr. Jackson-Paris. It has a nice ring to it, doesn't it?

One person taking the other's last name. Bonnie Jones and Rebecca Allen get married; they become Bonnie and Rebecca Allen. Although it seems odd to some people, those who have gone this route claim it works for them. This way, one of you gets to keep the name you grew up with, and the two of you end up having the same last name, which is particularly good if you have kids. The drawback, of course, is that you must decide who loses the name. (If one of you is named Buttafuoco, this may be an easier call.)

Adding your spouse's name to yours. This was actually pioneered by a famous nongay couple—John Lennon and Yoko Ono. When they got married, John took Yoko's last name as his legal middle name and vice versa—making him John Ono Lennon and her Yoko Lennon Ono. The one drawback to this is that both of you still have different last names.

Choosing a new name altogether. This means that the family has a common name, only it isn't a name that either of you has had before. It's kind of exotic to be able to pick a whole new identity for yourselves—like they did for movie stars in the fifties; however, it can be confusing to your friends and family for a period of time. ("What's their new name again?")

To legally change your name, you first need to make an appointment with a superior court, which you'll probably find at your county seat. They'll lead you through the steps, and when it comes time to explain why you want to do it, we recommend that old standby, the truth: "We're changing our names because we're married."

If you do change your name, don't forget to change your driver's license, credit cards, passport, Social Security, etc.

THE AFTERMATH

I like to end the ceremony by presenting the couple to the congregation—which gives them a chance to tell everyone what the new names will be. There is a new tradition that I think is just great, where people are choosing a third name for themselves. A couple I married had both been on a Buddhist path and they wanted it to be a common name, so they chose Bell, for a mindfulness bell, so that every time they heard the name it would remind them of what was the deepest concern and commitment to them. They both kept their surnames and each added Bell.

—THE REVEREND
MARY GRIGOLIA

SHE'S NO LADY, SHE'S MY . . . WIFE?

Regardless of what you do about your names, you'll still be faced with the problem of nomenclature. What *do* you call this person now? Do you refer to him/her any differently than you did before you had a ceremony? Personally, we'd like to wave a magic wand and come up with a whole new word to describe a partner for life with whom you share sexual intimacies, a word that doesn't carry the baggage that comes with *wife* and *husband,* one that doesn't have the sexual overtones of *lover,* one that isn't as legalistic sounding as *partner.*

We took a straw poll on this burning issue, and although we're not claiming to be Gallup, it appears that *spouse* is the terminology of choice for married gays and lesbians; some do use *husband, wife, partner,* or *life partner,* and some change the word according to the situation and whom they're speaking with. Then there are always the old standbys—*significant other, companion, sidekick, soul mate,* and even "Jason's other mother" for you coparents. But most people do seem to want to indicate that a new step has been taken in their relationship.

Photo: Michael Arden

AFTER THE DELUGE

Even if you've been living together, marriage is going to change you. Suddenly, your relationship takes on new weight and import, both to you and to the world, in ways that you never thought possible. Every time you go to fill out a form, you'll stop at the "Marital Status" box and think about it. "Let's see, no, I'm not single . . ."

If you weren't living together before you got married, you've got a real ride ahead of you. Learning to live with another person is

WOMAN:
His wife? He told *me* he was gay.

JIM DIAL:
Uh . . . I was referring to his wife . . . Hank. I use the term *wife* because I'm so comfortable with alternative lifestyles.

—FROM AN EPISODE OF
MURPHY BROWN

always such an eye-opener. ("You mean you do the dishes right after you're done eating? Really? All the time?") And regardless of whether you've lived together before, you kind of have to start writing a new script—because it's easy to get complacent and sloppy once you've made a long-term commitment. Keeping it fresh may be your greatest challenge. But it will pay off in a big way.

You now also have a life with a family that consists of (at least) two people. Not that you need to be joined at the hip, but the fact of the matter is that before, all you really had to concern yourself with was getting your own life headed in the right direction; now you have to coordinate that with another per-

Photo: Michael Arden

son. Sometimes it's harder; sometimes that other person is a ballast for you and makes everything easier. But no matter how you look at it, you are the recipients of a beautiful, magical gift.

*About a year after Jane and I had our wedding ceremony, I got a form in the mail to fill out for my twenty-five-year high school reunion, and it had a blank for my spouse's name. Now, I really hadn't thought about coming out to my entire high school class, but when faced with the reality of that blank, what choice was there? Either we were married or we weren't, and if I couldn't fill her name in there, what was it all about in the first place? So I neatly penned in the name, and mailed it off, feeling quite proud of myself. A few weeks later, I got a call from someone named Joanne, who worked for the company that was organizing the reunion. "Um, Tess, I just have a little question about some of the information you sent us . . . Where it says spouse's name, you wrote . . . *Jane *Anderson?" "That's right, Joanne. Is there something wrong?" There was a *long *pause, then: "Oh, no, of course, there's nothing wrong with that. I think that's great. It's just that this information goes out to all of your classmates, and I didn't want you to be embarrassed. You know, my hairdresser is gay and . . . " and so on.*

The point being this: although I'm very out in my daily life, I really don't know that I would have bothered to put Jane's name in that blank if we hadn't actually had a wedding. The fact that we are married (in our eyes if not in the eyes of the IRS) has changed me—profoundly and irrevocably. And I couldn't be prouder.

—TESS

The last thing we want to say is, we wish you both the very best of luck, and many, many happy years together.

RESOURCE DIRECTORY

NATIONAL SUPPORT ORGANIZATIONS

Gay and Lesbian Alliance Against Defamation (GLAAD), 150 W. 26 St., #503, New York, NY 10001; (212) 807-1700; www.glaad.org
Works through the media to better educate the public about relationships and equal marriage rights.

Human Rights Campaign (HRC), 1101 14th St., Second Floor, Washington, DC 20005; (202) 628-4160; www.hrcusa.org
Lobbying, education and national polling efforts around marriage.

National Center for Lesbian Rights (NCLR), 870 Market St., Suite 570, San Francisco, CA 94102; (415) 392-6257
Works on child custody, foster parenting, and family diversity.

National Freedom to Marry Coalition, 120 Wall St., Suite 1500, New York, NY 10005; (212) 809-8585, Ext. 205; www.ftm.org
Dedicated to recognizing and legalizing same-sex marriage in every state.

National Gay and Lesbian Task Force (NGLTF), 2320 17th St. N.W., Washington, DC 20009; (202) 332-6483; www.ngltf.org
Serves as the national resource center for grassroots organizations facing battles on the state and local levels.

Parents, Friends, and Families of Lesbians and Gays (PFLAG), 1101 14th St. N.W., #1030, Washington, DC 10005; (202) 638-4200; www.pflag.org
The national headquarters, which can help you find a local chapter.

Partners Task Force for Gay and Lesbian Couples, P.O. Box 9684, Seattle, WA 98109-0685; (202) 935-1206; www.buddybuddy.com
Provides a wide and useful variety of free and updated information on marriage and gay and lesbian couples.

RELIGIOUS ORGANIZATIONS

Affirmation, Box 26302, San Francisco, CA 94126; (415) 641-4554
Lesbian and gay Mormons (Church of Latter-day Saints).

The Buddhist Association, Box 1974, Bloomfield, NJ 07003

Dignity Inc., 1500 Massachusetts Ave. N.W., Suite 11F, Washington, DC 20005; (202) 861-9917
Lesbian and gay Roman Catholics.

Friends for Lesbian and Gay Concerns, Box 222, Sunnytown, PA 18084; (215) 234-8424
Lesbian and gay Quakers.

Integrity Inc., Box 19561, Washington, DC 20036
Lesbian and gay Episcopalians.

Metropolitan Community Church (MCC), MCC International Office, 8714 Santa Monica Blvd., West Hollywood, CA 90069; (310) 854-9110
Fellowship of progressive gay Christians.

Presbyterians for Lesbian/Gay Concerns, c/o James D. Anderson, Box 38, New Brunswick, NJ 08903; (210) 846-1510

Unitarian Universalist Office of Lesbian/Gay Concerns, 25 Beacon St., Boston MA 02108; (617) 742-2100; www.uua.org

Unity Fellowship Church Movement, 5149 West Jefferson Blvd., Los Angeles, CA 90016; (213) 936-4948
A Christian black gay church with fellowships throughout the county.

World Congress of Gay and Lesbian Jewish Organizations (WCGLJO), P.O. Box 23379, Washington, DC 20026; www.wcgljo.org

HISTORY AND SOCIOLOGY

International Gay and Lesbian Archives, P.O. Box 69679, West Hollywood, CA 90069; (310) 854-0271
Lesbian Herstory Archives, P.O. Box 1258, New York, NY 10116; (718) 768-3953

BUSINESS AND LEGAL

American Civil Liberties Union (ACLU), 132 West 43rd St., Fifth Floor, New York, NY 10036; (212) 549-2500;
    www.aclu.org
    For gay civil rights or other libertarian questions.
City of West Hollywood, City Hall, 8611 Santa Monica Blvd., West Hollywood, CA 90069-4109; (310) 854-7332
    For application for domestic partnership registration.
Hawaii Equal Rights Marriage Project (HERMP), 1820 University Ave., #208, Honolulu, HI 96822; (808) 956-4666
    Played a major role in the court case and is working to educate people in Hawaii and other states.
Lambda Legal Defense and Education Fund, Marriage Project, 666 Broadway, 12th Floor, New York, NY 10012;
    (212) 809-8585; www.lambda.org
    Coordinates the legal and political groundwork for winning and keeping the right to marry. Lambda is
    now working on the Hawaii case, promotes the Marriage Resolution, and has published a vast amount of
    indispensable background and educational material on marriage.

BOOKSTORES

Most gay bookstores, certainly the ones listed below, will be glad to fill a phone or mail order for you.

A Different Light Bookstore, 489 Castro St., San Francisco, CA 94114; (415) 431-0891; Also at 8853 Santa Monica
    Blvd., West Hollywood, CA 90069; (310) 854-6601; and at 548 Hudson St., New York, NY 10014; (212) 989-
    4850. Books by phone (800) 343-4002; www.adlbooks.com
Lambda Rising, 1625 Connecticut Ave. N.W., Washington, DC 20009; (800) 621-6969; and 241 W. Chase St., Balti-
    more, MD 21201; (410) 234-0069
Oscar Wilde Bookshop, 15 Christopher St., New York, NY 10014; (212) 255-8097; www.nycnet.com/oscarwildebooks

TRAVEL

Atlantis, (800) 6-ATLANTIS
    Gay and lesbian packages at Club Med resorts.
International Gay and Lesbian Travel Association (IGLTA), Box 18247, Denver, CO 80218; (800) 448-8440
    Will refer you to gay and gay-friendly travel agents in your area.
Mi Casa, Su Casa, (510) 531-4511
    International home-exchange network for gay and lesbian travelers.
Olivia Cruises and Resorts, 4400 Market St., Oakland, CA 94608; (800) 631-6277
    Planners of women's cruises and vacations.
Royal Hawaiian Weddings, Box 424, Puunene, Hawaii 96784; (800) 659-1866
    Complete union ceremony packages for same-gender couples.
RSVP Travel Productions Inc., 2800 University Ave. S.E., Minneapolis, MN 55414;
    (800) 328-7787; www.rsvp.net
    Gay cruises and vacation packages.

WEDDING RESOURCES

Band of Infinity, 1004 N. Ogden Dr., West Hollywood, CA 90069; (800) 349-5911; www.bandofinfinity.com
Sequentially numbered rings that symbolically count how many gays men lesbians, friends, and supporters there are in the world; you can also get the same number on both of your rings.

Family Celebrations, P.O. Box 3700, San Dimas, CA 91773; (888) 335-5998; www.familycelebrations.com
America's first wedding and special-occasion catalog designed for gay men and lesbians. (See page 170 for more information.)

International Formalwear Association, 401 North Michigan Ave., Chicago, IL 60611; (312) 644-6610
"Formalwear Guide" is available for $1 and a stamped, self-addressed envelope.

Mirror Image Studios, P.O. Box 280-W, Lederach, PA 19450
Personalized wedding cake toppers; they will create just about anything you can imagine.

National Limousine Association, (800) NLA-7007
Referrals of limousine companies in your area.

Precision Software, 65 Washington St., Suite 202, Santa Clara, CA 95050; (408) 241-4727 and
(800) 688-9337
Manufacturers of "The Wedding Workshop."

Sacred Rainbow, Shadow Grafix Inc., 1950 Cheshire Bridge Rd., Atlanta, GA 30324; (404) 872-5492;
www.shadowgrafix.com/rainbow
On-line source for commitment ceremony invitations.

Wired Wedding, Jones-Mack Software, PrideNY@aol.com
Gay and lesbian marriage/union ceremony software package.

Zebra'z, (800) 788-4729
Personalize your cake toppers with individual brides and grooms in a variety of ethnic and racial backgrounds.

RESOURCE DIRECTORY

WORLD WIDE WEB

The Web offers gay men and lesbians virtual on-line communities on which they can hook up, exchange views, and politically organize. (And, yes, for the marriage-minded, you can find everything from advice on floral arrangements to ideas on how and where to register.) The key is to be adventurous, to experiment, and to allow yourself to get lost on-line to find what you want. For the uninitiated, start with a search engine—Lycos, Excite, Yahoo, and Alta Vista are all terrific, and all list gay and lesbian topics organized by subject (i.e., gay/lesbian/marriage). There are also entire books devoted to the gay Net. (We like *Gay & Lesbian Online* by Jeff Dawson, 1998 edition from Alyson Books, but we may be prejudiced; Alyson is our publisher too).

If you're just starting out on the Net, there are a few basic on-line resources you might find helpful as you hook up. Keep in mind that the Internet is a living, breathing, ever-changing organism, and it's possible that today's site will be out of sight tomorrow. But as a starter kit, here are some established on-line communities offering local links, gay-specific search engines, chats, forums, and virtual events. Happy hunting.

Gay.com—www.gay.com
Out on the web—www.outontheweb.com
Geocities—www.geocities .com
Queer Living online—www.qmondo.com/queerliving
Family Q—www.studio8prod.com/family
Pride Media—www.pridemedia.com
Queer Resources Directory—www.qrd.org
Planet Out—www.planetout.com
Outwork Gay and Lesbian Business Network—www.outwork.com
Same-Sex Marriage home page—http://nether.net/~rod/html/sub/marriage.html
LeGal's home page (Lesbian and Gay Lawyers)—www.interport.net/^le-gal
Freedom to Marry—www.ftm.org
Homorama—www.homorama.com

SUGGESTED REFERENCES

GAY HISTORY AND SOCIOLOGY

The Big Gay Book: A Man's Survival Guide for the '90s, by John Preston (Penguin Books, New York, 1991)
Families We Choose: Lesbian and Gay Kinship, by Kath Weston (Columbia University Press, New York, 1991)
Gay American History: Lesbians and Gay Men in the U.S.A., by Jonathan Ned Katz (Meridian, New York, 1992)
Gay and Lesbian Stats: A Pocket Guide of Facts and Figures, edited by Bennett L. Singer and David Deschamps (The New Press, New York, 1994)
The Lesbian Family Life Cycle, by Suzanne Slater (The Free Press, New York, 1995)
Making History: The Struggle for Gay and Lesbian Equal Rights, 1945-1990, by Eric Marcus (HarperCollins, New York, 1993)
Out in All Directions: Almanac of Gay and Lesbian America, edited by Lynn Witt, Sherry Thomas and Eric Marcus (Warner Books, New York, 1995)
The Question of Equality: Lesbian and Gay Politics in America Since Stonewall, by David Deitcher (Scribner, New York, 1992)
Same-Sex Unions in Premodern Europe, by John Boswell (Vintage Books, New York, 1995)
Straight From the Heart: A Love Story, by Rod and Bob Jackson-Paris (Warner Books, New York, 1994)
Virtual Equality: The Mainstreaming of Gay and Lesbian Liberation, by Urvashi Vaid (Anchor, New York, 1995)

MARRIAGE AND RELATIONSHIPS

Daddy's Wedding, by Michael Willhoite (Alyson Publications, Los Angeles, 1996)

The Intimacy Dance: A Guide to Long-Term Success in Gay and Lesbian Relationships, by Betty Berzon, Ph.D. (E.P. Dutton, New York, 1997)

The Lesbian Couples' Guide, by Judith McDaniel (HarperPerennial, New York, 1995)

The Lesbian and Gay Book of Love & Marriage: Creating the Stories of Our Lives, by Paula Martinac (Broadway, New York, 1998)

The Male Couple's Guide: Finding a Man, Making a Home, Building a Life, by Eric Marcus (HarperPerennial, New York, 1995)

On the Road to Same-Sex Marriage: A Supportive Guide to Psychological, Political, and Legal Issues, edited by Robert Cabaj and David W. Purcell (Josey-Bass Publishers, San Francisco, 1997)

Recognizing Ourselves: Ceremonies of Lesbian and Gay Commitment, by Ellen Lewin (Columbia University Press, New York, 1998)

Same-Sex Marriage: The Moral and Legal Debate, edited by Robert Baird and Stuart Rosenbaum (Prometheus, New York, 1997)

Same-Sex Marriage: Pro and Con, A Reader, edited by Andrew Sullivan (Vintage, New York, 1997)

Together Forever: Gay and Lesbian Marriage, by Eric Marcus (Doubleday, New York, 1998)

PERIODICALS

The Advocate, 6922 Hollywood Blvd., Tenth Floor, Los Angeles CA 90028; (323) 871-1225; www.advocate.com

Curve, One Haight St., Suite B, San Francisco, CA 94102; (415) 863-6538

Frontiers, 7985 Santa Monica Blvd., Suite 109, West Hollywood, CA 90046; (800) 769-3877; www.frontiersweb.com

Genre, 7080 Hollywood Blvd., Suite 1104, Hollywood, CA 90028; (213) 896-9778; www.genremagazine.com

Girlfriends, 3415 Cesar Chavez St., Suite 101, San Francisco, CA 94110; (800) GRL-FRND; www.gfriends.com

Hero, 8581 Santa Monica Blvd. #430, West Hollywood, CA 90069; (310) 360-8022; www.heromag.com

In the Family, PO Box 5387, Takoma Park, MD 20913; (310) 270-4771; www.inthefamily.com

Out, Box 15307, North Hollywood, CA 91615-5307; (800) 792-2760

BUSINESS AND LEGAL

Gayellow Pages (national edition), Box 533 Village Station, New York, NY 10014; (212) 674-0120; www.gayellowpages.com

Comprehensive symbol-coded listings of gay businesses, entertainment, and political organizations.for the United States and Canada

Getting Organized: The Easy Way to Put Your Life in Order, by Stephanie Winston (Warner Books, New York, 1991)

An Indispensable Guide for Gay and Lesbian Couples: What Every Same-Sex Couple Should Know, by Steve Bryant and Demian, Partner's Task Force, Box 9685, Seattle, WA 98109-0684; (206) 935-1206

Legal Affairs: Essential Advice for Same-Sex Couples, by Frederick Hertz (Henry Holt and Company, New York, 1998)

A Legal Guide for Lesbian and Gay Couples, by Hayden Curry and Denis Clifford, edited by Robin Leonard (NOLO Press, Berkeley, 1996) www.nolo.com

Legally Wed: Same-Sex Marriage and the Constitution, by Mark Strasser (Cornell University Press, Ithaca, 1997)

The Rights of Lesbians and Gay Men: The Basic ACLU Guide to a Gay Person's Rights, by Nan D. Hunter, Sherryl E. Michaelson, and Thomas B. Stoddard (Southern Illinois University Press, Carbondale and Edwardsville, 1992)

Spousal Equivalent Handbook: A Legal and Financial Guide to Living Together, by George G. Truitt and Johnette Duff (Sunny Beach Publications, Houston, 1991)

ETIQUETTE AND WEDDING BOOKS

Bridal Bargains: Secrets to Throwing a Fantastic Wedding on a Realistic Budget, by Denise and Alan Fields (Windsor Peak Press, Monument, CO, 1993; (800) 888-0385)

Ceremonies of the Heart: Celebrating Lesbian Unions, edited by Becky Butler (Seal Press, Seattle, 1997)

Dear Abby on Planning Your Wedding, by Abigail Van Buren (Philips-Van Buren Inc., Kansas City, Missouri, 1988)

Emily Post's Complete Book of Wedding Etiquette, by Elizabeth L. Post (New York: HarperCollins, 1991)

The Essential Book of Gay Manners and Etiquette, by Steven Petrow (HarperCollins, New York, 1995)

Lesbian and Gay Marriage: Private Commitments, Public Ceremonies, edited by Suzanne Sherman (Temple University Press, Philadelphia, 1992)

Miss Manners' Guide to Excruciatingly Correct Behavior, by Judith Martin (New York: Warner Books, 1993)

Modern Bride Guide to Etiquette: Answers to the Questions Today's Couples Really Ask, by Cele Goldsmith Lalli (John Willy & Sons Inc., New York, 1993)

Places: A Directory of Public Places for Private Events and Private Places for Public Functions, by Hannelore Hahn and Tatiana Stoumen (New York: Tenth House Enterprises.)

    Updated annually. Can be ordered directly from the publisher for $28.95, which includes postage, tax, and handling: Box 810, Gracie Station, New York, NY 10028; phone (212) 737-7536

Wedding Readings: Centuries of Writing and Rituals for Love and Marriage, selected by Eleanor Munro (Viking, New York, 1989)

Weddings, by Martha Stewart (C. N. Potter, New York, 1987)

Weddings by Design: A Guide to Non-Traditional Ceremonies, by Richard Leviton (HarperCollins, New York, 1993)

TRAVEL

Answers to Most-Asked Questions About Cruising, A brochure available from Cruise Lines International Associations, 500 Fifth Avenue, Suite 1407, New York, NY 10110; (212) 921-0066

    Just send in a self-addressed, stamped envelope.

Fodor's Gay Guide to the USA, by Andrew Collins (Fodor Travel Publications Inc., New York, 1998)

Gay Travel A to Z (Ferrari International Publications, Phoenix, 1998, www.q-net.com)

Our World, 1104 North Nova Road, Suite 251, Daytona Beach, FL 32117; (904) 441-5367; www.ourworldmag.com

    Monthly magazine devoted to gay travel around the world.

Out and About, 8 W. 19th Street, Suite 401, New York, 10011; (212) 645-6922; www.outandabout.com

    Unbiased and timely newsletter for gay and lesbian travelers.

INDEX

INDEX